ADVANCE PRAISE

MAN *of the* TREES

"Richard St. Barbe Baker saw, years ago, what many of us are only now realizing, that environmental degradation is threatening our life support systems. He is celebrated by the environmental movement, including environmental activists like the late Professor Wangari Maathai, for his vision of a healthy future."
—Wanjira Maathai, Chair of the Board, Green Belt Movement

"There are many books written by Baker on his life and work. However, given the impact of his life and the prophetic nature of his call to arms to save the earth though all means possible from military-style all-out attack to people-centred social forestry movements, I have long wondered why there were none written by others. At last, Paul Hanley has addressed this omission....I thank Paul Hanley for seeing this project through to completion and for making the life and work of Richard St. Barbe Baker better known globally."
—Tony Rinaudo, World Vision Australia

"Paul Hanley's beautifully written biography of St. Barbe Baker reaffirms the everlasting legacy of a great earth healer; yes, that is what he was, a great earth healer. Whoever is interested in the right relationship between people and planet earth should read this book. It is a source of spiritual nourishment and timely reminder for practical actions."
—Satish Kumar, Founder, Schumacher College

"The Centenary of the establishment of 'Watu wa Miti' (Men/People of the Trees) in Kenya in 1922 clearly emphasizes the vital durability of the foresight of its founders Richard St. Barbe Baker and Josiah N'jonjo, who as environmentalists had a clear comprehension of the important ecological, social and economic roles of trees in the lives of ordinary people...Hopefully this book will stimulate a renaissance of the vision of Richard St. Barbe Baker and Josiah N'jonjo and trigger a reawakening of positive attitudes of society towards trees."
—Roger Leakey, Vice Chair, International Tree Foundation

"My friend and mentor Richard St. Barbe Baker was a genius at figuring out how to seamlessly integrate tree planting into the cultural DNA of millions of people from all walks of life and all corners of the globe. This book is part biography and part handbook for engaging a new generation in conserving and restoring the world's forests."
—Hugh Locke, President, Smallholder Farmers Alliance – Haiti

MAN *of the* TREES

RICHARD ST. BARBE BAKER
The First Global Conservationist

Paul Hanley

University of Regina Press

Printed and bound in Canada at Marquis. The text of this book is printed on 100% post-consumer recycled paper with earth-friendly vegetable-based inks.

Cover design: Duncan Campbell, University of Regina Press
Text design: John van der Woude, JVDW Designs
Copy editor: Marionne Cronin
Proofreader: Kristine Douaud
Indexer: Patricia Furdek
Cover art and frontispiece: Richard St. Barbe Baker holding a tree. *University of Saskatchewan Library, University Archives & Special Collections, Richard St. Barbe Baker fonds, mg071_baker_m1_holding_a_tree.*

Library and Archives Canada Cataloguing in Publication

Hanley, Paul, author
      Man of the trees : Richard St. Barbe Baker, the first global conservationist / Paul Hanley.

Includes bibliographical references and index. Issued in print and electronic formats. ISBN 978-0-88977-566-4 (softcover).—ISBN 978-0-88977-567-1 (PDF).—ISBN 978-0-88977-568-8 (HTML)

1. Baker, Richard St. Barbe, 1889-1982. 2. Conservationists—Biography. 3. Forest conservation—History. I. Title.

SD411.52.B39H36 2018   333.75'16092   C2018-903899-3   C2018-903900-0

10 9 8 7 6 5 4 3 2 1

University of Regina Press, University of Regina
Regina, Saskatchewan, Canada, S4S 0A2
tel: (306) 585-4758 fax: (306) 585-4699
U OF R PRESS web: www.uofrpress.ca

We acknowledge the support of the Canada Council for the Arts for our publishing program. We acknowledge the financial support of the Government of Canada. / Nous reconnaissons l'appui financier du gouvernement du Canada. This publication was made possible with support from Creative Saskatchewan's Creative Industries Production Grant Program. This publication has also received generous funding from the D. F. Plett Historical Research Foundation.

Contents

CHAPTER ONE
CHILD OF THE TREES—1

Fortunately, fortunes change; The temple of the woods; A life mission takes shape; To kill bears with a spade; Baker's Southern Wonder; A practical proposition; No collars at all; Gentling horses; Charlie Eagle and Beaver Creek; Breaking land, felling timber

CHAPTER TWO
CALL TO THE FOREST—25

War or peace?; Back from the dead; Call to the forest—and social activism; Back at school; A lucrative dream; Ghosts of Bakers past; Lost in the bamboo; A paradox; The Treeless Place; Dance of the trees; Sacked for taking a blow; Uncle Dick

CHAPTER THREE
SOCIAL FORESTRY—61

Sustainable yield in Nigeria; A brief idyll in Europe; Igi Oka; Education or catastrophe?; Baba Wa Miti

In 2015, I was greatly touched to have been asked to open the United Nations Paris Climate Conference, where I also addressed the participants on the importance of conserving the world's forests. In addition to protecting existing forests, I argued that to mitigate climate change we would need to restore the forests lost since 1950. I also spoke of the importance of supporting Indigenous people in their efforts to protect forests in ways consistent with their cultural traditions

Reading the biography of the 'Man of the Trees', it occurs to me that I could have been invoking Richard St. Barbe Baker, who had made similar appeals as far back as the 1920s. As Assistant Conservator of Forests in Kenya, he had recognized the emerging trend of deforestation and desertification. More than that, he had taken action to address these problems. His approach was to collaborate with Kikuyu elders and youth to replant trees lost to unsustainable logging and slash and burn farming. Since Kikuyu culture was built around ceremonial dance, he sponsored the first Dance of the Trees and with Chief Josiah Njonjo launched the Men of the Trees, destined to become one of the first international conservation organizations.

I had the great pleasure of meeting St. Barbe Baker in 1978, shortly after becoming Patron of the Men of the Trees, now known as the International Tree Foundation, and it was through this organization that I was able to plant an avenue of lime trees at Highgrove in memory of St. Barbe Baker. Needless to say, I felt entirely sympathetic to St. Barbe Baker's objectives and was eager to lend support to this pioneering grassroots movement with branches throughout the world. Many of the ecologically sensitive practices I have promoted throughout my adult life had been championed by St. Barbe Baker before I was born. Newton's aphorism, about standing on the shoulders of giants, clearly applies to St. Barbe Baker, a giant of the global conservation movement who foresaw the environmental crises we face today.

St. Barbe, as friends called him, was a true pioneer. Long before the science of climate change was understood, he had warned of the impact of forest loss on climate. He raised the alarm and prescribed a solution: one third of every nation should be tree covered. He practiced permaculture and agroecology in Nigeria before those terms existed and was among the founding figures of organic farming in England.

In my book, "Harmony: A New Way of Looking at Our World", I argued that the global environmental crisis is symptomatic of a deeper crisis of perception. We would benefit from re-examining the traditional wisdom that identified and celebrated a sacred presence in Nature and within people, and by combining that with the best of contemporary science. In his books and lectures, St. Barbe Baker had said much the same.

Behind St. Barbe Baker's prescience was his deep spiritual conviction about the unity of life. He had listened intently to the Indigenous people with whom he worked and seen a similar sensibility in the then new sciences of ecology and silviculture.

It is now clear that had we heeded the warnings of St. Barbe Baker and other visionaries, we might have avoided a good deal of the environmental crises we face today. It is not too late. We can save our forests and reclaim the deserts if, as the motto of the Men of the Trees – *Twahamwe* – puts it, we "pull together as one." This spirit of collaboration across different parts of the scenery, and by the public, private and N.G.O. sectors, is absolutely vital if we are to achieve the solutions we so desperately need. Richard St. Barbe Baker's message is as relevant today as it was ninety years ago and I very much hope that it will be heeded.

Introduction

BY JANE GOODALL

I first learned about Richard St. Barbe Baker when a friend gave me a copy of one of his books, *My Life, My Trees*. Before I was even halfway through reading it I was wondering why on earth I had not heard of this incredible man before, and as I learned more about him I became increasingly impressed by his life and his accomplishments. Indeed, he has become one of my true heroes, for he was, without doubt, one of the greatest advocates for the protection and restoration of forests ever. And, without doubt, he blazed a trail for many twentieth-century conservationists.

One of the things I learned about him was that his love of trees and forests began in much the same way as mine when we were children and, by a strange coincidence, both growing up in Hampshire. I had a particular affection for a beech tree in our garden. I spent hours high up in his branches where I felt closer to the birds. I thought of "Beech" almost as a person and with him I shared my most secret thoughts. When Baker was about five years old he went off into the forest alone and also developed a special relationship with one particular tree—which just happened also to be a beech tree. She became, he says, a mother confessor to him, his "Madonna of the Forest." He would stand close to her and imagine he had roots digging deep down into Mother Earth and that up above were her branches, reaching up to the sky. After such an experience he believed he was imbued with the "strength of the tree." (How interesting that I thought of my beech as a 'he' while Baker's was a 'she'!)

Baker seemed imbued with extraordinary strength. After serving in the First World War he became a forester, and for the rest of his life worked tirelessly to help protect forests around the globe, starting in Kenya. He was one of the earliest foresters to realize the terrible harm that was being done to the planet through deforestation. This realization impelled him to act, and act he did. For the better part of eight decades, he campaigned to restore forests and reclaim deserts all over the world, including in many parts of Africa. He supported reforestation efforts in all the countries bordering the Sahara and extended his efforts to the Middle East, Europe, North America, India, China, Australia, and New Zealand. It is estimated that billions of trees were planted during his lifetime and since then by people he inspired and by organizations he founded or advised and assisted.

Some of his dreams—such as a worldwide tree-planting campaign or a global children's green movement—were too far ahead of their time to be realized while he was alive. But he planted seeds of hope that would flourish through the efforts of many others. Today, the Billion Tree Campaign has planted more than 15 billion trees and almost all groups in the youth movement I started, Roots & Shoots, which involves hundreds of thousands of young people, from kindergarten through university, in 100 countries, choose to plant trees as part of their effort to make this a better world.

Baker's life was inspirational and I hope that this book is very successful so that thousands of people will come to learn about his amazing work. And that they will then be prepared, in Baker's own words, to "dedicate their lives to the service of the earth."

Prologue

I met Richard St. Barbe Baker in 1976. He was a vigorous eighty-five. To me, at twenty-four, he seemed the archetypal sage: snow-white hair and gentle face, worn by long years of travel; compassionate wisdom and utmost confidence; zeal undiminished after decades of relentless effort to save forests on six continents.

He even used a staff.

He had invited himself to the University of Regina, in my home-town, to lecture on trees. Apparently he was a world-renowned conservationist, yet none of my circle had heard of him. There was an aura about him, but who was he? People seemed a bit confused. Was it his name? Was he considered a saint? Someone called him *Sir* Richard.

I was part of the Earthcare Group, a university seminar on bio-dynamic agriculture. It seemed the place to send a 'Man of the Trees.' An impromptu talk was organized. Little did we know that Dr. Baker was well known in the biodynamic movement launched by the Austrian philosopher Rudolf Steiner, whose ideas Baker had helped introduce to Britain; or that he was a close friend of Herbert Koepf, whose book was a course text; or that he was considered, along with Sir Albert Howard and Sir Robert McCarrison, among the founding fathers of organic agriculture in England. He never mentioned these credentials.

After studying his life I now see that his short visit to Regina was classic Baker. That night we met at an apartment he had 'comman-deered.' The hosts seemed delighted, if a little surprised, when dozens squeezed in for a fireside chat. Baker was a storyteller par excellence. We were rapt as he told us of the first dance of the trees in Kenya, of the fight to save the redwoods, of his campaign to reforest the Sahara. His enthusiasm was infectious.

I also met Hugh Locke that night. Hugh's story is a good example of the influence Baker often had on people. Originally from small-town Saskatchewan, Hugh was about to move to London to take a second degree in architecture. As we walked home that night, he told me he had decided to combine his studies with offering to be Baker's assistant. He did, and eventually this work morphed into a career in international development. Later, Hugh co-founded Haiti's Smallholder Farmers Alliance. Using social forestry methods pioneered by Baker in Africa, thousands of Haitian farmers are now planting over a million trees a year, overcoming poverty while restoring the landscape. Baker is still planting trees, through many proxies.

Also among the guests that night was the provincial minister of the environment, listening intently. Who invited him? Baker always courted government officials, the higher the better. He aimed to meet the top dog and had met dozens of heads of state, royals, aristocrats, chiefs, and ministers. His message was always the same: Plant Trees to Save the Planet!

Today, most environmentalists—most people, perhaps—have heard of Al Gore, Wangari Maathai, David Suzuki, Jane Goodall, and other world-renowned conservation activists. Though not so well known, Baker was arguably the first such 'global conservationist' and most certainly a pioneer of the modern environmental movement.

Born in England in 1889, Baker had a long connection to Saskatchewan, where he had made a stab at homesteading in 1909. He later became conservator of forests in Kenya and Nigeria in the 1920s, an international forestry advisor, popular lecturer, and best-selling author. He was dubbed "Man of the Trees" by the famed American broadcaster Lowell Thomas, who predicted Baker would someday marry a tree. (Trees did figure prominently at his weddings.)

The day after our gathering at the University, I joined Baker at the Indian Head Tree Nursery. The nursery, opened in 1901 to produce trees for the treeless Canadian plains, was turning out millions of saplings a year for shelterbelts and wildlife habitat. As we toured the place, we noticed that herbicides were being used to control weeds. Baker mentioned that the last time he had visited the nursery they weren't using herbicides. When was that? our guides asked. 1910, he said. Without a hint of criticism, he simply noted he had never used a herbicide in any nursery or forestry situation in over eighty years as a tree planter. It really was eighty years: he planted his first trees in his father's nursery as a toddler. (No doubt, Baker turned over in his grave when the Canadian government shut down the Indian Head Tree Nursery in 2013.)

Baker was well ahead of his time in advocating sustainable forestry. He predicted the local and global impacts of deforestation and desertification decades before these were widely acknowledged. In 1922 he started the first international ENGO (environmental non-governmental organization), The Men of the Trees, which in its heyday had members in 108 countries. In 1936 he launched *Trees*, which after eighty years is considered the oldest environmental journal still being published. In addition to kings and presidents, his extraordinary networks of contacts included leaders of thought, visionaries, eminent scientists, artists, eccentrics, crackpots, and ordinary people everywhere who loved trees. He had a particular affinity for Indigenous people, especially in Africa, where he was the first European inducted into the secret society of Kikuyu elders.

Like his uncle, the explorer Sir Samuel White Baker, St. Barbe (as friends called him) had a taste for adventure, which he indulged in every corner of the world. A cowboy and lumberjack in Saskatchewan, he was among the first one hundred students at its fledgling university. In the 1970s, his alma mater awarded him an honorary doctorate, presented by an old friend, John Diefenbaker, the university's chancellor and a former prime minister of Canada.

After recovering from wounds sustained in the First World War and completing his forestry training at the University of Cambridge, Baker began his career in Africa's tropical forests. At one point, the territory he administered was as large as France. An early advocate of racial equality, he was blacklisted by the colonial service for his interventions on behalf of Africans, after which he began his cease-less planet-wide travels to promote forest conservation.

In his twenties and thirties, he pioneered now familiar develop-ment concepts such as social forestry, permaculture, agroecology, fair trade, and ecotourism. In his forties, he succeeded in manoeuvring the warring factions in Palestine into a collaborative reforestation scheme. In his fifties, he campaigned to save California's redwoods. In his sixties, he crossed the Sahara on a ground-breaking ecological survey. In his seventies, he traveled the length of New Zealand—more than 1,500 kilometres—on horseback. In his eighties, he took up the study of Chinese, intending to cross the Gobi Desert on a Mongolian pony. In his nineties, he finally made it to China.

His greatest obsession was the idea of reforesting the Sahara by way of a military-style campaign requiring an army of twenty-two million tree planters. Twice he traveled around that desert—and once through the middle of it—visiting every Saharan leader to promote the project. Queen Elizabeth recognized his efforts to save the world's forests by awarding him the Order of the British Empire.

That's it in a nutshell. But as you read about his life in detail, what emerges is a portrait of an indefatigable conservation hero full of paradox. Baker was a sylvan Don Quixote, a forester who rarely had a steady income, often surviving on the largesse of others. He was at once humble and self-aggrandizing; was equally at home in a thatched hut or a mansion; was by turns paternalistic and progres-sive, conventional and eccentric, soldier and peace activist.

By today's norms, readers will find aspects of his early attitudes toward Africans antiquated, even offensive. No attempt is made to whitewash his comments from the 1920s. By 1966, in his book *Sahara Conquest*, we see he has rejected the "scramble for colonial power, which unfortunately characterized the latter part of the nineteenth century" and embraced the African liberation movement. As his story unfolds, we see the gradual transformation of his consciousness as he sets aside the Edwardian values of imperial Britain and becomes a world citizen and an ally of Indigenous people. Significantly, he recognized in the traditional cultures of Indigenous peoples he met in Canada, Africa, New Zealand, India, and elsewhere, keys to rectifying the dominant mechanistic worldview that sanctioned the systematic destruction of the ecosphere.

Serendipity was his currency. He had a way of being in the right place at the right time to nudge others, whether presidents or popes, to action.

Or did he? At times, his stories strain credulity. Did he really plant the seed that became Roosevelt's Civilian Conservation Corps? Did he deliberately exaggerate his role? Did he consciously craft his own mythology?

Clearly, he was a visionary, a charismatic speaker, an engaging writer, a great campaigner. In 2006, when the United Kingdom's Environment Agency proposed the one hundred greatest eco-heroes of all time, there is Baker. He is ranked below figures such as Rachel Carson and Al Gore, but, curiously, above the Dalai Lama, Charles Darwin, Mahatma Gandhi, and even Gautama Buddha!

Some things *are* certain: He started planting trees as a child and never stopped. He mobilized thousands to plant and protect billions of trees. And the thousands he inspired carry on his work.

Dr. Baker's epitaph can be distilled to the words of his favourite poet, Henry Van Dyke:

He that planteth a tree is a servant of God,
He provideth a kindness for many generations,
And faces that he hath not seen shall bless him.

CHAPTER ONE

Child of the Trees

Bumbling about the nursery, stopping now and then to sniff buttercups, a child drenches a bed of pine seedlings from his little watering can. Now he salutes his "troops," popping off the seed coats of the tiny "soldiers" with the flick of a sharp twig "sword."

He races through the damp yard and gardens. Roses are in bud. The cattle are fat. Fowl flap and scatter as he runs past. With the Queen on the throne, the colonies rich and vast, "The Firs" on sunny Beacon Hill on the fringe of a pine wood in the south of Hampshire is secure, blessed in its soil and the mildness of its weather—a blessed spot to be born and tend trees.

Richard plays childhood against this bucolic backdrop, with the suffering and sinister world, its dark satanic mills, well beyond the hedgerows. Home is innocent, pastoral, Arcadian, a world of country parsons, farm folk, God-fearers. Embraced in a fair wood of oak, beech, and pines, it is a green and pleasant land.

FORTUNATELY, FORTUNES CHANGE

Charlotte Purrott, the only daughter of the local squire, had refused to marry John Baker, a man who could not provide in the manner to which she was accustomed. Baker, being of inauspicious means, was more intent on serving the Evangelical Revival of the times than pursuing the family tradition of a Cambridge education and life as a wealthy country gentleman, an ambition further interrupted when he was cheated of the family fortune by its trustees.

When Miss Purrott's father also lost his money, this time in a business venture, she wrote John Baker:

Dear John,
My father has lost all his money. Please marry me.

He did. And so Richard was born, on October 9, 1889, to a father who had taken up his hobby, nursery work, to make a living. Richard grew up drinking in the world of trees and tree care with his mother's milk.

His was a loving Christian home earnestly dedicated to the virtues of the time: pious worship, hard work, and the Arcadian ideal—a simple harmony with God's creation, His reflection seen in nature, an honest agrarian life.

Beside the work of planting, tending, and selling trees, John Baker involved himself with missionary work. He built a Mission Hall seating three hundred people in his own garden and set to work filling it with people from the neighbourhood. The work attracted missionaries from abroad, including the likes of General Booth, the founder of the Salvation Army, as frequent guest speakers. The Mission was a haven for all. The poor and unemployed were welcomed to coffee suppers, paying for their meal with an attentive ear to the sermons, the singing, and the illustrated talks on *Pilgrim's Progress*. It was a life rich in speculation about scripture and the Second Coming.

Richard St. Barbe Baker grew up among trees. He played with them, made friends with them, talked to and hugged them, planted and tended them, absorbing silviculture in a garden world. He later recalled:

When I was two I had my first little garden. The first things I grew were nasturtiums and soon after that with the help of my Nanny I scratched my name in the soil and sowed white mustard seed. A week later I was proud to spell out the letters of a green RICHARD.

At four with the help of an old sailor I rigged up a little flag made from a larch that grew in the wood. I was proud of my flagpole which I had barked and painted myself; it was the centre of the little garden. Each morning I hoisted a flag and each evening I took it down, carefully rolled it up and tied it correctly ready to hoist and 'break' the next day. At the entrance of my garden I stuck two withies and made an arch just big enough to allow me to pass under it. In a months time to my

Charlotte and John Baker.

great delight they started to grow leaves. It was a great thrill, for until then I had not grown anything more ambitious than nasturtiums and mustard.

When I was given a wheelbarrow I used to collect leaves from an oak wood at the end of the garden. I dug a little pit up to my waist and gradually filled it with layers of leaves, covering this with road scrapings and stable manure from our pony, and finally topped it with inverted slabs of turf.

I watched my father bud roses in the summer and graft pears and apples in the winter. He allowed me to tie the buds in with

Richard and his sister, circa 1897.

wet raffia grass from an iron bowl. I became quite expert at this and soon I was allowed to prepare the bud myself. If the graft on the apple stock had not taken there was a chance to bud it later. I loved doing this and vied with the gardeners in getting the best results. On Saturday evenings instead of playing cricket, as a great treat I was allowed to help my father sow tree seeds in long narrow beds I had helped to make. As the little pine seedlings came up they wore a little 'cap' which they seemed to be raising in salute. I was fascinated by the regiments of tiny seedlings and I protected, weeded and watered them. Their care was more important to me than any game.

While other children played with toy soldiers, Richard marched about the seedbeds, saluting the new trees and popping off their seed "caps" with his toy sword. He moistened the soil with a little watering can, making hundreds of trips from the rain barrel to the seedlings. Near the house there was a sand pit to play in, a little desert which he set to reclaim, shaping contours and 'treescaping' with leafy twigs dropped about by squirrels or the wind. These he placed strategically in avenues leading to a castle, complete with moat and drawbridge.

There was something unusual about this lad. Tree love was in his blood. Years later, traveling and lecturing on trees, he liked to tell the following story—the reverse of the young George Washington myth—to American audiences. Once when he was five, his father discovered that a number of young cherry saplings were missing and that Richard had a guilty look about him. "Where are the cherry saplings, Richard?" "I cannot tell a lie, Father," answered Richard. "I planted the cherry trees." He had found some little trees and couldn't resist the urge to settle them in the earth. He'd apparently done a decent job of it, too.

THE TEMPLE OF THE WOODS

In 1894 he had an unforgettable experience that, at the early age of five, altered his perception and, in his words, "I believe more than anything else influenced the way by which I have come."

His old nurse, Perrin, was a true Hampshire native, married to a forester whose charge adjoined the Baker estate. Perrin would take Richard walking through these dark woods—which seemed to him to be so full of romance and adventure—to visit her cottage, where the weekly batch of bread was baked in a brick oven. He watched her remove the sweet-smelling loaves from the oven: "To me Perrin was a sort of High Priestess officiating at the altar and the scent of the burning gorse seemed like incense to me."

The surrounding woods were extensive and, to a small boy, strange and inviting. One day he asked and then begged Perrin to let him go off into the woods a ways. Reluctantly, she allowed him to set out, accompanied by warnings about adders and the little people. He set out exultant to explore this great forest, at first keeping to the path, but soon was in the taller trees where the path petered out and led into bracken, the ferns luxuriant and well above his head. He was lost but it did not seem so to him. Rather, he had entered a fairyland. He wandered dreamily, losing all sense of time and place. High above, through the green canopy of leaves, light entered the forest in shafts, illuminating the morning mists and casting subtle shadows on the fronds that touched him as he walked on, penetrating deeper. His senses heightened; he saw, felt, smelled, and heard the forest, its every light, texture, fragrance, cry, and murmur, new but not a threat, rather an invitation, a splendour of trees.

Although I could only see a few yards ahead, I had no sense of being shut in. The sensation was exhilarating. I began to walk faster, buoyed up with an almost ethereal feeling of wellbeing, as if I had been detached from earth. I became intoxicated with the beauty around me, immersed in the joyousness and exultation of feeling a part of it all.

Soon the bracken became shorter, and before long it was left behind as a clearing opened where the dry pine needles covered the floor of the forest with a soft brown carpet. Rays of light pierced the canopy of the forest, were reflected in the ground mists and appeared as glorious shafts interlaced with the tall stems of the trees; bright and dark threads woven into a design.

I had entered the temple of the woods. I sank to the ground in a state of ecstasy; everything was intensely vivid—the call of the distant cuckoo seemed just by me. I was alone and yet encompassed by all the living creatures I loved so dearly.

The overpowering beauty entered into his very being; his heart brimmed with an inarticulate thankfulness at being alive; his universe said YES and he agreed with his own small voice. Strange to say, it seems that he was adopted by these trees, or born a second time, now to forest parents, a child of beeches and pines. Merging with the trees he became root, branch, and heartwood. In the temple of wood and light, he is leaf and seed.

This early mystical experience became a core and centre of his life. He lived it, relived it, and recreated it for others—and for the forest. "In the wood among the pines, it seems that for one brief moment I had tasted immortality, and in a few seconds had lived an eternity. This experience may last forever."

Emerging from his reverie, he followed another path and was soon back in the world of Perrin, fresh bread, and the washing hung on the line, but everything seemed changed: the bread smelled that much sweeter, the clothes now bright flags flapping in the breeze. Back home, he sensed his parents' affection as never before. "I was in love with life; I was indeed born again, although I could not have explained what had happened to me then."

The woods now held a new fascination. He sought out the mystery place but couldn't find the same experience. Instead, he explored the forest. He picked out a certain tree, and when he was feeling unhappy or if something had gone wrong during the day:

I would leave the house, run down the little lane, cross the meadow and visit a particular beech tree in the wood. That beech tree with smooth bark was a Mother Confessor to me— my Madonna of the Woods. Standing by the friendly beech, I knew in my heart that my troubles and my grief, as well as all that pleased me, were but for a passing moment. I would imagine that I had roots digging down deep into Mother Earth and that all above I was sprouting branches. I would hold that in my thought for a few moments and then come back with the strength of the tree and a radiant heart, knowing that that was all that really mattered.

A LIFE MISSION TAKES SHAPE

Richard was the eldest of five children, three boys and two girls. He became responsible at an early age, helping about the place. His father was kindly and a natural ecumenist. People of all walks of life, and not a few contacts of various backgrounds—Hindus, Muslims, and Jews—frequented the house. The house was open to all and a string of visitors, often seeking a bite to eat or food for the sick, aged, and needy, would arrive first thing in the morning, to be greeted with a cup of tea.

On wet days one of Richard's jobs was to grind the grain. John Baker came by his name honestly: he was a master baker. He also gave seasonal work to many people in his nurseries and in the winter months opened a gravel pit to provide work. All these people were welcomed at the Mission Hall to its simple suppers and lectures; these gatherings, especially those that dealt with the Holy Land, engraved themselves on Richard's memory, affecting his future.

John Baker had been moved by a religious fervour aroused by Miss Chenevix Trench, daughter of a prominent archbishop. At the age of eighteen he had carried on her work in his Mission Hall, which soon became a unifying force in the neighbourhood. He attracted Christian missionaries of all denominations and held monthly prayer meetings that attracted three hundred people, Richard's mother leading the singing and father giving the address.

Once General Booth himself came to the service as a special guest. He held forth both afternoon and evening.

Back in the house after a simple supper to which I was allowed to stay up, as a special treat, the General began to lay down his rules for the salvation of the soul. According to the General a soul was allowed to backslide twice, but no more. 'Surely God will forgive seventy times seven,' protested my father. 'No Mr. Baker.' The General was emphatic. He had his own conditions for salvation in his army.

Richard's encounter with General Booth had a profound effect on him. As a ten-year-old, his encounter with the Salvation Army influenced his decision to enter church work in Canada and later in England, to become active in social service to poor workers, the unemployed, and youth, an interest that remained with him life-long. Additionally, Baker's interest in a military approach to conservation may have been influenced by the soldierly bent of the Salvation Army.

TO KILL BEARS WITH A SPADE

Baker's family had long been interested in biblical prophecy and, in keeping with the times, speculated on the date of Christ's return. One prominent visitor who joined in the speculation and calculations was the Reverend Melville Churchill. Together, over a cup of John Baker's fine coffee, made from freshly roasted and ground beans to which a tiny piece of butter, half the size of a small pea, was added just as it came to a boil, he and John Baker concluded that Christ should have returned in 1844. Although they never predicted the Second Coming, Melville did accurately predict that his cousin Winston would some-day be prime minister.

Richard's home, though intensely pious, was more open and tolerant of others than was the case with demanding evangelists like General Booth.

The Bakers' religiosity went back many decades. Their fore-fathers were ministers of the church and scholars as well. Richard's great-grandfather, rector at Botley, Hampshire, for fifty-two years, was the "old-fashioned type of sporting pastor." He promoted the manly art of boxing, would "beat the tar out of highwaymen," and happily walked dozens of miles to preach. His son, Richard's grand-father, was also an athletic pastor who lived to walk, undertaking all his pastoral visits on foot, often using his walking stick to plant acorns in the hedgerows as he went. "Sometimes when my father and grandmother were driving in the chaise they would meet my grandfather returning from some visit," Richard later wrote. "For fun, he would start running backwards in front of the fast-trotting pony and at every dozen strides or so would jump backwards over his walking stick!"

There was an innate sense of adventure in the Bakers. Richard's uncle, Samuel Baker, was an intrepid explorer who had been co-discoverer of the source of the Nile. There was a strong gene for swashbuckling and big thinking, and a family lore of hunting stories, the sporting life, exploration of the wide world of the colonies, the frontier. Richard was brought up on stories of Samuel Baker and the letters of his great-uncle Richard, who went to Canada "where he cleared the bush and shot wild bear."

Baker later recalled: "As a boy of ten I used to find it thrilling to listen to letters read to me by my father, which he too had enjoyed as a ten year-old. Long passages of these letters had dealt with philosophical and religious questions, often in an introspective vein, but every now and then there would be a spicy bit about bears. It was then that I really sat up and took notice."

One incident left an indelible impression on the young boy. Uncle Richard told the story of his neighbour who, hearing grunts in the night, pulled on a sheepskin over his nightshirt, and rushed out into the cold only to find a large bear lifting the prize sow out of the pen. No weapons at hand, he had grabbed up a spade, and hitting the bear a resounding blow on the head, killed it. It fell dead at his feet.

Dead at his feet! I kissed my mother and said good night to her and my father. Looking out from my bedroom window I could see my young trees in the moonlight. I searched in all directions, but there was not even a shadow that remotely resembled a bear. "I will go to Canada one day," I thought, "where I can kill bears with spades!"

Machismo aside, the Bakers had soft hearts and there was a strong tendency to vegetarianism that accompanied their love of animals. Father John Baker was near to being a vegetarian; his father had been one. Only one meat meal was served each week in the Baker home, mainly for the benefit of the staff, but Richard was, or claimed to be, a dyed-in-the-wool vegetarian from day one. His first and only challenge was to get past the fourth commandment.

Around the age of five, father served son a slice from the weekly joint of beef. Richard consumed the vegetables and left the meat, but father insisted, on principle, that his son be obedient and clear his plate. Richard refused and was sent to his room with the beef to 'think about it,' his father checking in occasionally to see if any progress had been made. A flash of insight came to him; he went to the window and in a loud whisper called the kitten, which saved him by gobbling the meat. On next check he could report that the meat was 'gone.' He never could admit to his father that he had disobeyed him, but his father never served him another slice of meat.

Although a number of his early statements and friends' accounts contradict later autobiographies, Baker claimed to be a lifelong vegetarian and became an activist in the vegetarian movement.

BAKER'S SOUTHERN WONDER

If he was to "kill bears with a spade" in Canada, he had first to grow up and get an education. Richard's first school was in the neighbouring village of Bitterne. Holidays were taken up with work about the nursery, where his father was raising thousands of small forest and ornamental trees from seed. Richard helped with bed preparation, seeding, weeding, and transplanting until the trees were ready for dispatch by rail. As soon as he could drive, he was trusted with delivering loads of trees to the new planting being developed in the neighbourhood.

John Baker was scrupulous in his tree management. He had himself been at this work since the age of three when he planted apple pips in little flowerpots in the playroom, tending and watering them for two years. Then, assisted by the gardener, he planted them out. Decades later, Baker's Seedling and Baker's Southern Wonder, which had originated from the pips he had planted as a child, were two varieties in demand among British growers.

John's caring attitude secured him a good clientele. Richard would accompany his father, observing him as he escorted his clients about the nursery, listening as he advised them on their choice.

"To my father, each tree was, as it were, a person. He knew them every one; many of them he had tended for as long as ten or twelve years before they were ready to make their departure to their final home." John Baker would send out his man to help with the planting out, and again a year later to inspect, making sure the trees were 'happy' in their new environment.

The father would also take his son out inspecting and felling timber. He would carefully select a mature tree and calculate the direction of the cut to avoid damage to younger trees. Although he carried a measuring tape, he rarely used it as he could estimate the cubic contents of a tree at a single glance.

Here was a bit of a quiz, a game for father and son: "Now, my boy," John would say, "how many feet do you think there are in that tree? I would make a guess and often be a long way out, but with infinite patience he would correct me and help me develop the judgment that is so valuable to a forester."

On Sundays Richard would walk the lanes, getting to know the trees of the district, and would report back to his father on all he had seen. He and his brother, Scott, would walk and ride their bicycles, their 'bone-shakers,' through the county and the New Forest.

There was a friendly old chestnut tree at the bottom of the garden that provided a summer retreat for the children. Easy to climb, it was made to hold a platform that, once erected, served triple purpose as table, fruit store, and lookout. "It was probably not more than 40 feet above the ground, and yet to our childish eyes it seemed as though we were on the roof of the world." From this eagle's nest they could view the gardens, the gardeners at work, the neighbours—every sight and sound were plain. "My brother and I used to sit on one branch leaning back on another, pleasantly shaded from the sun and sheltered from showers by the dense canopy of the leaves."

Fifty years later Richard, remembering that tree, could say: "Looking back on the years that have passed, it is difficult to estimate the tremendous influence of that tree friendship upon my whole life. Although I was not fully conscious of it at that time, that close contact with that very vital tree, when as a growing boy I was developing rapidly, stimulated my whole being and generated balance and poise."

Inspired, encompassed by these branches, Richard wrote his first essay on trees at the age of ten. The fragrance of that tree remained with him throughout his life.

A PRACTICAL PROPOSITION

The Bakers' passion for trees was also a practical proposition: besides growing and selling them, they put them to use, not only for beautification, shelter, and as a playground, but also for food and timber. All the lumber required for his father's buildings and repairs came from trees on the property. Richard watched and later assisted the sawyers who cut the planks and beams by hand.

There was an artistry in their work. Each log would be treated so as to yield the best with as little waste as possible. By comparison, the circular saw of today is grossly extravagant, often sacrificing as much as twenty-five percent of the valuable timber in the sawdust. Oak was always cut on the quarter, so that the flowers or rays might be shown to the best advantage. When it was wanted for posts or palings, they would cleave it with axe and wedges. Wood converted in this way is much more valuable than sawn timber, besides being more natural and, therefore, more beautiful. Compare the oak paneling in an old manor house with the modern imitations of today. Homes were built to last, and afford an inspiration to succeeding generations.

Richard acquired his values from this time and carried them throughout his life: an understanding of quality, vocation, artistry, and the value of work as a form of worship. Such values seemed antique as the priorities of the age changed to quantity of production, efficiency of destruction, thoroughness of exploitation, and commercial expediency.

He learned to work like a navvy alongside the men, acquiring the practical skills for his life's calling.

Meanwhile, his schooling continued. In 1902, at the age of thirteen, he was sent to Dean Close School, Cheltenham, a school with evangelical tendencies. The Fleckers, whose son James Elroy, Richard's school friend, became a well-known British poet, headed the school. Richard entered school life at Dean Close with enthusiasm. In sports he enjoyed cricket, but was not a very dependable bat; he was a moderate bowler, but soccer was his sport of preference and he usually played outside right. His main exercise was running and he was encouraged to take up cross-country, which also got him out in the woods.

His major interest as school was not sports, however, but carpentry. At home he had already become fairly accomplished at carpentry, but now, under the expert guidance of 'Uncle Page,' the school instructor, he learned the joinery, which stood him in good stead, not only after his move to Canada, but at several times during his life when he supported himself through woodworking.

Holidays were often spent on wooded estates in the vicinity, and much time was devoted to forestry work, accompanying the owners, foresters, and local tree and woodland management authorities.

NO COLLARS AT ALL

At Dean Close, Richard received his second 'call' to Canada when a man came to talk to the students about the dominion:

> It was not what he said but what he did that impressed itself on my mind. He wore a tail coat with stiff shirt and collar and ready-made tie, and at one stage in the lecture he caught hold of his collar and shook it savagely and said, "Out in Canada we don't have to wear these durned things, we wear soft collars, or no collars at all." My mind was made up, I must go to Canada.

The chance to kill bears with a spade and without a stiff collar to boot!

His preparations began. At five every morning he got up and went to Southampton to learn how to make horseshoes. He joined a friend's camp in the forest, living and working outdoors, sleeping under the stars, and getting fit for the Canadian bush. His upbringing had equipped him with the practical skills for homesteading; his camping friend helped to toughen him up. After a day of carting fruit from the orchard, washing clothes, grinding grain, and baking bread—and on Sundays conducting services at mission churches—the young men would put on the gloves and box the evening away. Their coach was "a fine specimen of muscular Christianity and although I had a longer reach he made me hop around. I was always grateful to him for putting me through my paces in preparation for the North-West...."

After years of thinking about emigration, Richard learned that his father had become favourably disposed towards his plans. Despite his desire that his son take over the family business, John Baker had been faced with the prospect of selling land to pay for Richard's education. It was timely, then, when Bishop Lloyd, who had been chaplain to the expeditionary force against the Métis resistance and later to the Barr colony, and for whom the Canadian city of Lloydminster was named, returned from the prairies seeking young volunteers to go west to 'blaze the trail' for the Church and to minister to the scattered settlers. The young volunteers would enrol in Emmanuel College, the school of divinity at the new University of Saskatchewan in Saskatoon. His mother approved. The way was now clear.

But how would he finance his travel and education?

Since the age of twelve, when he had noticed a neighbour manipulating a frame of comb, Richard had been an avid beekeeper. He had traded his apple trees—to encourage him in budding and grafting, his father had given him five of every hundred trees—for a stock of bees. From used Quaker Oats crates he built his own equipment. He increased the stock by catching swarms, and by the age of sixteen was an expert with sixteen productive hives, the best of which yielded 240 pounds of honey in a single season. When he was twenty he sold the hives, bought a ticket for Canada, and sailed from Southampton. This was the start of three and a half years "in the hard school of the open spaces."

GENTLING HORSES

In the late summer of 1909, Baker took the train to Saskatoon, Saskatchewan, where he would be one of the first hundred students at its fledgling University. By enrolling in arts and sciences he kept a promise to his father that he would continue his education. However, having little money, he had to combine work with his academic career. In Saskatoon Baker found both opportunities to work and an attitude to life unheard of in the old country. This was a whole community that was starting from scratch. If you wanted something you had to make it or make it happen.

First off, Baker needed a place to live. With two other students he built a shack on campus (claimed to be the first student residence in Saskatoon). Baker got his first paying job as a part-time sports reporter for the local paper. With the wages he bought a meal ticket at a Chinese restaurant, so one meal a day was assured.

Baker was an excellent horseman and during the long summer vacation he traded large Hudson Bay blankets to the Indigenous people for wild mustangs that he then rounded up, gentled, exercised, and fed. When fully trained he sold them to doctors and other professional men for their sleighs and buggies.

Baker was a real Englishman, a tenderfoot, but as a boy he had read everything he could on the North American West and his romantic

Student residences on the bald prairie, University of Saskatchewan, circa 1910.

image of cowboys was fully alive. On one of his trips to explore the West he found himself at Pleasant Valley, Alberta—cow country.

Baker fancied himself a good horse trader. One day he arrived at a farm after a round-up, looking for a deal. The farmer scratched his head and said, "Do y'r see that cuss over there? If you can ride him you can have him as a present."

I had already broken in wild cayuses and secretly fancied myself as a bronco-buster. In England, before I could walk, I could ride. The "black devil" soon showed himself to be tough and as clever as a demon-possessed monkey. Finally, after sweat-inducing exertions, I managed to get him in the corral. Quickly, I roped and hauled him onto the rails where I tried, at first in vain, to quieten him. At last, when he seemed quietened, I pitched my stock saddle on his back and he bucked high in the air. The saddle bucked higher. I pitched it on again, clung to the girth and managed to cinch it. In a second I tore the ropes clear of the rails

Baker's paradise: on horseback in the forest.

and flung myself on the horse's back. He lunged forward and the
bit slipped on the left side. Flat on my back, I gazed at the sky.

My audience of cowpunchers guffawed loudly. Their laughter
hurt; it was the spur I needed. I got back in the saddle and away
went the bronco, bucking, cavorting, furiously snorting and
whinnying. With all my strength I pulled backward and quickly
slipped to one side. Down he went in the deep snow, greatly sur-
prised but unhurt. As he scrambled to his feet, I caught the saddle
horn and off we went again, he on his equine fandango with me
desperately trying to hold on and think ahead of him. Bored by
the dance, suddenly he accelerated into a wild pencil straight gal-
lop, fast as the wind it seemed, unheeding of the man on his back.
I held on. Out of the corral and for about twenty miles his career
continued and then the pace slackened. He was utterly exhausted
when I hauled on the reins outside another farm.

The following day Baker rode back, past the cowpunchers and
the ex-owner, on what proved to be one of the best horses he had
ever ridden.

Life wasn't all frontier exploits. With a cohort of just one hundred
students, college life in Saskatchewan was an entirely new experience to an English student used to well-established schools. Not only
did he operate the first student residence, which doubled as a livery
stable, he also played hockey and was a champion long-distance runner. He was elected to compose the school yell, which combined the
school colours with the name and motto of the university:

Saskatchewan, Saskatchewan, Varsitee!
Hi hickety ki yi! Hi kickety kee!
Deo et patri! Deo et patri!
The green, the white! Ki yam i yam i kee!
Sas-s-s-s-s-skatchewan!

As a sophomore Baker had the privilege of initiating freshmen,
one of whom would later become prime minister of Canada, a
staunch supporter of Baker's, and who, much later, as chancellor of

the university, would bestow an honorary doctorate on him. This was, of course, the young law student, John Diefenbaker. Making the connection with Diefenbaker, a future national leader, was typical of Baker. Throughout his life he chanced to meet influential, famous, powerful, or gifted people with unusual frequency, encounters he never failed to take advantage of, sooner or later, on behalf of his great cause, forest conservation.

CHARLIE EAGLE AND BEAVER CREEK

Life on the prairie was an education. He met, traded and dealt with people of all nationalities, but St. Barbe was particularly attracted to Indigenous people and quickly made friends at the Moose Woods reserve (now Whitecap Dakota First Nation), about sixteen miles south of Saskatoon. It was the home of Charlie Eagle, who Baker described as "chief, religious leader and school master." Their friendship helped train Baker in living off the prairie. He sat around the fire or the stove and took in the stories passed down from elders to children—the moral tales, lessons of nature, hunting stories, instructions in arts and crafts, the humour—all woven into a never-ending epic that went on night after night.

> I learned much as I sat by the fire with the children of Charlie Eagle's tribe. The Crees* accepted me as a member of the family. I felt at home with them. In the summer we organized a joint picnic with the Canadian homesteaders and had flat racing. The Indians rode bareback. Our horses were generally better bred and could go faster on the straight, but on the corners the Indians gained every time. The holiday was a great success and became an annual event.

Associating with the Indigenous people was a significant experience for Baker. Within a few years, his collaboration with Indigenous Africans would become a central element in his life's work.

---

* In fact, they were Dakota, not Cree.

Beaver Creek, not far from the Whitecap reserve, became his "Canadian retreat." After a few "exhilarating" (read -40°C) months in his shack on campus, he heard of an abandoned homestead for sale at Beaver Creek, fifteen miles from the college. With dreams of starting his own ranch, Baker borrowed a buggy and set off one Saturday night to prospect the place. On the way he learned something of the domestic ingenuity of bachelors living on the lone prairie:

In a light-hearted way I had set off without calculating the time I would spend on the road and the effect it would have upon an extremely healthy appetite. Five miles out of town darkness fell rapidly and my hunger was ravenous. The night was cold and the pony, resentful of my nocturnal absentmindedness, jogged sullenly on his dreary way. Although I was still a tenderfoot, when I saw a light ahead I knew what to do. It was the usual social practice to call anywhere for a bed and something to eat. Canadians are hospitable people. The pony also sensed the nearness of a farm and quickened his pace, just as keen as I was to get cover for the night. As I drew near I saw a wooden house with a barn beyond. The house was owned by two bachelors

Baker's mentor and friend Charlie Eagle, far right, with a group of men at the Moose Woods Reservation (Whitecap Dakota First Nation), August 1910.

and they were glad to see me. I stopped the buggy in the yard and walked over to the open door. "Put up your horse, son," said one of the men, "reach down some hay and come right in yourself." I bedded down my horse and went back to the house.

"Reach out and help yourself!" one of the bachelors said, indicating the table with a steaming saucepan full of corncobs. My hosts dug in their forks and took out a cob, smothered it with butter and bit off the corn. I soon got the knack and between us we finished off the lot. It was an enormous meal and, for my part, I was quite satisfied. Each of the men took out a plug of tobacco and shaved bits off into their palms, filled their pipes and lit up. We talked together for hours before we went up to bed.

They used only one large room upstairs, the others were stacked with stores and equipment. I shook out my buffalo rug, spread it on the floor and prepared for sleep. The two men clambered into the large bed in the middle of the room. I stayed asleep until I was wakened by a kick in my side. "Say, you'll be cold there on the floor," said one of the men, "get up and come in here with us!" It was cold on the floor and, unwrapping my rug and throwing it on the bed I clambered in beside them. It was warm and comfortable and I went off to sleep again immediately. It seemed scarcely a moment before I was awakened once more by another dig in the ribs. "What is it this time?" I asked wearily. "Keep your feet up, you're kicking the bread!" I wondered whether I was dreaming. "The bread did you say?" "Sure, the dough! It's in the foot of the bed keeping warm. You want it to rise, don't you?" I tucked my feet up as far as I could and slept soundly until morning. I was learning quickly.

Baker arrived at the homestead the next day. It wasn't the best of farms by any means, but by then the prairies had already worked their magic on him.

There was ample compensation in the wonderful sense of freedom of these flat prairies and wide stretches. On cloudless

nights it was never dark; the Milky Way lent the earth a soft
white light. I learned to love sleeping in the open, learned to
close my eyes on the softness of the night and open them again
to the alarm of sunrise.

He secured the homestead and during the summers camped on the
banks of Beaver Creek. Vacations were spent helping out neighbouring
farmers, gentling horses, or joining local fishing or trapping parties.
St. Barbe, who claimed never to have eaten meat, speaks in his earlier
biographies of learning how to hunt, trap, and live off the land from
the Indians. However, the major components of his diet were dates
and whole-wheat bread made from flour ground from his own crop of
wheat, as well as the odd meal at a Chinese restaurant.

At that point in his life, Baker had not yet become the ardent animal rights advocate he would later be. "I did not think then of the
cruelty I was inflicting by trapping wild animals. I am particularly
glad that I never was tempted to kill a beaver." He had a fascination with beavers and considered them fellow foresters; he spent
many hours watching and learning from them. It seems fitting, and
somehow not surprising, that Beaver Creek has since become a conservation area and nature interpretive centre.

During this period of his life, Baker was also active in church work,
helping to build up congregations from isolated settlers clustered
around central schools and mission churches. He would often ride
long distances on Sundays, leading church services in the Saskatoon
area. The thought of a career in the church remained a strong con-
tender for some years.

BREAKING LAND, FELLING TIMBER

St. Barbe's experience in Saskatchewan began to awaken his understanding that all was not well with the world. He came to understand
that the idyllic farm life of Arcadian England was the exception
rather than the rule. Not everyone was growing and planting trees;
many more were cutting them down—or ploughing them under. And
he was participating.

He sat on a gangplough behind six horses, breaking four and a half acres a day. He was heartbroken by what he was doing. The prairie sod built over centuries was peppered with tiny willows that he ripped out and turned under. Without adequate provision for soil protection, the new settlers were setting the stage for the dust bowl of the 1930s.

One way to protect the soil was by planting shelterbelts to reduce wind speed, thus lessening erosion. St. Barbe visited the new government tree nursery in Indian Head in 1910; the nursery distributed trees free of charge to farmers, at first mainly to provide farmstead shelter and heating fuel, but also for field shelterbelts. His visit to the nursery contributed to the conservation vision forming in his mind. (When he returned to Indian Head some seventy years later to see the nursery producing over six million shelterbelt trees a year it was another confirmation of his early sense of the vital role of trees in farming.)

Life in Canada was good, but he was drifting, and at twenty-three his future was still undetermined. In the fall of 1912, with a few weeks left before school was to start, he signed on as a lumberjack in the forest camps north of Prince Albert. The sawmill at Big River was the largest in the British Empire at the time. The loggers were clear-felling trees over a wide area, stripping all the timber:

This area had been virgin forest and one evening, as I surveyed the mass of stricken trees littering the ground, I wondered what would happen when all these fine trees had gone. The felling was wasteful and I felt sick at heart. The first snow had fallen and it was too much trouble to fell the trees below the line. They wouldn't bother to push the snow away to reach ground level and the waste of timber was appalling.

The experience left an indelible impression on Baker. He returned to Saskatoon and the university determined to study trees and afforestation and to qualify to work as a forester.

The agricultural college at the university and the Experimental Farm in nearby Sutherland were experimenting with trees, and St. Barbe became involved, promoting field shelterbelts. As for forestry training, he soon discovered it would be long and arduous, but also that there was no forestry school anywhere in Canada at that time. The nearest school was in Seattle, Washington. To Baker this seemed a long way off, and the combination of his desire to see home and family and the inclination to follow the generations-old family tradition of studying at Cambridge led him to sell his valuable fur coat, made from "musquash" he'd shot and trapped on the Vermillion River, as well as his buggy and sleighs, cayuses and broncos, and buy a ticket home via Winnipeg, Chicago, and New York.

Winter had already come when he departed, aiming to be home for Christmas. After a few days sightseeing in Winnipeg, he took the train, the "big potato," east. His short time in the big cities gave him a foretaste of future American experiences.

When his ship the *Olympic*, the more fortunate twin sister of the *Titanic*, drew alongside at Southampton on the morning before Christmas, 1913, his father was waiting to meet him with the pony trap.

I was so glad to see him that I didn't mind his embracing me. He was an emotional man and had a habit, when deeply moved, of throwing his arms about us, which in my younger days used to embarrass me. We drove back to West End and I spent a wonderful Christmas with my family. That was one of my happiest Christmas holidays, after a long absence in a strange land, for it was spent with my father among the trees both he and I loved, while we talked over all past happenings and planned for the future.

And what a future it would be.

CHAPTER TWO

Call to the Forest

WAR OR PEACE?

Now home, Baker had some decisions to make. "I was being torn in two directions—I had a sense of mission toward the Church and I had a sense of mission to the Earth itself, to help restore the tree cover and play some part in halting the march of the deserts."

He spoke to his parents. Both his grandfather and great-grandfather had been parsons, Cambridge-trained. Although his father was a grower of trees, he was himself inclined toward the ministry. On the other hand, his mother felt that the work to heal the earth was another expression of the religious impulse, part of the social gospel. A debate raged, but within a few weeks he was at Ridley Hall, Cambridge, studying theology.

In his spare time and on vacations, he threw himself into charitable work in the East End of London. When, in time, the Bishop of London offered him a position in the church, he was torn again. Ordination had always seemed a possibility and he had served the church, whether in the missions in Canada, at home, or in London, all with a view to gaining a wider experience in church work.

It was 1914, Baker was twenty-five, and war was declared. No decision need be made for a few years. At Cambridge he had already joined King Edward's Horse, the King's Overseas Dominions Regiment, a largely ceremonial show unit representing men from the dominions and colonies. They trained in two pre-breakfast drills a week.

Up to this point war had been something hypothetical. Suddenly, it was upon them. The officer in charge had fired up the men with the idea that "there's a war coming; now is the time to choose the pals you want to die with." They did, roping in their best friends to join up.

Again, Baker was caught between two opposing tendencies. Given his swashbuckling sense of adventure and bravado, he had the inclination to defend king and country. On the other hand, as a Christian and theology student, he had taken to heart the Sermon on the Mount.

If the teachings of Jesus meant anything and if we were to take up His Cross and follow Him, it would mean throwing up my cavalry training and becoming a conscientious objector to war with all the deprivation it would entail. My tutor, however, explained that the Sermon on the Mount was a counsel of perfection and obviously we could hardly expect to be able to live up to it yet. Besides, Jesus himself fought the moneychangers in the Temple and would wish His followers to steel themselves for the fight against evil. He said: "I came not to bring peace but a sword."

Somewhat bewildered, the young divinity student decided to go to the summer camp with his regiment. Two days before war was declared, he was in camp at Canterbury at the old Cavalry Depot, in the midst of mounted sports, when everything was stopped. The major told them they were on the brink of war and that if they wished to they could volunteer for service oversees.

This was August 1914. There was no more time for philosophical speculations. One had to choose on the spot to fight or back out; despite reservations, he joined his friends in the fight.

Baker's duties during the war years were numerous. Initially, he had been involved commandeering horses throughout the British countryside. When he was commissioned as a second lieutenant to the Royal Horse and Field Artillery he had expected to be sent to France and the front, but instead was assigned to Ireland, where he was in charge of eight hundred "wild Irish reservists" and six hundred horses. They were to be equipped and trained for overseas service and taught to ride.

As riding master, he was very much in his element. These were happy days with time for hunting, tennis, and, of course, the required kissing of the Blarney Stone (which worked its magic). Before sailing for France in the early days of 1915, he had trained five hundred horsemen.

During one of his first actions in France Baker identified a German observation post in a church tower. He felt rather squeamish when

Captain St. Barbe Baker, circa 1915.

the artillery blew the church to bits on his advice. However, for this success he had been given a few days leave. "Of course I accepted. In London I was invited to a tea party by some friends, all anxious for the latest news from the front. One old lady who confronted me said: 'Isn't it terrible that those Germans are firing at churches behind our lines?' I kept very quiet."

BACK FROM THE DEAD

During the spring horse shows, Baker won the Corps Cup on his colonel's horse. Back at the front, he was rewarded with the important task of building a fighting post for the colonel in preparation for an offensive. In the middle of the job the Germans sent over forty heavy shells in five minutes and twenty-seven men were buried in the mess.

The corpses were extracted from the rubble and lined up in a temporary mortuary. One of the soldiers went through the line ripping off dog tags. One 'corpse' started to bleed when the tag was ripped off and was delivered to a hospital instead of a grave. In the Duchess of Westminster Hospital at Le Touquet-Paris-Plage, the 'corpse' of Richard Baker woke up from the first of several near-death experiences.

For a few days he could feel no pain. He seemed outside his body, watching with interest, yet unconcerned, as he was skilfully pulled back to life. Recovery was like being thawed out: the freezing doesn't hurt, it's the warming up again that kills you. Physical as well as mental anguish set in, including remorse for his share in the killing. In the fury of war he had taken a hefty toll of German lives. "In my war madness I used to carve a notch for each 'heart-shot' on an old bow I had found and with glowing pride I had filled it from tip to tip. In the hospital, from each notch the eyes of those officers I had killed seemed to look sadly out at me. Their ghostly spectres haunted me." The vision of a dead war buddy come back to console him saved his sanity. Later, Baker recorded this impression in a poem about a dead soldier returning from the other side to comfort his mother.

Following the stretch in hospital he returned to service, first to Ireland on light duty. He found Ireland in the midst of the Easter Rising and himself in charge of quelling disturbances in Cork, which he accomplished with considerable panache—and zero casualties on either side.

Having done his bit to help settle the rebellion, Baker was leading a route march with thirty-six young officers in training when his horse crossed its front feet and came down, rolling on him with the gun team on top, resulting in a fracture of his thigh.

In the summer of 1917, still recovering from this accident, he was stationed near Southampton, receiving horses from conditioning depots to take on to France. He made fifty-eight crossings of the English Channel and conducted eighteen thousand horses to Le Havre. On two occasions his ship struck mines and sank.

Eventually he became fit enough to be promoted to the Remount Depot at Dieppe, where he was employed taking horses up the line. "This was done under the cover of night and we usually managed to hand over before dawn and get the horses dispersed to their units before the German planes were up. However, on one of these trips to the front, a dive bomber dropped a string on the train, which was blown up just as we were shunting back—that was the last time I was smashed up."

Baker was sent to recover at a beautiful wooded estate, where he was able to help the woodsman, as well as fellow officers who had suffered loss of limbs. In April of 1918, he was invalided out with the rank of captain.

In 1962, Baker published an illustrated book, *Horse Sense: Horses in War and Peace*, a recollection of his many adventures with horses.

CALL TO THE FOREST—AND SOCIAL ACTIVISM

During this final convalescence, St. Barbe had time for serious reflection. On the battlefields, in the mud of Flanders, during the long waits for dawn before the expected attack, or going over the top himself, he vowed that if he survived he would devote his life to forestry. His war experience had deepened his sense of mission, of greater purpose in life. His first activities as a social activist, aside from church work, began in the post-war period before he entered the forestry program at Cambridge.

While still in hospital, he had read the book *British Destiny* by Daniel Dunlop. He wrote to Dunlop, and the author came up to see him with an invitation to visit whenever possible. "Talks with Daniel Dunlop opened my eyes to the fact that we were losing more lives through the ignorance of health in our great cities than we were on all the fronts put together. War slew in its thousands, but preventable disease in tens of thousands." In response, St. Barbe became involved with Sir Percy Allen of the British Institute of Social Services in an effort to garner support for the establishment of a Ministry of Health.

Inspired by his contact with Dunlop, who had helped organize the Federation of British Industries, St. Barbe took on the task of approaching "industrial magnates and captains of industry," urging them to become active in providing exercise and sports programs in the workplace and to appoint welfare officers with some monies to be spent on the prevention of illness among workers and their families.

Once the health ministry was established, he entered forestry studies. The lessons learned approaching prominent business and political leaders were not lost on him.

Baker was also actively concerned with unemployment, prompted by his experience with fellow veterans, many now disabled. During one of his convalescences he had been sent to Cambridge by Canadian officials to investigate possibilities for Canadian veterans to take a course in agriculture or forestry while waiting to be repatriated. This incident is worth repeating; it was one of the first examples of what would become Baker's signature approach, so often repeated in conservation work, incorporating both audacity and luck.

Having been shown around the Cambridge experimental farm, the vice-chancellor asked him what he thought. "I told him that I was disappointed. You have merely 400 acres of poor or indifferent land with a mere pittance of 400 pounds a year from the Government. You are carrying on the most laborious experiments, which in Canada would be done in less than a week in test tubes." Baker was sent away with a suggestion and a letter of introduction to Sir F.E. Middleton, the government's director of agriculture: "Tell him what you told me," said the vice-chancellor.

Several weeks later, Baker happened to pass by the director's office in London and, taking a chance, went in. He met the director for twenty minutes and was sent away. Not long after, Baker heard that a considerable sum had been appropriated to the experimental farm and that they were now able to prepare for an influx of servicemen ready to study scientific agriculture. Baker never forgot the lesson learned: be bold and confident and aim for the top dog.

During this period he was also asked to give evidence at the hearings of the Rural Reconstruction Committee of Great Britain with regard to the advisability of forming a Forestry Commission. At this time, veterans, especially officers and those who had suffered injuries in the war effort, were given a measure of respect, and Baker's concern for returning veterans was well received. He was always proud that he had played some small role in establishing the senior forest authority in the country, even before he had received any forestry training.

BACK AT SCHOOL

In the fall of 1918, Baker at last entered forestry school at Cambridge, already having some background in arts and sciences from the fledgling university in Saskatchewan and some divinity training at Cambridge. He had practical experience in his father's nursery and as a lumberjack in Canada, in addition to his training as an amateur naturalist in the countryside around his childhood home and in the woodlands and forests of England, Canada, and France.

Nevertheless, settling down to university at the age of twenty-eight, with a whole generation of young men at his heels and after an early life of practical work, war, and adventures in the colonies, was not easy. "In my blissful ignorance I had imagined that forestry was something you do in a forest, and I had even hoped that it was something you learned how to make someone else do." He soon found that to get anywhere in the forestry world you had to take an honours program in the sciences, and on top of that, become proficient in the principles of silviculture, forest botany, entomology, management, resource utilization and protection, as well as practical forestry. "As far as I could see, the only subjects upon which we were not required to pass a searching examination were knitting and the care of teething infants!"

He had a feeling that the life of a simple woodsman, saving all the time and expense of an education, was a more suitable lifestyle—unless he could reach the top of his field. With that in mind, he threw himself into his studies, literally burning the midnight oil—much to the consternation of his frugal landlady—and with very black coffee as a pillow.

He was fortunate to have the most able professors, of wide experience and well traveled. One of the most influential was Herbert Stone, author of *Timbers of Commerce*, who had a well-catalogued collection of some four thousand specimens of wood. Stone's ability to inspire students, and his technique of approaching the subject from the point of view of a fellow student, always conveying the impression that they were engaged in research together, rubbed off on Baker and became invaluable to him in training foresters throughout his life. "Many were the problems sent to him by timber merchants and industrialists throughout the country, and he would let me share in unraveling them, and would sometimes give me the responsibility of tackling a conundrum unaided and so instilled confidence."

Baker was particularly interested in the economic utilization of timber and made a study of the manufacture and uses of plywood and plastics. He also specialized in principles of forestry, silviculture, and tree genetics.

A LUCRATIVE DREAM

One of the knotty problems Baker had to face was money. All he had was a war pension, and that had been reduced to forty-two pounds a year. So it was with some trepidation that he had entered Caius College, uncertain that he would be able to meet the various financial obligations presented to the student. His financial woes were solved early one foggy November morning.

"I dreamed that I saw an aeroplane evolving into a home on wheels. It was quite clear to me how the parts could be utilized." Great stores of aircraft materials left from the war could be turned into caravans (the British term for a vacation trailer), not only for holiday use but also for temporary housing for returning veterans frustrated in their search for accommodation.

Serendipitously, when he sat down for breakfast and a read of *The Times*, there was an advertisement inviting tenders for surplus aircraft materials. He checked the time of the next train and headed off to buy materials, designing and making up a list of the items needed for a prototype en route.

At the materials dump, he was asked what he wanted: "'To begin with,' he replied, 'a couple of airplane undercarriages,' to which the man in the office exclaimed: 'A couple! This is the Government Disposals Board. This is the smallest lot: thirty-six of them.' Even though they were parked quite close to each other they took up quite a big space in the hangar. The tender form in triplicate had been placed in my hand, together with an indelible pencil, and I wrote down the price I would have given for a pair. 'What else do you want?' Some plywood, please, I mildly answered. 'That's the smallest lot,' said he, pointing to a stack of beautiful plywood 12 feet long and 4 feet wide, almost touching the top of the hangar. Again I put down on the tender form the amount I estimated I would have to pay in the open market for enough to make a couple of caravans."

At this point Baker let his imagination go and signed tenders for hydroplane floats, bales of Holland fabric, aero-engines, propellers, and a dozen or so ailerons. Visions of amphibious and flying caravans danced in his head.

Apologizing for taking the gentleman's time and expecting never to hear from him, Baker returned home. Ten days later he had a card from the station master at Cambridge informing him that ten truckloads of aircraft materials had arrived and that he would be charged demurrage if it was not removed within twenty-four hours!

On the way to his first class he paid a flying visit to a friend, a maker of motor bodies, asking to put some plywood in his shed, brushing aside any questions. He called the stationmaster with directions. After his first lecture, he raced to the local inn and commandeered some sheds to store the thirty-six undercarriages. "By five o'clock that afternoon when I called on my motor body friend, everything had been delivered and with a piece of charcoal, I designed the first caravan trailer to be mounted on aeroplane undercarriages!"

The caravan had a Pullman roof with six pivoting ventilators and a wide window at the back, allowing a rear view for the driver of the tow car. A trap door in back gave entry to an ice chest and food store. A large cupboard under the chassis held camp beds and tents for six extra guests. Inside there was a gypsy cooking range with insulated double pipes going through a cupboard to make a warming oven; a sink fed with water from a roof top tank; a writing bureau; and a Russian divan that could be strapped up during the day.

St. Barbe had built the first mobile vacation trailer. He formed a company called NAVARAC CARAVAN Company, using the same style of advertisement as Rolls Royce. The first NAVARAC was unveiled in June 1919, generating much interest. The local newsreel representative took note, and the next evening a film was distributed to movie theatres around the country. Baker began turning out caravans at £300 a crack. Sales were brisk. The workshop became a hive of activity. "When the Government held an exhibition of aircraft materials at Olympia, simple fool that I was, I put it on exhibition, and thus gave the idea to makers of aeroplanes who had accumulations of aircraft

The NAVARAC alongside a traditional caravan.

material and were exploring ways of utilizing it. Soon a dozen or more were turning out caravans of improved patterns—streamlined and much lighter in weight than the NAVARAC."

Baker lost an opportunity to make a fortune, but he had paid his way through forestry school and given employment to a few craftsmen. The idea of caravans later became part of his vision of pastoral revival: he envisioned holiday campers planting trees and gardens; he composed a Caravaner's Code of the Countryside and a Caravaner's Creed; and he continued to promote conservationist caravanning through the years.

Much later, in 1969, he published his *Caravan Story and Country Notebook*, around the time that a group in northern Scotland were actually fulfilling his dream in a little garden caravan colony they called the Findhorn Community. It was destined to become the mecca and model for New Age communities.

During his first university vacation, he was attached to the Horse Guard Headquarters lecturing staff of the Army School of Education. He gave several lectures a day to camps of service men waiting to be demobilized. Up to a thousand men came to a single lecture and St. Barbe gained experience that he would use to good effect in future. His main topic was trees, of course, and the opportunities available for men to enter forestry and become forest settlers.

Baker was also active in the Cambridge Debating Society and once went up against Winston Churchill on the question "In the opinion of the House it is not advisable to hang the Kaiser or make Germany pay." Baker's side won.

Another interest was the Raleigh Club, for which the membership qualification was to have been "off the beaten track." When his turn came to speak of his adventures, Baker presented an illustrated lecture on northwestern Canada. Speaking of the mushrooming growth of Saskatoon, he said that when he arrived circa 1909 there were only eleven thousand people, and when he had left three and a half years later there were forty-seven thousand. "Ever afterward when I met a member of the Raleigh Club I would be asked: 'Been back to Saskatoon lately, Baker? What's the population now?'"

The other club Baker joined, and to which he returned continuously through the years, was the Naval and Military Club, his home away from home. More of its members had died in the war—over six hundred—than those of any other service club in London. His caravan, parked outdoors, became a rallying point for friends who had served overseas.

With all of these side interests and schemes for making a living, Baker did manage to receive his forestry diploma, graduating at the top of his class. As soon as he completed his training he applied to the Colonial Office for the post of assistant conservator of forests in Kenya. To his bitter disappointment, he was turned down on medical grounds. Although he was gradually recovering from his war injuries, requirements for service at the equator were very stringent.

He protested and reapplied for examination, but as the office offered little hope, he prepared to set off with his caravan to explore the forests of Europe, perhaps to continue his education at the forestry school at Nancy. But just as he was about to depart he received a telegram asking him to return for a further examination. He passed and almost at once received orders to set out for Kenya.

GHOSTS OF BAKERS PAST

Illustrious, adventurous, unusual relatives were part and parcel of Richard Baker's familial mythology. Ghosts of relatives past called him in various directions, to Canada or Cambridge, to war, and to Africa. A curious mix himself—Edwardian gentleman and rustic, conformist and eccentric, conservative and progressive—Baker came by his traits honestly. His bear-killing uncle was a mild example.

His great-great-great-grandfather had been a soldier by profession and a sailor by inclination. Six-foot-six and hefty in proportion, he sailed around the world three times with a hand-picked crew of "tough and desperate men" who, chosen for this reason, agreed to die before being defeated by Spanish pirates. When they were attacked, Major Baker slew fifteen pirates himself, seized their ship and personally delivered it to the Admiralty in London.

The Bakers' African connection was supplied by no less that Sir Samuel White Baker, an explorer, officer, naturalist, writer, and abolitionist, who once served as governor general of the Equatorial

Nile Basin, but also held the title of pasha and major general in the Ottoman Empire. He is mostly remembered as an explorer of the Nile and the interior of central Africa, and as the 'discoverer' of Lake Albert. He was a friend of King Edward VII, but shunned by Queen Victoria because of his relationship with a white slave girl whom he had rescued and eventually married.

While Samuel Baker believed in the sacred destiny of the empire under Divine Providence, he also respected Indigenous people and fought against the slave trade. As governor, he had forged strong bonds of trust between local people and the Crown, a trust often betrayed by those that followed him.

Richard Baker had inherited some of the attitudes of his illustrious relative. He respected Africans, their customs, beliefs, religion, and mode of government, as well as their human rights. Initially, he had an idealistic view of British justice and believed that, in principle, British colonial rule would be fair-minded and potentially a useful force in African development. He thought that adopting sustainable forest methods would lead to a lucrative trade that would benefit Africans, particularly through employment. In time, Baker would become disillusioned with colonialism and the colonial authorities' lack of support for fair and sustainable forms of development.

How do we assess someone enmeshed in colonial service in Africa in the 1920s, given contemporary standards? Certainly, Baker was not free of paternalism. In fact, by current standards many of his views at that time would be considered antiquated at best. Against the attitudes typical of the time, as we will see, his views were often enlightened and progressive, and ultimately they made it impossible for Baker to continue in colonial service

Clearly, Baker loved Africa and he did all that he could, over the next sixty years, for its preservation and development. For someone in colonial service in the 1920s, his methods were often radically progressive, presaging the grassroots, community-based social forestry practices that would come to be appreciated much later. In his book *The Origins of the Organic Movement*, Phillip Conford argues that Baker, Sir Albert Howard, and Sir Robert McCarrison, all considered founders of organic farming in Britain, were deeply influenced by their experiences working in the colonies. Each respected the intelligence of local farmers, paid close attention to Indigenous agricultural practices, and then sought to test their efficacy according to Western scientific principles that would legitimize their more widespread adoption.

LOST IN THE BAMBOO

On the way to his first post in Kenya, Baker was fortunate to make friends with a government official who was a scholar of Swahili and who devoted two hours daily to teaching Baker, with the result that he arrived with enough language to get by—at least to deal with his servants, who spoke no English. But this also proved to be to his advantage, as they taught him enough of the language that he was soon fluent and passed oral exams in colloquial Swahili after only three months.

He arrived late in 1920 in Mombasa, gateway to Kenya and its rich hinterland.

> *I went up to the sundeck and leaned on the rail, looking ahead into the mouth of the harbour. My first impressions were of a deep iridescent blue water with green trees dropping down from the hills to the very edge of the sea. It was a magnificent sight, full of promise of the rich tree-covered land beyond. West of Mombasa lies the Nika country through which it is necessary to climb some six thousand feet to reach Nairobi, capital of Kenya. Here are some of the finest congregations of big game in the world: Kongoni, with their comical gait; Thompson's gazelles, with ever wagging tails; lions and zebras.*

He was first assigned to the highlands and stationed at the headquarters in Nairobi. While waiting to be posted to a district, he began his work as assistant conservator by making a collection of Kenyan wood and sending samples off to his old friend Herbert Stone at Cambridge for analysis of their commercial potential.

Life in Nairobi was pleasant enough and he was able to associate with the settlers, who were kind and hospitable. But he was, of course, anxious to set out on safari, to meet the Africans, and see the countryside. His first opportunity came soon and proved to be an initiation by fire. He was given the assignment of exploring the possibility of using giant bamboo as a substitute for wood in the manufacture of quality paper. This bamboo, unlike the Indian variety, had soft nodes, so showed promise as a substitute for esparto grass, a basic material used in papermaking, of which there was a shortage.

The first few days of the trip were fairly easy as he and a couple dozen carriers negotiated the fringe of the Aberdare forest without difficulty.

As we penetrated further I realized this was no routine trip. I saw after a few hours that it was impossible to survey and chart the area from the forest floor. Only an aerial survey would be suitable. The bamboos grew thickly over a vast area and our progress was made more difficult by the steadily rising terrain. The average height of the bamboos was fifty feet and they were too thick and close together to walk through without continual sideways movements. We moved painfully forward in an eerie greenish half-light that filtered through the dense screen of canes.

After two days in the forest I knew we were lost. The compass was accurate, but virtually useless as I had no idea of the extent of the forest and there were no maps of the area. We had followed old elephant trails that meandered and it would have been impossible to plot our exact position with or without maps. After the third day my carriers began muttering among themselves and I knew they suspected we were lost. If they were once certain we were lost, without any knowledge of the extent of the forest, they would give up hope and lie down with packs and equipment to die. I chose the thickest of the bamboo canes, about sixty feet high, and began to climb it, hoping to get above the curtain of canes all around us and to plot the nearest high ground, from which we could find a way out. I climbed twenty feet until I felt the soft, sappy cane bending beneath me. Even the thickest cane would not bear my weight.

I decided to press on all the time not striking camp at night. My carriers would then have less time to brood; action might keep their minds off their unhappy situation. We kept on until well after dark. The experience of going through the bamboos by the light of a hurricane lamp was uncanny. My carriers were afraid; my own nerves shrieked as dark, shadowy forms scuttled away in the undergrowth. The swaying hurricane lamp cast eerie shadows and we spent half the time keeping in touch with one another. After two more hours of the weird night trek I called a halt. We were fit to drop where we stood. I sent some boys off to gather dried bamboo culms and light a fire to keep the beasts away.

We had reached the limits of fatigue, I dared not ask my bearers to pitch a tent or even fetch further supplies for the fire and we slept in its dying embers. I awoke at dawn and saw that, although they had rekindled a blaze, they were chattering among themselves trying to persuade their leaders to approach me. This was no time for me to discuss our serious situation and I told them that we would start again within an hour. But this time we should not follow elephant trails but press straight ahead on a compass bearing.

That meant hard work with the machetes, clearing away the canes, squeezing and torturing our bodies through the dense curtain of bamboos. We started off and after two or three hours I saw, to my joy, that the canes were getting smaller. The going got tougher and tougher as we climbed far more steeply than before. But the green eerie light was getting brighter and at last I saw clear light ahead. We came out on to open mountainside where I could get my bearings. We were through the forest and I could see that the return journey would be easier as, with the height of the mountainside above me, I could climb a few hundred feet and map out the compass course for the homeward journey, selecting the easiest paths through the forest.

*Now as I looked about I saw a different world. A world
that I had never seen before. Wherever I looked I saw beauty.
A great expanse of beautiful lilies made a carpet of scarlet
velvet set on a lush green such as I had seen before only on
boggy, water-logged land. There were gigantic lobelias and
huge groundsel, twelve to fifteen feet in height. [From Dance
of the Trees]*

It was a fairy-like glade. About his feet were clusters of everlasting flowers with golden centres, like those his mother used to pick
at home toward the end of the summer and keep for the winter.
Home was a long way off and yet, as he touched these flowers, for a
flickering second time and space vanished and he was once again on
that sunny hill, and drying on a sheet of *The Times* at his feet were
those same flowers. The ground was deep in a damp moss and he
was surrounded by phantom growths of giant heather with gnarled
and twisted stems all draped with lichens. A morning haze hung low,
but as he came to higher ground it suddenly cleaved and, as if bidden
by magic, perhaps eighty miles away appeared the peak of Mount
Kenya, *Kerenyage*, Possessor of Whiteness. Gaping chasms held the
snow that had blown clear of the dark shoulders. Just as quickly, it
disappeared and he was never given that gift again.

This was Africa then. Beauty, unbelievable if you haven't seen it,
but enmeshed in tests and difficulties, danger and opportunity. They
spent many days collecting specimens.

*The return journey was not without its discomforts and diffi-
cult moments.*

*It is alarming enough to come upon a mass of elephant dung,
waist high, still moist and steaming and to realize that somewhere just ahead of you or even behind you were elephants. But
often we would hear a deep rumbling, like distant thunder, and
soon I realized that this was the rumbling from their stomachs.
You may guess how I felt, knowing that the huge beasts were
within twenty or thirty feet, probably scenting us and listening
for our every move, standing ready to charge at the sign of any*

interference. Unlike buffalo, elephant tread delicately. They can
move with great speed, almost without a sound.

But they were never attacked, despite crossing the Aberdares four
times in different places. During two months safari on foot, Baker
and his companions covered some thousand miles, felling twenty
thousand bamboo stems, providing accurate estimates for future
exploitation on a sustained yield basis. The samples were sent to
England and proved suitable for high-quality paper; the potentiali-
ties for future paper supplies almost surpassed comprehension. That
expedition was a more-than-interesting introduction to life as a forestry officer in Kenya.

A PARADOX

His next safari was to the Solai Forest to demark a timber concession for a settler, who was to be one of the first exporters of pencil
slats made from *Mutarakwa*, an African cedar. Baker had noticed
that this wood was similar to the Virginia cedars commonly used to
make pencils. He had been walking through the bush and found a
tree recently felled by the Kikuyu, noticing the smell, which reminded
him of pencils. He tasted the chips and whittled them. Again, it was
like pencil. Samples were taken and sent to Herbert Stone.

This safari was an easy one. The men were happy because there
was plenty of game and in these days Baker enjoyed shooting,
despite his professed vegetarianism. On this safari he got to know
more about the Kenyan trees and studied their mode of growth. "It
was fascinating to unravel the story of the past and see how many
trees valued for their timber required nurse trees of lesser growth to
improve soil conditions and enable them to reach maturity. It was
here too that I noticed for the first time coffee growing wild, drawn
up in dense forest, and not the typical bush of the coffee plantations.
To the forester such exploration and discovery provides the most
exciting adventures of all."

His next assignment was to the coast, an entirely new experience,
vastly different from the highlands. The area from the border of

Tanganyika to Italian Somaliland was extensive, mostly sea frontage and mangrove swamps, whose trees provided the main local sources of fuel and building materials.

Besides identifying species and their potential uses, he was responsible for assigning timber concessions. Baker soon realized that his job as conservator was really one of supervising the rape of Kenya's forests. He began then to think of means for implementing a conservationist policy for sustained yield.

Behind the coastal forest was a desert, Nyika, sparsely populated, but abundant in game. Here he was to demarcate a new forest reserve. One day while hunting he had the misfortune of being scratched by a poisonous thorn. "I soon ran a high temperature and had the symptoms of lockjaw. My followers improvised a stretcher and carried me fifty or sixty miles to the nearest trail while a runner took word to the district officer at Melinde." Fortunately, a vehicle was available to bring him back. His life hung in the balance, but under the care of a surgeon who had the antidote, he was brought around after a few days.

Attending him were two men who Baker referred to as "faithful servants." Ramazani Bin Omari was a nephew of the sultan of Zanzibar who travelled with Baker during the whole of his stay in Kenya. The other was a Nyamwezi "boy" from Tanganyika who refused to leave Baker's employ. Following a safari he had been paid off and Baker moved to a new headquarters five hundred miles away. Three weeks later he showed up and insisted on returning to Baker's service.

"I have no work for you," I said. "When I travel in these parts I have Swahili carriers. Surely you will not be happy away from your home and people." However, he begged to be taken on even as a 'small boy.' It seemed quite incongruous that this big fellow, over six feet in height and with an enormous build, should wish to attach himself to my establishment in such a junior capacity. However, I was impressed by his devotion and gave in, and found him invaluable on safari. It was he who carried my spare gun or camera, and would sometimes carry me, too, across rivers, even though they might be infested by

crocodiles. He was just another of the faithful ones who ask for nothing more than the privilege to serve.

This was the attitude of the colonial officer to the native African: crossing crocodile-infested waters on their backs, losing them in impossible bamboo forests, calling strapping men 'boys.' But Baker himself was a paradox. The superior attitude that was his British inheritance was matched by his affinity and rapport with the Indigenous people he met, first in Canada and now in Africa.

He would come to know Africans intimately, participate in their religious practices, and study their culture. In the forests he would learn to string the big bow with the *kamba* from the back of the wild buffalo; he picked up the hunting language of the forest dwellers, learned to make fire with two sticks in the approved way, received gifts of tree seeds when people learned of his weakness for planting them; he was initiated into their mysterious psychic communication, exchanged news and stories with the headmen of villages and the *dhow* captains and crews. And, eventually, he sacrificed his power and position for them.

Was he more colonialist or ally of the African? I'll let the reader judge.

THE TREELESS PLACE

Baker's major posting was to Muguga, The Treeless Place, seventeen miles from Nairobi. It was here that he came across the nomadic methods of farming that had devastated northern Africa. "The Romans had created a dust bowl in almost two million square miles of North Africa," Baker later wrote, "wheat mining to satisfy the demands for free bread and circuses!" Imperial Romé had deforested the land to prepare the soil for grain cropping, but in this semi-arid and drought-prone region, ground cover is essential to hold the soil in place. Centuries of exploitation took their toll. "They were followed by wave after wave of Arabs with their goats," observed Baker. "These animals kept the natural tree cover from returning and healing the scars made by the Arabs, who had removed the soil protecting trees with machete and fire. The goats were ready cash for the

Arab and they accumulated their wealth in their flocks and herds, driving them before them as they invaded the forest."

The nomadic farmers St. Barbe encountered in the highlands of Kenya were thought to have moved south into the land from Ethiopia; they had bartered food for land with the original forest dwellers, "the forest protectors—the men who lived by the bow instead of the hoe." When these farmers decided to make a new farm, they went into the forests and selected a suitable area. The trees were felled and burned with the aim of getting an enriched soil on which to grow food. When the site was exhausted and spent, they went elsewhere and used the same technique again.

> *This was nomadic farming at its worst; destructive and wasteful methods such as these had created the Sahara Desert. As the seasons went by the trees fell to fire and axe and the forests retreated. This is an equatorial region. The sun beat down.*
>
> *Then came the giant steam engines using prodigious quantities of wood. Indian fuel contractors were kept busy felling large areas of beautiful and valuable trees, such as cedars and olives, and destroying a delectable land that had survived centuries of nomadic farming through crop rotation. Into the cleared land came thousands of white invaders from north and south, from east and west, with tractors and ploughs to hasten destruction with fertilizers and monoculture.*

Add to this the fact that Indigenous farmers had slowly to shift from a subsistence to a cash economy in order to pay taxes and to give portions of their crops to landlords, the pressure to increase production always mounting. It seemed that Baker could see, as plain as the African day, what was coming. He looked forward sixty years, to the droughts and devastating famines, to the hopelessness of a people utterly defeated by injustice, towards nature's ultimate retribution after millennia of mistreatment. "There was but one hope, and that was to restore the indigenous forest. I demarcated a wide area and had it gazetted as a forest reserve. Cultivators were used to clear the rubbish and plant young trees between corn and yams so as to leave a potential forest behind them. Thousands of transplants were needed and the department grant for reafforestation was negligible."

Baker had no help in this from his superiors; indeed, the head conservator of forests was not a trained forester, had done nothing to conserve soil, forest, or wildlife, and had never developed sufficient interest to visit Baker in the field.

Baker had been observing the model of nature, its ability to perpetually grow and replenish, as well as the sustainable methods of farming that mimicked natural systems. Groundnuts and peanuts could be grown, for example, between trees that provided a natural form of irrigation. Each morning the plants opened out to form a living mulch, and when they closed at night the soil around them was cool, which resulted in a heavy dew. "It is, in fact, the same principle as the old English dew ponds," observed Baker. "This wonderful plan of Nature will only function when surrounding trees provide relatively cool conditions during the day in the upper air and give off enough moisture to produce a dew fall."

Baker began to envision a form of dryland agriculture that depended on the intercropping of trees, including food and shelter trees, and traditional annual crops. The trees provided a microclimate conducive to the growth of annuals and at the same time protected the soil from erosion. Trees were also a fuel source.

Already Baker had begun to experiment with the production of vast quantities of *Mutarakwa*, the pencil cedar trees. The problem had been seed germination. Both his practical and theoretical training proved useless as it was impossible to germinate the cedar seeds by the usual method, the husks being remarkably tough. So he had first to figure out how nature did the job and noticed that it was done with an intermediary: wood pigeons. When the birds swallow the seeds, their gastric juices partially dissolve the tough husks. Where the pigeons leave their droppings, the cedars grow. The pigeons usually roost in olive trees, so the cedars spring up among the olives. Later, the olive tree enjoys the light shade cast by the cedars.

Following the lesson of nature, Baker soaked the seeds in acid and turned the seeds out on zebra skins. He had his men rub them to loosen their outer coating. The first nursery of seedling boxes, on the platform of the Kikuyu railway station, became a minor tourist attraction. Here were some eighty thousand germinating trees. But with no money, how could they be established?

DANCE OF THE TREES

The only solution was to enlist the support of the people themselves, but farming by axe and fire was traditional among the Kikuyu. He would have to tread carefully. "The tribes would not readily tolerate a white man who asked them to break with their tribal traditions," he observed. "I wanted them to plant trees. I had to have their assistance, particularly as my financial grant for this work was so small. I wanted them to use better systems of farming which would give bigger yields over longer periods and would directly conserve the amount of virgin forest they destroyed each year. The problem was difficult and I almost despaired of finding an answer."

One evening, he sat on his veranda listening to the beat of the drums and watching the young *morans*, or warriors, assembling for a dance:

The lives of these people were closely linked with their tribal dances. From the very womb of their mothers they have known rhythm. It was the N'goma or dance that brought the parents together; they danced through their courting days and danced through the months of early married life, following the various seasons, sometimes by day and sometimes by night, with or without ceremony, dancing for the sheer joy of living. Song and dance is the spice of life among the children of nature. They held ritual dances when the beans were planted. They danced when crops were harvested; for marriages, births and deaths. Each dance was different and had its own form, style and meaning. I sat there, watching the last rays of sun glinting on their spears, marvelling at their shiny bronze bodies, admiring their fine head-wear and proud bearing.

His thoughts went back to the days of the war when he had seen the African Labour Corps unloading the ships at Boulogne and gaily picking up enormous loads to the rhythm of song and dance, "impossible loads that would have taken four of us to lift, let alone carry. I had watched them from my horse boats at all hours of the night and early mornings whenever I was waiting for the tide to serve. It had set me thinking what we spoilt children of western civilization had lost through becoming sophisticated as we develop our self-consciousness. Among the primitive people song and dance is the mobilizing force for action, whether love-making, picking up a load or planting beans."

It was then that the inspiration came to him like a flash. "I shot up from the chair and gripped the veranda rail. I would create a dance for the planting of trees, a ritual ceremony for forest conservation, for better farming, for the battle against the encroaching desert! I hurried into the bungalow and scribbled away at my pad until it was too dark to see anything but the white blur of the paper."

To digress a moment, here we see that Baker had adopted the romantic notion of Africans as 'primitive' 'children of nature,' who had not been 'corrupted' by civilization. The 'noble savage' or 'nature's gentleman' represented humanity's innate goodness, as opposed to the 'spoilt' Western sophisticate. While obviously patronizing and paternalistic, this outdated attitude is perhaps the best that could be expected from an agent of the British Colonial Office in the 1920s. That said, Baker also shows an unexpected appreciation for Kikuyu culture and a desire to foster collaboration rather than force compliance.

Viewed from today, images of dangerous warriors, fair damsels, and colonial meddlers in the following description of the first dance of the trees will seem archaic. But Baker's intention of combining sustainable development with culturally sensitive innovation may rightly be seen as an early application of social forestry practice, a development approach that would emerge in the 1970s.

Baker's first step would be winning popular support for his idea of a dance of the trees, starting with community leaders. He immediately launched a series of talks and discussions with the chiefs of various tribes. He asked them for their advice; he put his plans before them; cajoled, even threatened them with the disastrous ecological consequences of their current practices; and begged them to set up a council of chiefs and elders to discuss the problem within the next few weeks. Baker set off on long lecture tours and used every means at his disposal to capture grassroots support.

"There are many dances," the chiefs said. "You must first enlist the support of the young *morans* or warriors...they in turn will capture the hearts and willing hands of the people. But for the trees! Trees grow without the aid of man. We are not sure that the *morans* will create your dance."

Thongo Thongo was the senior captain of the dances, which the young warriors staged. They went from village to village showing off their prowess. As soon as Baker met Thongo he knew that he would help.

"Thongo," I said, "you have dances for the bean planting and dances for the harvest. Your land needs more trees; your crops will be better, and trees will safeguard your land for your sons. I want you to make a dance of the trees and take your people into the forest where they can plant more trees."

Thongo shook his head doubtfully. "Miti (trees); shauri ya Mungu, Trees are God's business, trees just grow!" "Yes," I replied, "but you are cutting down the mother trees and you do not give God a chance. Here is my idea! This is what I want you to do." I told him that in three weeks time I should hold a big dance at my camp. This was an ideal place, for it was situated at Muguga. All that remained of the forest in that area, which had been cut down and burned, was one sacred Mugumu tree, left to collect the spirits of trees that had been felled.

Talk of mother trees, tree spirits, and helping God may seem quaint in the era of scientific materialism; however, it is instructive to note that recent observations confirm some of the Kikuyu notions about plant communication, which Baker had accepted. For example, University of British Columbia forestry professor and ecologist Suzanne Simard has shown experimentally that trees communicate via fungi, with certain trees functioning as repositories of information—as mother trees.*

As encouragement, Baker offered a prize of a young bullock for the best *moran*. Then the winning warrior would have the right to choose the prettiest girl in the dance, and to her Baker would give a new necklace. These attractions proved irresistible; the young men and women were agog. Each day the drums beat out the story of the great meeting to be held at *Muguga*.

His supervisors in Nairobi heard, as they were bound to do, of these activities and did not entirely approve of his plan; more than one was "actively apprehensive of the dangers of bringing thousands of warriors together in a moment of great emotion."

His greatest support came from a good friend, Bill Lancaster Jenkins, the American consul general. As Baker outlined the scheme to him, he immediately saw its potential. In every possible way, he lent aid and it was entirely fitting that he was with Baker on the afternoon of the great dance, held Sunday, July 22, 1922. His other European guest was Dr. Conviccione, the Italian consul.

The young warriors assembled over a twenty-four-hour period, until there were three thousand of them camped around Baker's bungalow. Further back was the encampment of the visitors, spectators, and hangers on, at least another two thousand men and women. The young men were adding the last touches to their war paint and tossing head plumes. "All morning messages reached me: 'Can we start now?' But to each I said 'Wait!' Bill and I lunched on the bungalow veranda and it was early afternoon before I gave the signal for which they had waited." Baker described the scene in his 1956 book, *Dance of the Trees*:

> *Rank upon rank passed us. The tribal drums beat a slow muffled rhythm. The rays of the sun glittered on their spears and sparkled off the metal decorations of the swaying drums. I caught my*

---

* Peter Wohlleben's book on this topic, *The Hidden Life of Trees, What They Feel, How They Communicate—Discoveries From a Secret World*, which summarizes the science of tree communication via the "Wood Wide Web," became a surprise bestseller in 2015.

*breath at the splendour of the sight and my stomach tightened as
I realized I was responsible for it all. Clan by clan they marched
past, and fell in by the solitary Mugumu tree. With me were the
twelve senior chiefs and a young chief, Josiah Njonjo, who was
to act as my interpreter. I was to speak to them in Ki-Swahili,
and Njonjo would translate my words into Ki-Kikuyu.*

*First the bullock was paraded for their approval and with
it were shown the beads for the prettiest maiden. A chatter of
delight arose at the sight of the sturdy animal and the heavy
necklace brought giggles from the girls. Now I had to speak
to them and I knew the possible consequences of what I was
about to say. "You are here young men of the Kikuyu to listen
to me. You are handsome young men and fine dancers. But do
you know what the Masai say about you? They say you are an
inferior people. They call you the destroyers of the trees!" There
was shocked silence—the Masai were their hereditary enemies. The next few seconds were tense and I could feel almost*

Warriors assemble for the first dance of the trees.

*physically the change that came over them. The smiles faded
from their faces and on every side I saw animosity, hostility.*

*I continued, raising my voice slightly: "The men of the Masai
are right! You cut down the trees and you burn the wood. Your
women have to journey two or three days to collect sticks to
cook your food. You have destroyed the forest." They listened in
sullen silence. All I could hear was the breeze moving through
the lone Mugumu tree. "The white man wants to give you better houses. But for that there must be more wood. The white
man has brought you the gari ya moshi, the train that brings the
good things into your land, and the gari ya moshi eats wood.
You must now take action. You must now be the forest planters, make the tall trees grow once again in your land, to provide
wood for your homes and people....Listen well to my words! I
want volunteers. They will give me a solemn oath to plant and
tend trees through the years. You shall be Watu wa Miti (Men
of the Trees) and the Masai will respect and envy you."*

*The young men were silent. I noticed their knuckles tensed
white around their spears. The few elders around me murmured
"Namwega, namwega—good, good!" The feeling of tension
began to ease and the captains of the N'gomas fell into earnest conversation with their clansmen, and gradually a general
hum of agreement arose. Soon, a few hundred of them stepped
forward and announced that they would be the band of the
Watu wa miti. I picked out fifty and presented them with brass
disks they could wear on their wrists, held in place by goatskin
straps made gay with green and white beads. This was their sign
of fellowship, and I rapidly made it plain that there was great
honour in wearing the brass insignia of Men of the Trees; it was
not lightly to be earned. During my term of office in Kenya, the
discs cost me 250 pounds, which came out of my own pocket.*

*By now the smiles had returned, and it was time for the
dance. The chiefs, with my assent, gave the signal to begin.
Slowly the dance began, their feet stamping rhythmically to
the beat of the drums. They beat faster, louder, and the bronze
bodies swayed. They advanced, retreated, lifted their spears to*

shoulder height and lowered them again. A low murmur came from the watching people. It swelled and faded with the beat of the drum, the drums that had often called them to war. But this was for peace! Drums for the planting of trees! I watched them evolve the dance before me, a dance that in future would take place only when their tree-planting ceremonies had been fulfilled, a peaceful dance to a peaceful drum.

The line broke up and they fell into ranks. From either side the girls came and took up their positions, joining hand in hand in lines and opposite them drew up a rank of men half a dozen paces away. Again the drums sounded and they began to dance. With a tripping movement the girls moved toward the morans and retired with three long steps and a kind of curtsy. Then the morans made their three clear strides and retired in the same fashion. Each movement became faster, until all seemed to be moving at once. At each advance they chanted and were answered with an echoing chant. They were beautifully drilled. It was a great jamboree, three thousand people in step together, with unbroken rhythm.

At a signal from the drum a magical movement took place; the sides facing one way turned and were at right angles to where they had been before, this enormous crowd moving as one. There were many simple variations, but the theme was always the same. This was the first dance of the trees.

To the Italian ambassador, this event was stunning. He said, "Baker, this is marvellous. This is the *Fascista* of Africa. You must meet my friend Mussolini"—a chilling comment from today's vantage. (Of course, this was long before the implications of fascist ideology were generally understood. Baker's Men of the Trees, like his contemporary Baden Powell's Boy Scout movement, would be racially inclusive and international in scope.)

Baker and the American consul were to pick the winners, but it was near impossible. Finally, they decided to award two bullocks. The two delighted warriors now had to choose the two prettiest women, the best dancers. Again they couldn't decide, so two women were chosen and another necklace promised. Now came an unexpected part of the festival. The two men took their bullocks and staged an impromptu rodeo.

The discs became a popular item and were only obtained through difficult trials, adding solemnity of the vows of the Men of the Trees. Later, the Kikuyu evolved a password for use among the members: *Twahamwe*, which, roughly translated, means "pull together." When a young man was admitted to the society he agreed to a three-fold promise: to do one good deed a day—this borrowed from Baden Powell and the Boy Scouts; to plant ten trees each year; and to take care of trees everywhere.

Here was what St. Barbe needed: a willing army of forestry volunteers. Having succeeded in linking tree planting to a cultural norm, the dance, he had engaged youth in this development venture. Each evening, if they couldn't think of any other good deed for the day, the *morans* would come by Baker's bungalow and help with the

The first dance of the trees by the sacred mugumo tree.

planting out of tree seedlings. Before long, about eighty thousand cedars and olives from the stock that had been seeded on the railway platform were planted out in boxes in the first big tree nursery in Kenyan history.

But the way was not entirely clear. On returning from a safari to Tanganyika, Baker was met by Chief Njonjo, who appeared to be in great distress. "'The farm of boxes is broken,' he reported. Their nursery destroyed. It couldn't be. 'Bwana, come and see,' was Njonjo's reply. I borrowed a pony and galloped to the nursery. Where there had been a delightful nursery of trees ready for planting out was a tennis court!"

"Not a trace of the nursery remained, not a box or a seedling, nothing. I turned away, sickened. All that loving care and voluntary service, all those 'good deeds' wasted! How they must have suffered, these young farmers who had given up valuable time to help restore their native forests and to bring back the dew and the rain to water their vegetable crops. At my prompting they had created a fine nursery, only to have it destroyed by an unimaginative government official." They had come up against the stone wall of officialdom.

As Baker thought about how to protest this stupidity, Chief Njonjo arrived, having walked from the station. Together they looked at the tennis court. "You see what happened," Njonjo said quietly. "Now those young men who came to make the nursery have gone to bush and they will never do another thing for love." Baker took this as a challenge. He was suffering with his friend, but carried on with a new idea.

"You have some good land for nurseries on your territory. Now that your men know how to prepare the seed, there is nothing to stop you from having your own nurseries." Chief Njonjo called the men together: "*Baba wa Miti* (Father of the Trees)," as Baker began to be called, "has returned. He says the new white master must have his place to 'knock the rubber about' but we can have our own nursery here on my farm at *Kibichiku*." And they did, but this time they started a nursery of a million trees. Other chiefs vied with Njonjo to have their own nurseries, this time under the control and protection of the Kikuyu themselves.

Such was the African genesis of the Men of the Trees, which grew from this beginning to become an international movement with thousands of members working in 108 countries—arguably the first international environmental non-governmental organization.

SACKED FOR TAKING A BLOW

In the spring of 1923, Baker had been in Kenya for just over two years. He had built a good working knowledge of African forestry through extensive travel, catalogued multiple species, collaborated with English experts on wood utilization, established plans for forest management, and initiated several considerable tree nurseries. More importantly, he had also become a friend to the local people, particularly the Kikuyu. He had learned their language, their customs, and their beliefs, and had begun an important social and economic development program with them, one that respected their culture while promising to improve their economic status.

It was already a common policy of the colonial service to move an administrator or forester to another part of the colony or to another country if he was considered to have become too close and too sympathetic to the local colonized people. Soon Baker sealed his fate. He was accompanying his superior officer on an inspection of the Kikuyus when the officer struck a Kikuyu worker on the face with the butt end of his hunting crop. Baker protested but was ignored. Again, the officer went to hit another man. This time Baker stepped between them, taking the blow to his collarbone. Such behaviour was unheard of. Baker was dismissed from the service and sent packing to England.

This incident would change the course of his life.

Obviously, being sacked by the Colonial Service was hard on the career of a British forester, at least in terms of his ability to earn money—ultimately, it meant he lost some £35,000 in pensions. On the other hand, it forever cemented his relationship with the Kikuyu people, to whom his act was a proof of friendship. And, though his official services were now curtailed, he was free to enter into the arena of non-governmental activity, an opportunity he might otherwise have overlooked.

Even though he was dismissed from service, he was nonetheless honoured with a farewell dinner at Government House, given by the new governor, Sir Robert Coryndon. He then said his goodbyes and set out for home, taking, typically, the most difficult route.

Standing at the railway station in Nairobi were two trains: one heading for Mombasa, the coast, and a ship home; the other heading north to Kisumu, a city on Lake Victoria. The opportunity to see the land of Samuel Baker by returning home via Uganda and the Nile presented itself. He took it, thus stumbling into another adventure.

From Kisumu he travelled by lake steamer to Masindi, the capital of Bunyoro, a kingdom in western Uganda. Baker arrived on what was to be a great day for the country, when it was to be announced that former Omukama (King) Kabalega—who had been exiled to the Seychelles for twenty-four years—would be allowed to return.

King Dohaga in his palace by a portrait of Sir Samuel Baker.

When Kabalega was crowned in 1870, he set out to develop his new kingdom through trade. However, he resisted British attempts to colonize his kingdom, and in 1894 the British declared war on Bunyoro. For five years Kabalega was able to fend off the invasion, but in 1899 he was shot and captured by the British and exiled.

Sir Robert Coryndon, the former governor of Uganda, had arranged the amnesty. The occasion of the arrival of a relative of Sir Samuel Baker to officially announce the return of the old king was auspicious. Samuel and Florence Baker had visited Masindi from 1872–1873 and became Kabalega's first English contacts. However, the Baker expedition was later forced to withdraw because of the ruler's hostility.

The announcement of Kabalega's impending return was made in the parliament of Bunyoro, and Richard Baker sat on the throne of lion and leopard skins by the side of the current ruler, Dohaga, and listened to the speech from the throne. When the important announcement was made a mighty shout went up from the throng surrounding the parliament.

This parliament had actually preceded England's by hundreds of years and "once more it was forcibly brought home to me," noted Baker, "that other countries had no right to enforce their laws and customs upon the ancient civilizations of Africa."

Baker was of the view that African governors, chiefs, royalty, and elders were often truly aristocratic and, in some cases, had what he described as "psychic powers." They were sensitive to the people they met from other countries, especially those claiming to be their superiors, and expected a nobility of mind and deep level of understanding from them. They were often disappointed.

Samuel Baker was one of the few European explorers who had respected Africans and he had received their respect in return. Richard Baker, as his descendent, was presented with many gifts, including a pair of elaborately beaded leopard's claws that were thought to bring good fortune, particularly many children.

Sadly, the return of the king was not to be: Kabalega had died on April 6, 1923, shortly before reaching the borders of the kingdom.

Unknown to Baker, Sir Robert Coryndon was governor general-elect for a proposed three-nation state comprised of Kenya, Tanganyika, and Uganda, and Baker had been put forward as conservator of forests of the projected United East Africa. That idea was abandoned when Coryndon died suddenly in 1925 during the visit of the future King George VI and Queen Elizabeth to Africa.

On the final leg of this journey, Baker traveled briefly down the Nile River on the SS *Samuel Baker* and then the SS *Livingstone*. He then walked one hundred miles from Nimule on the northern border of Uganda to Rejaf in southern Sudan, from there took a paddle steamer to Khartoum, thence to Port Said and home to England.

UNCLE DICK

Upon arriving in London Baker went immediately to Boy Scout headquarters to propose linkages between the Scouts and his 'forest scouts,' the Men of the Trees of Kenya. This proposal was relayed to the BBC's first radio station at Marconi House to be broadcast on the

Baker began his career as a lecturer in England in the 1920s. For the next sixty years, his lectures throughout the world delivered one key message: "Plant trees to save the planet."

weekly Scout Bulletin. However, the announcer could not pronounce the African names so called Baker in to make the broadcast, which Baker claimed was among the first children's radio broadcasts.

The radio studio of the day was simple: sacking on the walls and a microphone on a piece of rubber sitting on a table. Baker swallowed his nervousness and made the announcement, ending with the story of the Men of the Trees mascot, a serval cat called Ching, who could be seen in the London Zoo. The following holiday thousands of children showed up at the zoo to see the now famous cat.

After the short broadcast, Baker was asked to become a regular on a new children's program and for the duration of his stay became 'Uncle Dick' to thousands of British children.

Taking advantage of various connections, Baker was able to initiate a branch of the Men of the Trees in England in 1924. In the same year, he also renewed contact with his family, especially his brother Scott, and travelled to Wiesbaden, Germany, to visit his younger brother Tom, who had married an Austrian. Germany being a leader in forestry, this was also an opportunity to catch up on the latest ideas in his field before returning to England, where trouble was brewing.

CHAPTER THREE

Social Forestry

In 1923, while Baker was back in London, a controversy arose between the white and Indian settlers of Kenya. The Indians, numbering some twenty-two thousand, were claiming equality with the British, who numbered only five thousand. A delegation of British settlers came to England to put the question to the government and asked Baker to approach the leader of the opposition, Ramsey MacDonald. Baker did approach him, but on behalf of the Africans who hadn't been considered in the equation.

He invited MacDonald to lunch. Instead, he was asked to join MacDonald and the shadow cabinet in the House of Commons. Baker started out the meeting by poking fun at the future prime minister. "Mr. MacDonald, I've often wondered why you represent Labour—I wouldn't think you've ever done a day's hard labour in your life!"

MacDonald looked at Baker curiously. Baker recounted the story of Tolstoy's heaven, where St. Peter welcomed those with work-worn hands into paradise; those with soft hands would be sent back "to do a job of work." MacDonald held out his beautiful, artistic hands for inspection. Baker slapped them. MacDonald called to his associates, "Here's a man who says I won't get into heaven."

Baker was invited to give evidence before a special Labour committee hearing presided over by Josiah Wedgewood, an authority on East Africa. Lal Bahadur Shastri, then a student at Cambridge and later prime minister of India, and Annie Besant, president of the Theosophical Society, represented the Indians. Shastri captured the committee's imagination with his descriptions of Kenyan conditions. Things looked to be going in favour of the Indian point of view when Baker asked if he might ask a question.

"Has Mr. Shastri ever been to Kenya?" The answer was no. Ultimately, the whole thing was settled along the lines Baker suggested. "I said that we should not turn over the Indigenous African people to anybody, because the British were trustees for the Africans and we must fulfill our trust and not betray them (the Africans) to the Indians or the Europeans."

SUSTAINABLE YIELD IN NIGERIA

Ribbing aside, Baker made a good impression and in 1924, when MacDonald became prime minister, Baker's dismissal was revoked and he was appointed assistant conservator of forests in Nigeria. As Baker recalled, "In this post I was fortunate to be responsible for the last best forest in tropical Africa. My territory was about the same size as the whole of France and ranged from the Rain Forest through the Orchard Bush to the Savannah types."

Baker was first stationed in Benin. He returned to Africa with his previous experience in Kenya under his belt, as well as further study and the support of the British Men of the Trees, formed while Baker was home—but more on that later.

He was now part of an international movement. More than ever, he was motivated by a sense of mission, that his was a special, unique, and visionary work. He had a growing awareness of the emerging science of ecology on the one hand, and the emerging ecological crisis on the other.

The field of ecology was new in the 1920s. It had developed largely within forestry, but was not yet incorporated into forestry practice. In fact, Baker's official role as forest 'conservator' in Kenya had little to do with ecological management. It had merely been to control felling by enforcing a minimum girth limit, to collect stumpage fees, and to divide the proceeds among the chiefs and the colonial department.

The forests were extremely valuable, conservation an afterthought. Baker was issuing felling permits for up to £25,000 a month, and single logs of rare mahoganies could fetch up to £2,000 in the Liverpool timber auctions—and remember, these are 1920s values. Yet little thought was given to the sustainability of this valuable resource.

Baker's efforts to advocate for forestry practice on a sustained yield basis met with opposition. The local chiefs usually responded with the argument heard in Kenya: growing trees was God's business; trees grow by themselves, without the interference of man. In fact, this was the general attitude of people everywhere. Baker describes the situation in his 1944 publication, *I Planted Trees,* providing an

Squaring a mahogany log to economize on shipping.

early articulation of the concept of 'sustainable development,' a term first used in 1980 by the International Union for the Conservation of Nature:

> *The management of a very large part of the world's area is still limited to a mere harvesting of existing timber supplies, and may be likened to the depleting of a coal mine. It is mere exploitation which overlooks the valuable characteristics of wood, namely, that it can, under proper conditions, be renewed. The only kind of forest management worthy of the name is concerned with the conservation and continuous utilization of the forest, hence the study of the science of forestry has become essential.*
>
> *We have been living in a fool's paradise too long. Vast areas that once maintained apparently inexhaustible supplies of virgin timber have been laid waste, and this destruction grows apace with the improvement of devices for logging, transportation and milling, backed by the enormous capital that is invested in them. In many instances such powerful technical and commercial organizations are wrongly oriented toward large-scale exploitation, for although it may bring immediate profit to the individual investors, it is anti-social, for in all too short a time it may be the means of exterminating whole populations.*

Given the universality of ecology's principles, Baker could now make use of his experience from Europe and Kenya, with appropriate modifications for local conditions. His study of the experiences of the Indian Forest Service was even more relevant. The first task was to take the principles of scientific forestry and launch silviculture experiments so that he might arrive at an appropriate forestry approach for Nigeria.

> *In recording the experiments it required meticulous observation and intimate knowledge, not only of the various species of trees of which the forest was composed, but also of the relation of trees to each other and their response to cultural operations.*

My work involved not only the task of increasing the timber yield, but improving the quality of the forest products and at the same time improving the soil. It was my aim to maintain a tree cover on these soils, which in consequence of their physical characteristics, could only be used for forests. It was important to devise ways and means of guaranteeing a well-balanced natural economy in respect to climate and water supply. I felt instinctively that the practical solution to my task lay in carefully maintaining the original balance of Nature while planning to harvest its products in such a way that the perfect balance might be maintained. I had no figures on which to base my calculations and had to start from scratch.

One of the most fascinating branches of my study was in the sphere of forest ecology—that is, the science of forest sites—which rests on soil science and meteorology together with their basic relations. It necessitates the investigation of all aspects of the relation between the physiological, mechanical and biological peculiarities of the site, soil, and ground space, and the growth of the forest. Its extraordinary difficulty in comparison with many other technical fields stimulated my endeavours, and I was able to arrive at conclusions which influenced the silvicultural systems which I eventually adapted to the requirements of the forests.

It is not enough for the forester to be a botanist or a wood technologist, or even to be familiar with plant and tree migrations and ecology. The forester must be a silviculturalist. That is to say, he must understand the special complexity of the biologic entity called "the forest" which by itself is a living organism comprised of other complicated living organisms; plants and animals as well as trees. Among other things silviculture deals with the nature of tree stands, that is, the biology of the forest. It is an applied science in the truest sense. In silviculture the biology of the individual tree is substituted for the biology of the forest types, for the tree stand is not merely the sum of the individual tree species comprising it, but an organic whole in which all other organisms of the forest also belong.

These were forests of mahoganies, the trees which were the dominant trees and those considered the most valuable economically. Not pure stands of course but a combination of species. Each of the mahoganies is surrounded by other trees, including the important family of legumes, the soil improvers. These I have observed to be good nurse trees for the mahoganies. The more important species of mahogany require the services of a succession of nurse trees throughout their life to bring them to perfection. Some of these provide just sufficient competition to coax the young saplings upward. Others do their work in secret under the surface of the soil, interlacing the roots, a sort of symbiosis, like the mycelium, which starts as an independent web-like growth, surrounds the sheath of the plant rootlets and prepares food that can be assimilated by the growing trees.

Baker was able to obtain a good impression of the life of the forest at the ground and lower levels where the competition for space, light and nutrients takes place. Much more difficult was an understanding of life in the treetops. When first in Benin he attempted to find a high vantage point from which he could observe the forest's canopy, but never found one. Later, when stationed at Sapoba, with the help of the local forest dwellers, he built a sturdy platform in the treetops.

It was like another world to recognize the crowns of trees I had known so well on the ground. How beautiful the whole scene was with tiny birds fluttering from flower to flower, butterflies camouflaged against their feathered enemies! I found myself wondering if the baby mahoganies I had entered on the charts of my quadrats, would ever reach these exalted places. Here the love life of the trees takes place with the tender ministrations of the birds, bees, and gentle breeze. So little is really known of the romantic world of the tree tops where the dance of life goes on, fertilization of flowers takes place, and seeds are formed and ripened in the sun's heat.

Perhaps the major problem Baker faced as a conservationist was the fact that, as the desirable mahoganies were being felled, the secondary species were becoming dominant. A large part of his silvicultural plan then involved finding uses for the secondary species so that they too could be harvested.

In his first memo to the director of forests he applied for two additional forestry workers to supervise harvests, making the case for the economic benefits of more careful management based on sustained yield. The second request was for permission to spend half the revenues he obtained from felling permits to replant and regenerate cut-over areas. Again, he met with the twisted rationale of officialdom: there was no point in increasing spending on reforestation as there weren't sufficient staff to supervise the existing work. Catch 22.

Baker kept pushing the case for sustained yield management and eventually met with success, but in the meantime he had to pursue conservation with a budget of just £100 per year. The problem of forest management and experimentation without support staff had to be tackled again. And again, he turned to local people for help.

I was fortunate to be able to obtain the cooperation of some headmen who were able to explain to their followers enough to enlist volunteers. These were all bushmen, illiterate forest-dwellers, true, but with intuition of a rare order seldom met with among more sophisticated peoples. Their intellects are not cluttered with the lumber of so-called "civilization", and in a remarkably short time they clearly adapted themselves to various tasks which I set them, showing a surprising intelligence and discernment with a sympathetic understanding of what was required.

What was required, above all, was a considerable army of workers. Each individual would have to be trained in one or more silvicultural observations and, most important, would have to be instilled with Baker's enthusiasm. "One of the most encouraging experiences in my forestry work in Africa was the quick response of the Indigenous tribesmen to any measure I was able to introduce with a view to benefitting their forests. In every instance I had first to learn before I could understand the best ways and means of procuring the response that was necessary to stem the tide of forest destruction."

A BRIEF IDYLL IN EUROPE

With these experiments underway, St. Barbe made a collection of all secondary species, and on his leave, returned to England to study their potential at Cambridge—also with a mind to completing a doctoral thesis. He also did further research at the Imperial Forestry Institute at Oxford.

But the lustre of the old school had faded. In comparison with the life and challenges of Africa, the university seemed to be "dead alive." Could these old men be the same brilliant lecturers he had listened to so intently?

On this trip home, he also attended the First World Forestry Congress in Italy. He had been instrumental in bringing it together by collaborating with the Italian ambassador to Kenya, who had

Cambridge School of Forestry class reunion, Baker seated second from left.

attended the first dance of the trees. In subsequent trips to Italy, Baker had launched a local branch of Men of the Trees in Genoa and built a network of contacts. The congress was a success, the first in a series that Baker attended on a regular basis.

While in Rome, Baker had a personal audience with Pope Pius XI. This came about because Baker had agreed to supply the wood for a church in Benin City and it was customary for the Pope to meet anyone who had built a church. At the end of the audience, the Pope gave Baker his blessing. Beside Baker was a hearty American Catholic who slapped the Pope on the back and said, "God bless you, Pope!"

A few years later Baker's book, *The Brotherhood of the Trees*, was put on the *Index Librorum Prohibitorum*, a list of books banned by the Catholic Church, by an overzealous Indian cardinal who suspected the book was intended to advocate secret societies. Baker was able to take advantage of having met the Pope to explain the true nature of the Men of the Trees to a church official. Hearing this story, the Pope was amused and had the matter investigated. Baker claimed to be the first man to have his book taken off the Index in his own lifetime. (I could find no evidence that the book was either on or off this notorious list.)

At the end of his leave, he embarked again for Nigeria with several guests, "two splendid Light Sussex birds with four hens apiece" that he had more or less smuggled aboard. They were intended as gifts for the king of Benin, the thought being that they might improve the native strains of poultry, not to mention relations with the local government.

The presentation cock was not the success that I had hoped that it might have been, for three days before my arrival the King of Benin had been warned by the head juju man that he would soon see a white cock and that he would die. That explained why, instead of greeting me with his usual cordiality, the dark skin of his cheeks turned to a pale greenish tint at the sight of the lusty bird. I was ignorant of the cause of my cold reception until the court interpreter whispered his story, upon which I pointed out with special pride how well marked and how many black feathers there were about that bird.

As he described the productivity of the English birds, the king's interest gradually overcame his fear and the gift was accepted despite the *juju* man.

Back in the forest, it was with great interest that Baker inspected the progress of the various silvicultural management systems he had initiated. "In that country trees grow apace, and during the few months that I had been away it seemed that there had been phenomenal growth. My lads, too, gave me the best of welcomes, and I listened at length to the various palavers and their family happenings."

A tense audience with the king of Benin.

IGI OKA

This was to be Baker's last tour of service on the west coast of Africa and it was full of adventure. Besides supervising work at the experimental station, he had a considerable area of forest to administer. Felling was controlled by girth limit and each log was to be stamped with a distinctive crown. There were one hundred different concessions ranging from nine to two hundred square miles. The exploitation by British firms was heavy, but the implementation of good management helped to alleviate stress on the forest.

More serious was the clearing by Indigenous farmers; their networks of small tracts already honeycombed the forest, eliminating valuable mahogany timbers worth millions of pounds. When the staple crops of yams depleted the soil, the farmer moved to a virgin area and the process began again. Attempts were made to direct the new farms to areas where the trees were less valuable, but the steadily increasing population of the southern provinces created demand for ever more land.

The solution Baker devised and implemented on a small scale was a progressive development model for the whole of equatorial Africa and suitable in various forms for a variety of climate and soil types. He called it *Igi Oka*, Tree Farms, a term easily translated into several dialects, that clearly suggested what it is. Baker described the scheme in *I Planted Trees*:

> *Fifty-two of my forest workers needed land in which to grow their crops, so instead of allowing them to select their own sites at haphazard wherever they might be inclined in the virgin forest, I persuaded them to a site adjoining the young plantations. We chose an area of twenty-six acres of inferior bush which in years gone by had been cultivated. This they cleared in their spare time and we divided it into half-acre plots, oil palms being planted first to make the boundaries of each allotment. In between their food crops they planted an economic selection of the most valuable trees available in the nurseries.... In among the mahoganies, as nurse trees, they planted soil*

improvers which also provide useful timbers. Besides these we also planted African walnut and Obeche for plywood.

In addition to these indigenous trees we experimented with Burma teak. I used to get the Forestry Department of Burma to supply us with quantities of seed, which was shipped to Lagos. For ground cover we planted Cassia siamea, a welcome exotic. All these were planted by the forest cultivators in between their food crops at a distance of six feet by twelve feet. When I inspected their allotments at the end of the season there were on the average 300 trees flourishing, and one allotment had 366.

Among the farm crops grown were corn, yams, gourds, okra, peppers, iklogie, beans and ground-nuts, the latter one of the best nitrogenous crops and great soil-improvers. Each year a new farm is allotted to successful cultivators, so that in time they will create considerable areas of new forest for the growing benefit of their country. I should add that as an incentive to obtain the best results I gave a small bonus to those farmers who succeeded in establishing not less than 500 trees to the acre. That number is sufficient to take possession of the land and provide the requisite silvicultural conditions to produce the best timber.

This approach—agroforestry by today's definition—provided a simple way to protect the land from soil erosion and ensure sustainability of production. It ensured agricultural production while at the same time providing timber and fuel, thus enriching the economy and community perpetually.

"It is not a measure that can be enforced by law," wrote Baker, "but requires the voluntary cooperation of the people. I believe it should be introduced by farmers of their own race who should be trained cultivators and act as distributors of the young trees raised in local nurseries."

Such methods were even more valuable in the drier northern areas of Nigeria, the destination of Baker's next and most exciting expedition to date. He trekked north with the purpose of demarcating a new forest reserve for the department.

It is a change after the monotony of the rain forest to escape for a while into the country where at least you can get a view....The forests around Sapoba used to cast an uncanny spell on those who live there too long. Apart from being extremely unhealthy and full of malarial swamps, in these parts there seems to be a miasma rising from the soil. There had been nights in Benin when I sat on the veranda of my bungalow with a feeling of tenseness, as if something were going to happen. On such nights the wind drops to a mere whisper and the forest sounds are silenced, while the leaves stand listlessly on the trees.

At Akure on the trek north, Sergeant-Major Belo Akure, a war hero who would act as guide and interpreter, joined him. All the territories were under 'native' administration, so it was the local chiefs Baker had to convince to support the forest conservation plan. All attempts of the kind had failed in the past. The chiefs would simply

Baker in a palaver on forest management with a village headman, both men assuming a relaxed pose.

say: "We will not reserve the land. Our forefathers made no reserves, therefore we will not." When Baker encountered the same argument, he argued with equal vigour. "But," the chiefs argued in turn, "for six generations the forest has remained much the same. Therefore, why should protective measures be taken?"

This was not true as there was little high forest left. In the end, Baker persuaded the chiefs that it was indeed in their own interests to preserve one hundred square miles of forest, despite the rather precise regulations. Old farming rights would have to be forfeited and the chiefs were tough negotiators, determined to keep anything they could and reluctant to give up anything. The negotiations required continuous palavers, and in the course of a few weeks they had to convince dozens of chiefs and hundreds of headmen and followers.

At night he would put up in a rest house built with mud and roofed with palm leaves or grass. He obtained eggs and yams to eat: "I used to have yam cakes for breakfast, yam mashed for lunch, yam cakes for dinner, and for a sweet, pancakes or banana fritters."

The greater part of the trekking was on foot but a pushbike could be ridden even along the narrowest trails, though it had to be carried in the rough spots and across rivers. Baker travelled with the aid of a compass, the length of his trips limited to the capacity of the trekkers hauling the loads.

It is hard to imagine what the carriers thought of Baker bringing along a gramophone, but the device was a great source of amusement to the local folk, an effective icebreaker. He had brought recordings of old English nursery rhymes.

These I found the most popular. One evening a native dance was given in my honour and I returned the complement by inviting the entire population of the village to my rest house for a gramophone concert. I, with my interpreter Igabon, translated the words for their benefit. One of these was "The Farmer in the Dell." We translated it into Hausa, and everyone sang it to the accompaniment of the gramophone. When I put on a jazz tune they suddenly became very serious, so I did not play it any more but gave them some more nursery rhymes. "Jack and Jill" caused great merriment; this we translated, and when it came to the part about "Jack fell down and broke his crown, and Jill came tumbling after," they just laughed and laughed and laughed.

In the next village, he was greeted with an enormous blast of trumpets from the chief's court band. The noise was almost deafening. One of the instruments played was like bagpipes, but had no bag—the player managed to retain sufficient wind in his puffed-out cheeks. Baker spoke of his pleasure to be there and then described Scotland's bagpipes, wishing that he had brought a highland piper with him. "He would have been a valuable asset to the expedition. I concluded my speech with an invitation to the chief and his headman and band to listen to a gramophone concert. What pleased them most of all was the imitation of bleating sheep in the nursery rhyme, Little Bo-Peep. I ventured one jazz record, which called forth the oft repeated comment, 'Sweet, extremely sweet.'"

During this tour he gave as many as 120 talks on forest conservation, sometimes to the older boys at government and mission schools, but usually to chiefs and headmen.

One of the most urgent problems he identified on this trip was the practice of nomadic farming, which contributed to desertification. The northern people were gradually drifting south and southwest themselves, as if pushed by the oncoming desert, until they met the stronger coastal tribes and were stopped. Without any new land to work, they often sat down, as if preparing to die out. Baker believed that he was witnessing some form of large-scale racial suicide. He heard stories of travellers who passed through tribes where women had refused to bear children or chiefs had absolutely forbidden marriage. "So pronounced was the lack of will to live, that many tribes had to be compelled by the French authorities to grow enough food to keep themselves alive, and the art of pottery and the making of agricultural implements have quite died out."

The French, who Baker admired so much for their forestry at home, seemed incapable of dealing with forestry in their African colonies. Recalling this situation some years later, he said, "In French

Equatorial Africa, I am informed, the population has sunk from 20 million in 1911 to something less than five million in 30 years—largely as a result of forest destruction."

EDUCATION OR CATASTROPHE?

What Baker was observing in northern Nigeria would eventually transform the whole north of the continent. Some sixty years later, northern Africa would be plagued by widespread droughts, accelerated desertification, famine, and serious shortages of fuel wood and water—an all-out socioecological crisis. Economic conditions continued to deteriorate. Had Baker's plans to mobilize the Indigenous population in sustainable tree farming been implemented on a broad scale, we might have witnessed an entirely different outcome.

The question was how to promote African development without introducing more of the worst of European civilization. Baker's vision revolved around forestry, of course. While he was not the kind of conservationist that believed in the preservation of nature to the exclusion of all economic activity, he recognized the connection between economics and ecological permanence. Baker's notion of 'profitableness' took on a new dimension:

> It cannot be too strongly emphasised that the degree of rationalization even in forestry is determined by what is profitable—that is, by economic factors. 'Profitableness' as I use it here is considered from the point of view, not only of the individual, but the society and, of course, the fertility of the land, which is the very basis of human existence. The rhythm of growth must be manifested by approximating the conditions found in the natural forest—that combination of tree species which by natural selection has survived to adapt itself to its surroundings through the centuries.
>
> Good forestry is not merely good management for perpetual timber production, it respects the "purpose of forests." In many parts of Africa forests are of primary importance in checking the destructive forces of Nature, such as violent winds which

cause the soil and sand and even stones to shift and drift. If created with knowledge and skill, the forest may not only conserve moisture and regulate stream flow, but actually increase the amount of precipitation in their vicinity. The established and correct practice of forestry in sparsely populated areas may be the means of reconditioning the land and saving whole populations from racial suicide.

In Baker's view, the forest not only provides forest products, it protects the primary resources of soil, water, and air, and affects climate, all of which help to build communities on a solid footing. And, for Baker, forestry was the means of reclaiming lost land.

Baker saw his experiments in Nigeria with forest ecology and management, but also with human ecology and social-economic organization, as the hope for Africa:

It remains for young Africa to turn the tide of destruction and, by means which are now at the disposal of all, to reclaim their paradise so nearly lost. It may be that some of my young African friends may think that I am exaggerating the evil consequences of old methods of nomadic farming. If they are living in the Southern Provinces of Nigeria they are fortunate, for there is still forest cover and in consequence an ample rainfall. But away to the north, even on the southern borders of the Northern Provinces, in many places the orchard bush is giving way to the savannah type, and still further north rainfall is insufficient to maintain tree growth apart from stunted thorns and a few inferior species.

The old French Equatorial Africa has already become a graveyard for dying races, resulting to a great extent from thoughtless forest destruction by past generations of shifting cultivators. In many of these parts the few poor tribesmen that still remain are constantly being pushed south by the drifting sands of the desert which is the heritage of past forest destruction. Let my young African friends take warning and co-operate in the task of stemming the tide of oncoming desert. No amount of talk,

*politics or legislation will remedy the dire plight of those who
have been caught in a wedge of the desert. It needs a great army
of foresters, devoted men fired with the ideal of "service before
self," men who through serious application to the work in hand
have equipped themselves for the field of their labours backed
by the knowledge that science can offer them.*

In Nigeria, Baker's sense of mission expanded exponentially. He
seemed to have an intuition that, coupled with his scientific training,
resulted in an almost prophetic capacity. Only with the advantage of
time can we begin to see the accuracy of his sense of the two paths
open to humanity—one of ecological intelligence and one of ecological suicide. As he often put it, quoting H.G. Wells: "Civilization is a
race between education and catastrophe."

He could see where Africa was heading, and we can now see he
was right. His sense of ecological relationships was far in advance of
his time. His recognition of the value of trees and the wider purpose
of the rainforest presaged what is only now accepted by science: that
biotic systems affect climate, with rainforests tempering the atmosphere, acting like a planetary lung, cooling the air, regulating carbon
dioxide and humidity, and reducing albedo.* It is only the destruction
of the rainforests that is finally awakening us to the understanding
Baker had already developed in the 1920s.

At this point in his service in Nigeria, he began to see himself as a
kind of global tree missionary with a mission to educate the world to
save itself from catastrophe. Africa was a microcosm: the world was
becoming a desert, only tree cover could hold and reverse the trend,
and it was his job to organize this global campaign. "Forestry for me
is not so much a profession as a calling. It demands sacrifices, and
nobody should live by it who is not prepared to die for it."

Baker began to envision a coordinated approach to development, centred on forestry but involving all aspects of the economic
life of Africa: crafts, agriculture, and the like. His vision, if rather
romantic and paternalistic, does presage contemporary movements

---

* Light reflected by the land surface.

for fair trade and eco- and cultural tourism, and even development approaches like the Millennium Villages Project.

I wished I could start a co-operative society among them. We must not try to impose worn-out methods in our African colonies. I learned of one well-known business concern that has lost something in the neighbourhood of 2,000,000 pounds sterling, solely because, in my opinion, it was trying to introduce a form of wage slavery, which the African native would not accept. I should like to substitute co-operation for the wage system, rather on the lines of the first Men of the Trees...this indeed might form the basis of an African co-operative movement, and follow on from afforestation to food production and the development of handcrafts. Many of the tropical and sub-tropical products would find ready sale in the home market. Labour would readily be derived from African pupils in co-operative schools of forestry and farming. The pupils would all be Men of the Trees, having first been initiated into the order by the usual ceremony. In return for their work, they would be provided with food, plus a small number of tokens per month which they could bank or exchange for extra luxuries of life if they so desired at our local depot or stores. At the close of each season when the books were made up, they, in company with those who had invested in the money for the establishment of the centre, they would share in the profits made from their labours. The association might also provide for the organization of centres where native tribes, under their own chiefs and our resident representatives, would be formed into groups of workers who would cultivate small holdings in their own tribal land of their own free will, and would be allowed to dispose of their crops to our local resident, who would ship them against instructions from London headquarters. In London there would be a corresponding headquarters with a co-operative depot to deal with the disposal of shipments and products received from our colonial centres, to purchase stores and ship them to our agents abroad, provide a centre in London at which our members in London would be able to obtain the

*best domestic supplies, such as coffee, tea, cocoa, nuts and sugar
from our own plantations, on the best terms.*

*I visualize a travel service for our members who wished to
visit outlying stations; permanent camps would be available
and provide quarters and servants....Subscribers to the Men of
the Trees at home would be given the opportunity of becoming shareholders in the trading branch of the organization on
the most favourable terms....This business side of the society
would be in a position to render service to associates in a hundred different ways. At the same time it would give them an
opportunity of rendering a practical contribution to the development of the African peoples on sound lines.*

*It should continually be borne in mind that the primary duty
of the Men of the Trees in Africa is to protect their native woodlands and ensure that whenever a tree is cut down or destroyed
a new one is planted in its place. This idea is sufficiently valuable in itself, but beneath it [lies] the foundation of a much
wider ideal. This is but a starting point for the introduction of
improved methods of agriculture and for the substitution of
fixed settlements and the introduction of crop rotation to take
the place of the old nomadic farming.*

*With the introduction of improved methods of agriculture,
living in fixed localities will become possible. Village life would
soon spring up around our co-operative farms and conditions
would become better suited to modern requirements.*

BABA WA MITI

On returning from the expedition to the north he received a letter
from one of his forest guides in East Africa, suggesting that he return
there, at least to visit. The Men of the Trees were continuing to meet
but were wondering where he was. They called him *Baba wa miti*,
Father or Master of the Trees. The guide had told the scouts that he
would be arriving in five months, a neat psychic trick since Baker
was indeed planning to spend his next leave in East Africa, but had
only thought about it and had not written to inform his friends.

During one of his leaves in this period of his African service, Baker had had the opportunity to visit South Africa and explore many of its forests. Now he began to make major plans for what would be the first trans-African automobile trip: visas from various colonial powers were obtained, a route mapped, and petrol dumps arranged. His arrival would coincide with a royal visit; he hoped to acquaint the British royal family with the Men of the Trees, thus enabling the work to take a leap forward. At the last minute, however, his leave was cancelled and he was told to acquaint a newly arrived forester with his work, and then to move to open a new station in another part of the colony.

Baker held to his philosophy of divine providence and did as he was told. When he arrived at the new station, he was surprised to find that the tribesmen ran away from him and it was some time before he could overcome their fear. Just as they were starting to get on well and had begun the planting of a nursery, the big rains broke. His hut sat in a dried-up creek bed and was flooded. He woke up to find water up to his camp bed and himself with a wicked fever. Pulling an overcoat over his pyjamas, he got in the car and drove 120 miles to Lagos with a temperature of 105˚. "The drive must have done me good, because when my temperature was taken it had dropped to 103 degrees," he noted.

Seriously ill, he was sent home to Britain on the next boat—to die, he thought. Three days out of Lagos there is a place known as 'The Graveyard,' where the temperature suddenly drops several degrees and where many are buried at sea. Baker, however, would not find his final resting place in this Graveyard. Again he was spared.

As soon as he arrived in London, he went to the Colonial Office, where he surprised the clerks, who from all reports expected him to die. Baker reported that he was ready to go back to work. If and when a position opened in a more congenial climate, the office replied, he would be reappointed. In fact, he never was. He was destined to move far beyond the confines of colonial service, and his next adventure would pave the way.

CHAPTER FOUR

Becoming Man of the Trees

IN PALESTINE

It was 1929. Baker was resting in Norway with the family of Lord Salvesen, president of the Royal Geographical Society, when he received a message from Sir John Chancellor, the former governor of Rhodesia and high commissioner-designate for Palestine. Chancellor had been speaking to a meeting of the society in Edinburgh about a recent trip to Kenya and the significant efforts to plant trees at Muguga, which he had discovered were the work of the Men of the Trees. Salvesen mentioned that Baker was staying with his family in Norway. Sir John asked if he would pass on a message; he wanted to talk to this planter of trees.

Within a few days they were sharing breakfast in London. Sir John described his observations in Kenya. He was impressed with what had been achieved there in forestry through the voluntary coopera-tion of the people. Sir John asked the head of the forestry service in Kenya what his budget for replanting was and was surprised to learn that it was £300. "You have planted a great number of trees on a mere £300!" "Oh," he was told, "we've got our natives well trained, you know." Baker laughed and filled in a few details, describing all that is involved in social forestry.

Chancellor asked Baker to go to Palestine. He had in mind that he might bring together the warring religious factions if he could convince them all to do something useful for their common land, such as tree planting. The idea appealed to Baker enormously. "Not only had it been my lifelong wish to see all men working together in harmony, but there could be few parts of the world that needed care of this sort more than the Holy Land."

Baker decided at once to accept the offer, but it was not an offer of work, only of voluntary service. Not being classed a rich man, he was out of work now and certainly had no money for travelling about. He put this to Sir John, who said that Baker had merely to get to Palestine and he would look after the rest. As always, Baker found a way: through the kindness of Lord Salvesen, who operated a shipping company, he was taken as a passenger on a cargo ship as far as Marseille and then on to Port Said. Aboard ship he had the opportunity to brush up his Arabic.

Arriving in Kantara in the early months of 1929, he was given an official reception and found a railway carriage reserved for him. He travelled to Jerusalem overnight and lunched with Sir John, who invited him to live at Government House for the duration of his stay in the country. They discussed their shared vision of re-clothing this land with trees—and the history that had made a near desert of the 'land of milk and honey.' It was a history of devastation by successive invasions over several millennia. The Romans had destroyed the forests around Jerusalem after the time of Christ; during the Crusades the Turks had taxed the olive trees, and to avoid taxation the people had burned them; and during the First World War, the trees were sacrificed for fuel. Add to this the unsustainable farming and forestry practices—plus grazing pressures over multiple centuries—and the destruction was near complete.

During the Palestine campaign in the First World War, General Allenby, the British conqueror of the Turks, had begun a program of tree planting to offset the destruction, but it had not been actively pursued. Chancellor hoped to change that, but felt the main obstacle was religious sectarianism. The hope was to somehow bring together the warring sects at a meeting to launch a Palestinian branch of the Men of the Trees. This was Baker's task, and no small amount of ingenuity and bluff would be required to pull it off. He was given a date for the meeting three weeks hence. At dinner that night he would be given an introduction to the grandees of Jerusalem.

Baker had another interest in visiting the Holy Land. He had developed a deep interest in the then little-known Bahá'í movement and hoped to personally meet its leader at the Bahá'í World Centre on Mount Carmel in Haifa. Before he began his 'diplomatic assignment,' he asked permission to visit Shoghi Effendi. The commissioner offered his car and driver, and Baker made a flying trip to Haifa.

It was on the death of his grandfather, 'Abdu'l-Bahá, in 1921, that Shoghi Effendi became Guardian of the Bahá'í Faith, but it was not until March 1929 that I had first had the great privilege of meeting him in person, although he had generously written to me about the time I was elected to serve on the National Spiritual Assembly of England. He had sent me an inscribed copy of The Dawnbreakers, *Nabil's narrative, translated by himself from the Persian.* The Dawnbreakers *soon became my most treasured possession, and I would read it again and again, and each time capture the thrill that must come with the discovery of a New Manifestation.* *

The Guardian welcomed St. Barbe at his home, the house of 'Abdu'l-Bahá, in the Persian colony on Mount Carmel, opening the front door to him before he had a chance to ring the bell. Together they visited the gardens which the Guardian was laying out around the Shrine of the Báb, which in the future would transform Carmel into the most beautiful place in that land. (Eventually, the Bahá'í sites and gardens in Haifa and Akka would be greatly expanded,

---

* Baker must have juggled events in his memory, as this book was first published in English in 1932. Also, there is no record of Baker ever being elected to the National Assembly of England, the governing body of the Bahá'ís in that country.

becoming among the most beautiful built environments in the world and a UN World Heritage Site. On occasion, Baker would be consulted on tree planting.)

Together, they reflected on the religious and historical significance of the region as they looked out from Carmel towards Akka across the Bay of Haifa. They thought of the prophetic life of Elijah, whose famous cave was located on Mount Carmel, and of Isaiah, who spoke of that mountain's significance in the end times; of the Crusades and the armies of Napoleon, which attacked the fortress city of Akka, one of the oldest human settlements still in existence; of the life of Bahá'u'lláh, confined in the nearby fortress of Akka, an Ottoman penal colony. St. Barbe recalled the thirty-fifth chapter of Isaiah, which envisioned a peaceable earth of the future: "The desert shall rejoice and blossom as a rose. It shall blossom abundantly, and rejoice even with joy and singing; the glory of Lebanon shall be given unto it, the excellency of Carmel and Sharon, they shall see the glory of the Lord, and the excellence of our God."

He explained his mission to Shoghi Effendi and the plan to bring together the religious factions in Palestine to plant trees. The Guardian produced an envelope that contained his life-membership fee for the Men of the Trees and promised to do much more, assuring him that he would indeed succeed in his mission and offering every encouragement. Baker left for Jerusalem, his first membership in hand before the Palestinian branch of the society had even come into being.

In retrospect this, I find, was the greatest moment of my life. I became charged with his vitality and was at once captivated by his personal charm and deep sincerity. Time was pressing; he gave me his blessing and I returned to Jerusalem inspired and feeling fit to cope with any situation that might arise.... In retrospect, my life was shaped from the moment that the Guardian expressed his confidence in me, by not only giving me his blessing but his practical support by graciously becoming a life member of the Men of the Trees.

This was the beginning of a long and fruitful collaboration between Baker and Shoghi Effendi, who sent Baker no fewer than thirty personal letters over the course of that span of years.

MEETING THE GRANDEES

That very evening Baker was introduced to many of the city's leading figures and the next day called in turn upon the grand mufti, His Eminence the president of the Supreme Moslem Council, who represented the major Arab landowners; His Worship the mayor of Jerusalem; His Beatitude the Latin patriarch, who represented the monasteries that had already done much valuable planting around those buildings; the bishop of Jerusalem and the Near East; the chancellor of the Hebrew University; the Greek Orthodox patriarch; and Zionist leaders representing the Jewish settlers. Each was given an invitation and each agreed to meet with the high commissioner and himself in three weeks time to discuss replanting the land. None was told that the other religious leaders would be present.

Next, Baker went to the heads of government departments and educational institutions, including the chief forest officer, twenty of whom promised to act on an executive committee. He then prepared an agenda and wrote his speech, giving these to the printers for publication, including translation into Arabic and Hebrew, in time for the gathering at the American colony.

This left Baker with three weeks to explore the country and to indulge his new hobby, filmmaking. His first subject was the archaeological expedition of Sir Flinders Petrie, who was unearthing the history of Palestine in "the uttermost cities of Judah." Unbeknownst to Sir Flinders, who hated the idea of having his work filmed, his secretary had Baker film from behind a blind. "During my three weeks at Tel Farah I slept on a camp bed in the 'skullery' where skulls from the graves were stored on shelves, and under my blanket I struggled with my four-hundred-foot reels of film, testing strips to make sure my camera was behaving. This was my first introduction to archaeology in the field and it was a privilege to live among Arabs who had hardly changed their way of life since Bible times."

Baker sent a number of articles about this work back to *The Times* for publication, and the film, called *The Cities of Judah, Lost and Found,* was later shown in lectures around the world. His interest in archaeology was mainly to discover some of the tree history of the region, and the digs did indicate a wealth of tree cover that was once the heritage of the Holy Land.

> *The three cities were built on a bare, rocky ridge and the nearby country stretched away in barren splendour. The work carried out by Sir Flinders was further proof of the old fertility of this ancient land. Where there were cities there must have been food and water; once this land had been tree covered, green and full of promise. When the trees went the water table sank; the land was denuded and the crops failed; finally the desert crept over everything. If I had needed a reminder of the importance of reafforesting Palestine I would have found it in the cities beneath the sand.*

Baker's filming schedule allowed for frequent trips around the tiny country. He was entertained in the Bedouin camps and, listening to their stories, gained an appreciation for the ancient legends that run through and reinforce the messages of the Holy Book, which he knew so well from his religious training. The Bible stories seemed to come alive on these travels and instil an ever-deeper sense of the prophetic significance of reafforestation in the Holy Land.

Baker's religious inclinations were balanced by his practical experience. His journeys allowed him to observe the natural history of the country, which was not dissimilar to that of North Africa or other areas around the Mediterranean:

> *In ancient times the forest cover came down the hills to the waterside, but it was cleared for fuel, building timber or for ship-construction; more of the forest land was cleared to make fields for cultivating crops. The browsing stock, goats, sheep and cattle—in particular, the goats—would not allow the forest to reclaim the land, but kept the young shoots browsed close to*

the earth. The exposed soil became susceptible to erosion and the numerous streams and rivulets running down the mountainsides in the rainy seasons carried the good earth away, spreading it over the coastal plains or washing it out to sea.

Erosion following forest destruction and soil depletion has been one of the most powerfully destructive forces in bringing about the downfall of civilization and wiping out human existence from large tracts of the earth's surface. The destructive agency of erosion following in the wake of forest clearing has been a much more potent agency for destruction than military conquests. Erosion does not march with blasts of trumpets or the beating of drums, but its tactics are more subtle, more sinister.

From Palestine we can look out on lands where once stood great civilizations and on those ruined cities now covered with desert sands. The great empires of Assyria, Babylon, Carthage and Persia were destroyed by floods and deserts let loose in the wake of forest destruction. When the mountains of Greece were cleared of their forest wealth, their noble culture vanished, and when in turn their colonists settled in the virgin forests of Italy, they took with them the same destructive methods which in turn caused the downfall of the Roman Empire.

Being in the Holy Land reinforced Baker's sense of mission, which he linked to the biblical vision of renewal: the desert shall bloom as a rose; the trees of the field shall clap their hands; instead of the thorn shall come up the fir tree; instead of the briar a fig; the spear would become a pruning hook. He sensed himself as a part of a divine plan, a plan of renewal, the building of a new world order that combined spiritual, social, economic, and ecological principles in a concerted effort to reverse the destruction of the past and build a new earth. This notion of tree planting as a prophetic act intensified, but it was always linked to a practical plan.

In Palestine at the time, there were fewer than eighty square miles of forests, including scrub and plantations. But there were six thousand square miles suitable for afforestation. At least twelve thousand acres, in Baker's view, should be planted each year with twelve million forest trees. It was not really an ambitious program; it was only about half the area being planted by the British Forestry Commission in a year. The whole of Palestine might be reafforested at the cost of a single day of war. This land of milk and honey might realistically be restored to its former productivity.

THE RUSE

After three weeks of exploring and acquainting himself with the land and its people, Baker returned to Jerusalem for the fateful gathering. First, he engaged heads of government departments to act as host, one-on-one, for each of the religious leaders. The hall was prepared with curtained cubicles on the sides, each just large enough for two.

When the grand mufti arrived, Baker introduced him to Colonel Humphrey Bowman, director of education and a brilliant Arabic scholar, who led the mufti into the seclusion of a cubicle. As each leader arrived he was entrusted to the care of an appropriate counterpart. In the meantime, the centre of the hall filled with guests, including officials and government administrators.

The high commissioner arrived at the appointed hour to begin the meeting. The curtains were drawn back. All the contending religious leaders were present—you might say trapped—with no way out. What could they do but accept the invitation to be seated in the main body of the hall?

Baker was introduced and commenced to speak, fully conscious of his responsibility and opportunity:

Here, for the first time in history, were gathered the principal religious, venerable leaders of East and West—"Never the twain shall meet." The truth of these much-quoted words of Kipling was being challenged. Clad in their patriarchal and ecclesiastic robes and insignia, they were waiting for a pronouncement from me. I was no ecclesiastic or patriarch. I was no high official in the administration of Palestine under the British Mandate, but simply a forester—a planter of trees. Here I was treading on "holy ground".

This was the city of Abraham, Jacob, Joseph, and Aaron, of David and Solomon. It was also the land of Ishmael and his descendants, who outnumbered all the others, and where Mohammed had made his pilgrimage. It was the city of Jesus. With the representatives of three great traditions in attendance, St. Barbe tried to express his sense of the importance of the occasion, of the prophetic significance of the place, and of the potential for renewal of the land and people through trees. He recalled the natural history of the land and its value, including the economic value of tree planting.

Then he called upon those present to found a branch of the Men of the Trees, explained its purpose and role, and drew their attention to the articles of incorporation that had been handed around. He had taken the liberty of nominating the high commissioner as patron and the leaders as vice-patrons, the heads of departments as the executive officers, and the chief forest officer as secretary-treasurer. Baker proposed to donate £1,000 to help start nurseries, and the high commissioner promised to match it. "When I sat down it seemed to me that I had been talking too long and yet there was no hint of movement. It seemed as if I were awakening from a dream. As I looked into their inscrutable faces it was hard for me to see how far my appeal had gone home....Then one after another, members of the audience rose in support of the idea of founding the Men of the Trees in Palestine."

Everything was adopted as Baker proposed:

> I took a deep breath and plunged among the distinguished Vice-Patrons of my newly-formed society; all these dear, devoted souls who for the love of God had hated each other, but at length had been brought together in the love of trees, and in united action to restore the ancient Land of Promise by tree-planting.

FEAST OF THE TREES

With the Men of the Trees now launched in its fourth country, in his remaining months in Palestine St. Barbe set to work to plant trees. Before he had left Britain, he had been thinking about some counterpart to the 'dance of the trees' that might be enacted here. He had come upon the idea of a revival of the Feast of the Trees, also called the New Year of the Trees, which had been celebrated in the distant past by eating the fruits or nuts of fifteen different trees that grew in the Holy Land. The feast had continued to be observed by the Jews in the diaspora on the 15th of Shevat, which occurs in the spring, but had been discontinued in the Holy Land. Baker had been pleased to learn that plans were being made by Jewish settlers to revive this festival and that this had the blessing of the high commissioner.

Unlike other Jewish feasts that are historical and religious, the Feast of the Trees is purely a celebration of nature and its revival was to include tree planting by children—a kind of Jewish Arbor Day. St. Barbe took part in the first recurrence:

I drove to Beit Vegan, the House and Garden Suburb of Jerusalem, and took part in the tree planting ceremony in which four thousand school children came out from the city of Jerusalem to plant avenues along the roads in this new residential quarter. So keen was the interest that sixteen thousand grown-up persons— parents, uncles, aunts and friends of the children—attended the ceremony. There was an arch of welcome, upon which had been described in Hebrew: "Welcome to the Young Planters." From the point of vantage where I stood I could see a long trail of people filling the winding road for a distance of four miles, an unbroken procession. My camera registered it, but upon inspecting the picture it looked like a trail of ants.

Soon they approached, with mounted police on Arab steeds as escort. They were a joyful crowd. The whole atmosphere was charged with a holiday spirit, and as they marched they sang songs of the forest and of tree-planting. After they had passed under the arch, the procession split into two streams, two thousand children taking up their positions along each of the two main streets of the new suburb.

Along the new roads holes had been dug, and four hundred trees were in readiness. To each hole were allocated ten children, who, with the assistance of their schoolmasters, set the trees, which were well and truly planted. As soon as they were all firmed in and carefully staked, the young planters were each given a bag of refreshments. Soon they were scattered into little groups and joined their parents, and along the hillside I saw small picnic parties enjoying the after feast.

For my part I returned to Jerusalem, and on the way saw old men sitting in sheltered nooks and on the steps in doorways, celebrating the feast in their old way by eating the fruits of the land. I was deeply impressed with all that I had seen, and I felt that it augured well for the future of Palestine.

Baker also noted that these ceremonies were taking part in all of the Jewish settlements. At Ben-Sheman he witnessed a similar event with five hundred children: "I wish I could convey the festive mood, the enthusiasm which accompanies these tree-planting ceremonies. It is not a drudgery or a task which has to be performed whether they like it or not. It is a joyous moment...."

This sense of drama and ceremony particularly appealed to St. Barbe. He would attempt to reproduce a joyous approach to tree planting wherever he worked around the world, throughout his life.

He could see that the Jews were developing a tree sense and wondered if this were also true among the Arabs. His contacts led to many meetings and lectures to Arab audiences around the country. In Akka he was invited to meet a large and representative gathering of Arab landowners. His topic was: "Some Economic Aspects of Re-afforestation."

His Arabic being rather rusty, he used an interpreter, but the expressions of the faces of the audience told him that his message was hitting home. At the conclusion of his presentation, an old man got up and told a story which seemed to Baker to sum up his message and demonstrate profound understanding, a story which the old man had first heard from 'Abdu'l-Bahá himself:

Once upon a time there was a king walking abroad and he saw an old man planting olive trees, so he stopped and said: "You are an old man to be planting olive trees. What profit will you get in your planting?" To which the old man replied: "Your Honour, others planted that I should eat. I plant that others may eat." The king was so pleased with this reply that he said to one of his servants: "Give this man a bag of money." Upon receiving it the old man held it high in the air and said, "You see, Your Honour, already my planting has brought me profit."

Alongside his efforts to promote tree planting, much of this first trip to Palestine was spent in the production of two additional films, one on the orange industry, titled *The Romance of the Golden Jaffa,* and the other to be called *The Rebirth of Palestine.* During the filming of the Jaffa story, Baker stayed at both Jewish and Arab groves. The film covered the story of the oranges, from budding to eating. St. Barbe was impressed with the history, legends, and cultural import of the orange; he retold the legend that Buddhist missionaries from the Far East had taken pips they had found in their travels back to their

Inspired by his experiences with children in Palestine, Baker emphasized hands-on conservation training at an early age. "Twigs," a tree planting program for children, was started by the Men of the Trees in the 1930s.

monasteries to improve the strain, then after several years, they had brought back the new cultivar to the land of its origin, this being the origin of the Jaffa orange. One night, he flew over the orange groves when they were in full bloom. Even from the height of two thousand feet, the scent was strong and fragrant.

AT BAHJÍ

Baker worked his way north to Bahjí, the gardens and shrine of Bahá'u'lláh, the founder of the Bahá'í faith,

> *where I heard were all manner of rare trees and plants which had been brought by pilgrims from distant Persia. I had set out from Acre [Akka] and passed under an old arch of a Roman aqueduct through a plantation of eucalyptus trees and soon arrived at the beautiful residence where Bahá'u'lláh had been allowed to retire after his years of imprisonment in the fortress of Acre. The Turkish authority granted this concession, and here at Bahjí he must have spent his happiest days. He was a planter of trees and loved all growing things. When his devotees tried to bring him presents from Persia the only tokens of their esteem that he would accept were seeds or plants for his gardens.*

Baker made his pilgrimage to the mansion of Bahjí, to the rooms once occupied by Bahá'u'lláh, where Baker's fellow alumnus from Cambridge University, E.G. Browne, the Orientalist scholar, had been given an audience with Bahá'u'lláh. Here, St. Barbe sensed the hidden source of promise for the rebirth of Palestine, and the world.

> *Here, indeed, I was standing on hallowed ground. Once again this land of destiny and promise was leading the way and summoning men of goodwill everywhere to unite in the service of humanity as a whole. "We desire but the good of the world and the happiness of the nations, [Bahá'u'lláh had said to Professor Browne],...all men as brothers. Let not a man glory in this, that*

he loves his country; let him rather glory in this, that he loves
his kind." Yes, I thought, humankind, humanity as a whole.
Was it not this for which I had been striving to reclaim the
waste places of the earth? These were the words of a planter of
trees, a lover of men and of trees. I began to read some transla-
tions from the Persian. "In the garden of the heart plant naught
but the tree of love." I was enthralled by the sublimity of the
language. Here was beauty personified.

It was a glorious evening as he returned along the tide-swept road
to Haifa, and as he looked up to Mount Carmel, clothed in sunlight,
he again recalled the words of Isaiah: "The Glory of Lebanon shall
be given unto it: the glory of Carmel and Sharon. They shall see the
excellency of the Lord, and the Glory of our God."

It came to him that this was the perfect scene for the closing of his
film on the rebirth of Palestine. He took his camera into the gardens
and scanned the landscape, settling on the pilgrims coming to the
shrines, coming from all races, cultures, continents.

As if drawn by a magnet, some inexplicable spiritual force had
welded all hearts into one. Was this the "New Jerusalem" of St.
John's vision? Was this the long promised "tabernacle of God
with man?" As these thoughts were passing through my mind,
the Guardian himself came from the direction of the Shrine of
the Báb, and walked in the garden. My camera followed him
for a brief moment as he walked deep in meditation, but did
not obtrude; that was enough, he was there in my film as a
living emblem of the fulfillment of the promise of the ages....
Surely it is as one great human family that we must go forward
into the future.

With these millennial thoughts in mind—thoughts that appealed
strongly to his religious childhood and training and to his natural
idealism and visionary nature, thoughts that expanded his sense
of the scope of his mission and the work needed throughout the
world—he set sail for England. Although he had established a new

branch of the Men of the Trees in Palestine, contributed to the revival of the Feast of the Trees, and produced material for three documentary films, there was much more to do for Palestine.

Baker's return trip was on a cargo ship called the ss *Highland Chief*, loaded with Jaffa oranges for the Christmas market. The trip allowed him to add another section to his film. Upon arrival in London he followed the trail of the oranges right through to Paddington General Hospital, where he had taken a few cases of oranges to give to the children as a treat. The film closed on the children eating mouth-watering sections of oranges, the juice running down their cheeks.

The Jaffa orange film was used extensively in his lecture trips in England and was also excerpted for newsreels. Within ten years, sales of Jaffa oranges rose from a half million cases a year to eleven million. Baker liked to think that his film "played some small part in that success." St. Barbe was indeed a visionary and idealist, but with his practical streak, knew that stimulating the commercial market would encourage tree planting at the source.

"To 'The Man of the Trees' — with best wishes Allenby."

His other obligation to Palestine was to raise £1,000 for the planting of trees, as promised. To do this Baker relied on what became standard practice for him: harnessing the influence of the famous, rich, and powerful. He stopped in at the home of Field-Marshall Viscount Allenby, who signed a letter to *The Times* that Baker had drafted, making the appeal to cover the costs of establishing tree nurseries and roadside plantings in the Holy Land. Also signing the letter were Lord Melchett, known for his generosity to Jewish causes, and Sir Francis Younghusband, the eminent explorer of Tibet and chairman of Men of the Trees. That appeal netted £850, an amount that was increased to £1,500 after Baker's 1930 lecture tour of Canada and the United States.

Following these lectures and a subsequent first trip around the world, Baker returned briefly to Palestine to inspect the work. He found that the high commissioner had, as promised, doubled the capital Baker had collected, established no fewer that forty-seven nurseries, and had inaugurated plantings between Jerusalem and Jaffa dedicated to the Men of the Trees.

It is noteworthy that Palestine/Israel is one of only two countries that ended the twentieth century with more tree cover than it had at the beginning. More than 240 million trees have been planted there, covering more than 250,000 acres, about 7 percent of the country.

Could a similar approach work elsewhere? He would soon find out.

CHAPTER FIVE

Save the Redwoods!

A SLIM WALLET

As soon as Baker arrived back in England he went to the Colonial Office to tell them that he was available for service. He needed a job. But this was the end of 1929 and the world was moving into a slump. Plenty of people were awaiting appointments with little or no hope. Governments were beginning to cut back severely and, as is their habit, to eliminate anything but those projects with the most immediate currency. Forest conservation was on the shelf.

Baker was now forty. He had been twice invalided out of the army, once fired from Colonial Service, once invalided home from Africa, and was unwilling, on philosophical grounds, to go on the dole. His prospects, and wallet, were slim.

"It was no good to sit down and wait for a job to come," he observed. "What a hope! Somehow, by some means, I must strike out afresh. Remembering the definition of a pessimist and an optimist—the pessimist sees difficulty in every opportunity, while the optimist sees opportunity in every difficulty—I thought, here was my chance." He would use the time to undertake a tour of the forests of the world. This would also provide an opportunity to return to a natural life in the woods, without having to clock on and off or live the monotonous life of the dole. The fact that he had no money for travel didn't seem to occur to him. He drew up an itinerary that mapped out the locations of his growing network of forestry friends worldwide, starting with the United States.

Since 1926, when he attended the First World Forestry Congress in Italy and met and talked to the American delegation, Baker had wanted to go to America to explore the forestry situation there personally. He had numerous invitations from American foresters to assist them in initiating a more extensive and progressive program of conservation and reforestation.

Before departure, there were a number of tasks to accomplish. Besides fundraising for Palestine, promoting Jaffa oranges, and the activities of the Men of the Trees in England, he spent some time advocating for unemployment relief work. Baker was dead set against the dole, since for many unemployed it seemed merely to entrench the problem. He was a great believer in initiative. He had in mind to promote a new wave of emigration to Canada, where the unemployed youth of Britain could find healthy and wholesome opportunities as farm labourers, and eventually own their own farms. He made arrangements with Canadian friends to find placements on Ontario farms and then set about to tour southern England's cities to lecture on opportunities in Canada.

He recruited fifty boys.* At a farm near Guelph, Ontario, a training centre was established and most of the boys found placements nearby. Many succeeded in their new venture. Baker's efforts in this direction opened another door. A contact, the head of the migration department of the Canadian Pacific Railway, was so surprised at Baker's success that when Baker asked if he might find him free passage to America, the way was found on an empty boat heading to Bermuda, via New York.

---

* More that 100,000 'Home Children' were sent to Canada from the British Isles between 1869 and the late 1930s. We now know that many of these 'Home Children' were poorly treated and abused.

Early in 1930, he arrived in New York with five pounds in his pocket, only to have four taken by customs for duties on his films on Palestine and his slides illustrating his lecture on *The Adventures of a Forester in Kenya and the Mahogany Forests of Nigeria*, which he had taken along with the lecture circuit in mind. He was in rough shape financially, but no worse perhaps than the many millions suffering from the Depression.

He put up in a modest hotel in Gramercy Park and spent the first morning contacting every newspaper and journal editor in the city in an attempt to have articles commissioned. No success. He decided to get a breath of fresh air, such as it was in New York. A few steps from the hotel door, he ran into an old friend from Kenya, Major Radcliffe Dugmore, who had made his reputation as one of the first and best camera 'hunters' and had become a very popular lecturer in America. It was he who had helped Baker learn the art of filmmaking and Baker felt much in his debt.

As it turned out, Baker was just the man Dugmore wanted to see, as it seemed that an American film producer had pirated a few spectacular scenes from his film and the major had come to New York to either collect his dues or sue. Baker could be a great help; having been with him in Kenya, he could identify his shots. Dugmore took Baker off to his club, the Players, were he was a popular member. They joined several members and guests for lunch, and before long Dugmore had Baker talking about Africa. He began to tell them about a small tribe he had found in the forests of East Africa:

The little tribe was one of the few unspoiled by western civilization. They had no currency and no taxes. They lived frugally by their bows, and had no recourse to forest destruction. They had no hoe among them. The best hunter was voted chief. They lived close to Nature: their wants were few, and such as they were, they were supplied by the forest. I argued that theirs was a very advanced civilization because they had eliminated all the unnecessary things from life. Moreover they were bilingual: they had a hunting language and a social language.

Although his guests seemed intrigued, Baker suddenly realized that he had been talking too long and monopolizing the conversation. Embarrassed, he got up and made apologies, saying he had another appointment. But someone followed him from the table. He asked Baker if he had ever written a book. No, not really, he replied, although he had written a number of popular and scientific articles for magazines and journals. "Well," said the man, who turned out to be the editor of Dial Press, "if you can write as well as you can talk, you ought to be able to write an exciting book. We reckon that we publish the best travel books in this little city. Come around and meet my partner."

They went to the offices and met Lincoln McVeigh. In short order, Baker was commissioned to write a seventy-five-thousand-word book, illustrated with his own photographs. He had five weeks to do it, with a $500 advance in hand and the promise of the same again on delivery of the manuscript! His luck had changed. He wasted no time starting on his career as a writer—which in time saw him publish over thirty books, including a couple of bestsellers.

Dugmore put him up as an honorary member at the Players for the duration of his New York stay. Baker hired three stenographer-typists; each worked four hours a day. He ate one meal a day, at midnight, and from dawn to dark dictated his book or made notes, subsisting mainly on orange juice. In ten days he had finished *Men of the Trees*, took another week to ready the manuscript, and went to Dial Press.

ANOTHER STROKE OF LUCK: LOWELL THOMAS

Baker was an unknown in America and Dial needed some way to introduce him. They decided to ask Lowell Thomas, the best-known broadcaster of his day, to write a foreword to the book. This was a stroke of luck for Baker, not just in terms of book sales, for it paved the way for a lecture tour.

Lowell Thomas had been the correspondent for *The New York Times* throughout Allenby's campaign in Palestine and was one of the best-known lecturers in England. Thousands packed halls to hear his talks about Lawrence of Arabia and Allenby's heroics. His book on Lawrence was a bestseller and he had quickly become the most popular broadcaster in the world. His broadcasts on NBC's *World News* were heard daily by seventy million people all over the United States and Canada, making him one of the most influential public figures of the time.

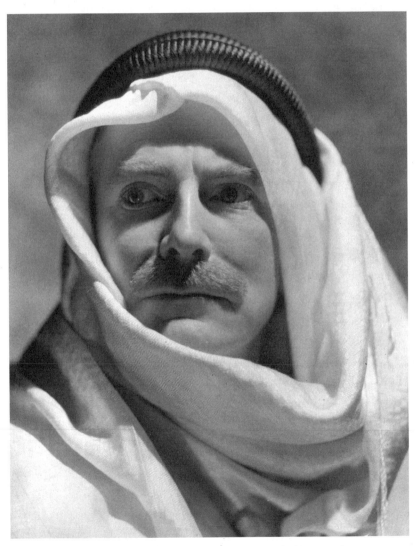

A portrait of Baker in Arab headgear by the renowned photographer Howard Coster.

Filled with thankfulness at his good fortune, Baker went to see Thomas. It turned out that Thomas already knew about Baker. "I followed your work in Africa ever since you started with those tribesmen," he told him. "I have always called you the 'Lawrence of Africa' for you have the same way of dealing with the people. Just as he got the best out of the Arabs, so you've got the best out of those Africa warriors. They did things for him and they do things for you."

Thomas asked for a simple lesson in Swahili, *jambo*—hello, *kwaheri*—good-bye, and the like, promising to "tell the world" about Baker and the Men of the Trees.

Baker's time in New York was well spent, but it was time to get on with the journey. The first lecture in a cross-country tour was slated for the Carnegie Museum in Pittsburgh, where he was more than surprised to find the hall packed. This was a time when people enthusiastically attended lectures of all sorts, when the famous Chautauqua Institute was at its height.

> I had a crowded and enthusiastic audience, and afterwards there was a long queue of people waiting to shake hands. I was not conscious of being particularly eloquent. I had talked quite simply of my life on the Equator, and of some of my experiences in the mahogany forests, and shown pictures of the big mahoganies. I had taken them, with the help of my pictures, to the Highlands of Kenya, and shown them slides of the first Dance of the Trees. I had introduced them to the forest-dwellers, the mighty bowmen....I had shown them ju-ju men in the act of casting a magic spell, but I was not prepared for all the ovation I had received.

And it seemed that half the people in the queue of well-wishers had a special gift for Baker: a copy of Joyce Kilmer's classic poem *Trees*, a gift he would be given again, and again, and yet again throughout his career as a public speaker.

There was an explanation for his success. "In the morning," noted Baker, "I learned that the great fellow Baker was not quite the drawing card he had begun to think. On the evening of the lecture, Lowell Thomas had come on the air for his nightly chat. Millions sat back to enjoy his half-hour and this is what they hear: '*Jambo*, everyone... that means, good evening! If you don't know what the language is—it is called *Ki-Swahili*, and I got it yesterday from a man called Richard St. Barbe Baker. Have you heard about Baker? He is the original Man of the Trees....'"

Thomas went on to tell something of Baker's story and to plug his forthcoming book: "Pittsburgh listeners remembered the advertisement in their newspaper that announced my lecture. And so, when Lowell Thomas had finished, they switched off their sets and came out to look for themselves. The talk from Lowell Thomas did me a vast amount of good, and later, when I was campaigning all over America, I found that I was known almost everywhere."

Thomas was the first person to call him the "Man of the Trees." The name stuck.

Before leaving Pittsburgh, Baker made his first broadcast on American radio, KDKA. In Nigeria it was the one station he could pick up clearly and tune into without too much interference. It was fun to tell its listeners about this odd connection with their favourite station, and perhaps talk to some Africans who might be listening.

GIFFORD PINCHOT, PRESIDENT HOOVER, AND THE LECTURE CIRCUIT

In Washington, Gifford Pinchot, the prominent forester, educator, and politician, and first Chief of the U.S. Forest Service (1905-1910), invited Baker to speak to two hundred members of the Society of American Foresters. There, he updated his contact list and was asked to contribute to a national forest conservation plan.

While in Washington, he was also granted an audience with President Hoover. Not being one to hesitate when opportunity knocked, he invited Hoover to be president of the Men of the Trees in America. Hoover replied, "Ask me again when I am through with my period of office." He did however pave the way for Baker, giving him introductions to the heads of government departments.

Over the next two years Baker visited much of the forested United States and in every case had the advantage of valuable help from

foresters, park superintendents, and officials, simultaneously forming a general appraisal of the American forestry situation.

In Chicago, he lectured to the Garden Clubs of America. He also
visited the first Bahá'í house of worship of the Americas, still under
construction. He describes this visit in his 1944 biography, *I Planted
Trees*: "At Wilmette, on the shore of Lake Michigan, I saw a wonderful temple in the early stages of its construction. A universal house
of worship built by those in all lands who are working for universal
understanding and peace, this temple is open to all sects and people,
and is dedicated to the Oneness of God and the oneness of mankind,
the union of science and religion, to universal education and the fundamental oneness of religions."

From Chicago, his circuit took him south to Texas and then
on to the Grand Canyon, which he found a terrifying experience.
Exceedingly beautiful, yes, but also a gruesome scar on the skin of
the earth and an object lesson in the results of deforestation.

He travelled across Arizona, sleeping under the desert stars. In
Tucson, he met Professor Douglas, who was developing the new science of dendrochronology, the study of natural history using tree
rings. He was able to tell Baker much of the prehistory of the southwest, and the influence of the Indigenous agriculturists of the area on
desert formation.

On to San Diego, where he had his first view of the Pacific Ocean.
"There were hitchhikers on the road, and by the time I arrived in San
Diego they were not only filling the car, but standing along the running boards and sitting on the wings." He stayed with a friend of the
renowned English horticulturist William Robinson, who had done
much to develop gardening in America. This friend introduced Baker
to the local tree life, particularly the citrus plantations.

Baker then headed north, where he had scheduled lectures with
the Pacific Geographic Society. He had again run out of money and
the lectures were his only income. Unfortunately, disaster struck
in the form of an earthquake and all public events were cancelled.
No lectures, no money. Baker was reduced to destitution. "I had to
eat, my last few dollars melted quickly away and there came the
day when I could afford only dates which cost two cents a pound

and were being fed to the mules because of the shortage of hay. They tasted good to a hungry man. After eating the dates I walked out to the Andreas Canyon to spend the night rent free under the California stars."

Once again, Bakers' propensity for running into the right people at the right time came into play. The next day he met a Dr. George Clemens of the Ministry of Agriculture, who had heard about Baker's efforts and now invited him to his home near Palm Springs. The next day, Clemens, Baker, and other guests made a trek to the Andreas Canyon. On the return trip, Baker and another fellow decided to try returning directly across the canyon, a feat that had often been tried and just as often necessitated a rescue of the fools who attempted it. But Baker was in fine shape after subsisting on dates and spring water and spent the next four hours in a harrowing adventure, saving his friend's life and having his own saved, but making it across nonetheless, to the amazement of the locals. The feat was well publicized in the local papers.

His lectures for the Pacific Geographic eventually came off, much the better for the publicity he had received. Three thousand turned out in Pasadena and four thousand at the Philharmonic Hall in Los Angeles! The lecture fees allowed him to continue on in somewhat better style. His journey led northward and he visited the Institute of Forest Genetics in Placerville. Their work breeding improved forest stock was on the leading edge of scientific forestry. Placerville had been the home of Luther Burbank, the plant wizard who developed more than 800 strains and varieties of plants during his career as a plant breeder. Baker was able to visit the garden where he had developed many of the fruit and nut trees we enjoy today. His ultimate goal, however, was the California redwoods.

THE CATHEDRAL OF NATURE

Claudia Skipworth Coles, the American who had first introduced Baker to the Bahá'í faith, also introduced him to the redwoods. "You can't call yourself a forester," said Claudia, "until you have seen the California Coast Redwoods." They had been calling him ever since.

At last the way was clear for the first of twenty pilgrimages to this "supreme achievement of tree growth," this "cathedral of nature," this forest mecca of massive trees, the largest and oldest living things.

It was in the winter that I first met the giants, when snow lay deep at their feet. The morning that I walked among them, there had been a fresh fall and everything was pure white. The trails were deeply covered, soft and dry. I knew for the first time the real meaning of the silence of the snows, the only sound was from the little avalanches from the upper branches as the piles of snow became too heavy a burden and gradually under the strain the branches bent and shed their load. This was happening on a hundred trees all around and so it seemed the snow was again falling. All was silent but for these snow slips from the treetops. The sun shone bright on myriads of glistening particles. It was an experience impossible to describe in mere words.

I had long wanted to meet the oldest living trees on earth, the Big Trees, called by the Indians, Wawona. They had first been described about 1852, and people doubted the truth of the reports of their size. There was nothing to equal them in bulk, for they were unbelievably huge, even when I found myself among them it was difficult to realize their enormous dimensions, and it was only when I had walked around one of the impressive trunks that I began to comprehend their magnitude. One of the first I approached in this way was close to thirty paces around the bole. It would take at least fifteen men with outstretched arms to have encircled its great trunk. It towered to a height of perhaps two hundred and eighty feet, but this was not the tallest.

This first glimpse of the redwoods was at the Bohemian Grove where the Bohemian Club produced "grove plays" in a natural theatre, the audience sitting on tree trunks. St. Barbe liked this idea immensely and thought to seek out some similar setting on a larger scale that could be a gathering place for tree lovers, a place of nature pilgrimage, a theatre, and a meeting place for "convocations of wisdom."

He slept overnight in a hollow redwood. Preparing his fire, he found a number of arrowheads—he was not the first to use this shelter.

The Big Trees had been an amazing revelation to me. In my wildest dreams I could not have imagined anything to equal them. I was overpowered by their ponderous weight and magnitude. Each tree was a monument, a living, growing evidence of a race of trees which, maybe, once covered the earth, and which by some freak of Fate had been allowed to survive in this one spot.

There were two redwoods, two sequoias, *Sequoia sempervirens,* the coast redwoods, which were the tallest trees in the world, but the overall giant was the *Sequoia gigantea.* They were named after the Cherokee leader, Sequoyah. St. Barbe describes the trees in his 1943 book, *The Redwoods.* "One of the remarkable characteristics of the tree is the thickness of its bark, which may be from one to two feet through. You can beat on it with your hand as hard as you like without injury to yourself or the tree, so padded, soft and spongy is its makeup."

Soon after Europeans first saw the trees in 1852, the bark was stripped from one tree to a height of thirty feet and it was exhibited in many places; eventually a room was built for it in the Crystal Palace Exhibition. The tree of course died, and Baker writes:

It took five men twenty days with pump augurs to bore it down, but so solidly did the trunk rest upon the stump that it refused to fall even after two more days had been taken up inserting wedges to upset its balance. But one noon when the men were at dinner nature took pity on man and brought the forest mammoth crashing to the ground with a force that caused the earth to tremble as from an earthquake. Such was the vulgarity of man [that], upon the stump, which measures twenty-five feet across, a pavilion was erected, a ballroom was opened and religious services were held there on Sundays, while on weekdays it was used as a dancing floor and for theatrical performances and concerts.

The 'Kingdom of the Giants' is on the western slopes of the Sierra Nevada, at altitudes from five thousand to eight thousand feet and in scattered groves along 250 miles.

When a visitor first enters any one of the thirty-two groves of the giants, he is not immediately impressed with the individual size of the trees, because everything around him is proportionately great. But let him approach one of these giants, place his hands on the trunk and look skyward into the treetops. Let him walk around the massive bole, count his paces or time his journey. It is then that a feeling of awe and wonder begins to descend on him. He may pick up a cone, examine one of the tiny seeds born from that same giant, which in turn had sprung from such another tiny seed four thousand years ago. It is the combination of the time factor with the impression of size upon the senses that makes the visitor slow to realize their magnitude.

Perhaps the largest tree was the General Sherman:

I was taken to this tree by the superintendent of Sequoia National Park and myself measured the base circumference, which was 101.6 feet. The height of the tree above mean base was 272.4 feet. It might have been taller in past times, but its head had become dome-shaped, buffeted by storms and burnt by lightning. The greatest base diameter was 34 feet...the height of the largest branch above the ground was 130 feet and its diameter where it left the massive trunk on the south side of the parent tree was 6.8 feet. It went outward and upward for 140 feet. This branch itself is larger and taller than most European forest trees.

And this tree demanded a recital of statistics:

The wood contained in the trunk of the tree would be enough to build three hundred bungalows. It would make a box of one-inch boards, if cut without waste, to house a luxury liner the size of the S.S. Queen Mary, or provide a roof of half-inch boards covering ten acres. There is as much timber in this tree as is found in about twenty acres of average pine forest. It would require at least ninety railway trucks and three engines to move the trunk alone. The total weight...has been calculated to be over six thousand tons. Just think of it, this mammoth tree, sprung from a tiny seed, smaller than the head of a match. Let us stand in awe and wonder.

The tree, or one of its neighbours of comparable size, is also the oldest living thing in the world. Its exact age is unknown, and could only be told by reading its rings, but is estimated to be as much as four thousand years, the closest to immortal of any living thing. Circles of trees sprung from one another trace back nine thousand years.

In *The Redwoods*, Baker recounts the biography of this tree: its life spans most of recorded history; it was alive when the temples of Karnak were built, four thousand years ago; when the Israelites were in Egypt, it was six hundred years old, a youth dominated by its neighbours, making slow headway; by the time of the first Olympiad in Greece, it had reached its full height, achieving full size as the Parthenon was being built; at the time of Confucius and Buddha it was throwing out great branches, each a mighty tree, in search of light; by the time of the decline of Greece, when Roman civilization was beginning its rise, it was by then over two thousand years old, having lived but half its span; Christ was born, His message grew into greatness; Mohammed appeared; the Crusades came and passed; Europeans arrived in North America; the Renaissance and then the Industrial Revolution came and passed. Ancient.

I had been deeply impressed, but I had not been prepared for the new experience that was awaiting me. I had turned west once again and was heading for San Francisco, where I crossed by ferry and set out along the Redwood Empire Highway, all shaded by the tallest trees on earth. I was now in the zone of the Coast Redwoods, for they formed an evergreen wall on either side. The farther north I went, the more beautiful they became, more perfect was the forest, less disturbed by the logging operations which have ravaged their realm in the more southerly regions. It is futile to try to describe the rapidly changing panorama of loveliness as I spun along, too quick to comprehend their meaning. It was not until I had arrived in the region of the redwoods at Prairie Creek that I had time to explore their treasures, for from there onwards my journey was more leisurely, and all the while it seemed they were increasing in beauty and stature.

This was some kind of paradise for the Man of the Trees. Trees mythic, fantastic, supernatural. The ground carpeted with tree ferns that towered above his head, with azaleas and rhododendrons, with giant irises ten feet tall. For others, such as John Muir, the great naturalist, these trees had also been a haven and mecca. Baker called the most beautiful grove the Grove of Understanding. Here he envisioned a great meeting place for the arts, for youth, for planning the future of the world. "Man can gain so much from his tree brethren," he wrote. "Could they but stand and stare or bask in the sunlight of those immemorial groves, sanity would surely return. If Thoreau could tramp miles through the deepest snow 'to keep an appointment with a beech tree or yellow birch or old acquaintance among the pines,' I would tramp hundreds of miles to keep a tryst with a Coast Redwood."

But while Baker stood in awe, seeing the great forests as meditative healers, as holy ground in which human understanding could flourish, many more stood in awe of the dollars that could be netted from sawing up as many giants as possible. Logging proceeded apace.

SAVE THE REDWOODS!

In the early weeks of 1931 he returned to San Francisco, to the offices of the Save the Redwoods League. Sir Horace Plunkett, first chairman of the Men of the Trees, had introduced Baker to Madison Grant, founder of the league, one of the earliest conservation activist groups, with a very specific purpose. Grant had invited Baker's collaboration in the efforts to save the trees before it was too late.

On his cross-country tour Baker had already talked up the redwoods and interested the Conservation Committee of the Garden Clubs of America in saving a grove of their own. Up to this point, the league had concentrated all of its activities on saving single trees or small groves in memory of individuals and families who had given money for their purchase. Baker was alarmed at the rate the trees were being felled. Of the original million acres, over half had already been cut and fire often followed in the wake of the loggers. Redwood lumber was particularly popular as a roofing material, and the lumber interests were powerful and influential.

To Baker, these groves were sacred and symbolic. When the Kikuyu cut down their trees they left one sacred tree to gather in the spirits of the fallen ones—a practice consistent with today's scientific understanding of tree communication. Were these 'ultimate trees' a sort of sacred tree for the world? Should they be preserved to take in the spirits of a vanishing species? If people could cut down these ancient beauties, was there any hope?

He felt that what was needed was to save *communities* of trees— they could not regenerate without a protective buffer environment. This was a radical concept at the time, more in keeping with today's understanding of conservation. Moreover, he was of the belief that the redwoods had an influence on the Californian climate, situated as they were in a belt within ten miles of the coast.

A sufficiently large area had to be preserved for the balance of nature to remain undisturbed. The trees had to be allowed to flourish and reproduce themselves in the atmosphere they had created. My immediate concern was to save a large enough area to retain the local climate and I felt that at least twelve thousand acres would be required to be effective.

He went to San Francisco and put in a plea with the Save the Redwoods League to make the salvation of larger stands their next project. They gave him their assurance, but money had to be found— the trees would have to be bought back from the timber concessions, public opinion would have to be tapped, a sense of urgency established.

There was little more Baker could do at present. Before he left San Francisco he developed his pictures, made slides, and equipped himself as best he could to tell the world about the great trees.

WITH THE MAORIS

With the campaign to save the redwoods on hold but not forgotten, St. Barbe sailed through the islands of the Pacific, no doubt meeting their trees as he made his way to the Antipodes. He worked his passage, splicing steel cable and lending the ship's carpenter a hand.

In New Zealand he travelled widely through the country and fell in love with the land and people—and the trees, of course. New Zealand seemed like a little paradise: fair, fertile, and visually stunning. Baker was profoundly impressed with the Maori people and took much time to learn their culture and something of their language. He was impressed with their conservationist ethic. In many ways they seemed not to distinguish between themselves and the land—all were brothers, sisters, children in nature, under the divine mother and father who gave birth to plants, animals, and the human race.

Baker thought that the 'civilized' world had lost something essential when it gave up its nature culture/religion, something that must in some form be regained if a right relationship to the earth were to be rebuilt. For if the plants and animals were our family, as in Indigenous cultures—an understanding he saw as very much in keeping with ecology—could we so easily countenance their destruction? The values and insights of these cultures were a treasure needed by the dominant industrialized societies for their own transformation and preservation.

Baker travelled to many of the beauty spots of the country, meeting trees and photographing scenes for his lectures. The most beautiful scenery was at Lake Matherson near Mount Cook—which would figure prominently in his future.

He wrote to Lowell Thomas about an amusing incident that occurred when he went to great lengths to get just the right shot of the glaciers visible from the lake. He lay down for some time on the ice of the Fox glacier, waiting for the sun to come out and reveal the perfect light.

I had not noticed that I was laying stomach downward in a thawed patch. As soon as the sun went in everything froze. The sun came out, I got my shot and was about to get up when I found that my loose tweed suit had become saturated and frozen in the brief time that the cloud had covered the sun. When I tried to get up I was stuck.

He had frozen solidly to the glacier. Fortune was with him, however. If not for a friendly Maori who rescued him, he might have been there forever, slowly carried to the sea at glacial speed.

Like the Kikuyu, when the Maoris wanted a tree from which to make a canoe, they would first ask its permission. From the first days of their arrival in New Zealand they had established a management system. There was an age or girth limit that controlled the felling, the trees especially valuable for canoes or other purposes were set aside under *tapu*—the origin of the word *taboo*—by the wise men.

But in modern New Zealand, all was not well. Forestry was neglected and large areas were being razed for agriculture, especially grazing; erosion was setting in.

New Zealand has become famous as a pasture country, but at what a cost! With a recklessness only surpassed in Australia and the United States, virgin forests have been swept away to make sheep runs, just as if there was not enough mutton in the world already. Indiscriminate burning, overstocking and devastation by rabbits have in places caused complete destruction of all vegetation. Fourteen million acres of forest have been felled and sown in grass, or allowed to revert to tufted grass. In the hill areas, where the forests should have been conserved, but where they have been replaced by grass, so inferior is its nature that it can afford but a precarious safeguard against flood. The washing of soil down the short river courses into the sea threatens to leave that country like an "emaciated skeleton."

So here too was a job to be done. Was there nowhere in the world where people were satisfied to live lightly on the land? When Baker arrived in Wellington, the capital, he was greeted by Sir Francis Dillon Bell, the first commissioner of state forests, whose son William had served with Baker in the war and had been killed in 1917. Bell had also briefly been prime minister, in 1925.

"Is it not a common experience," Baker observed, "that one only meets the next person in one's life if one is qualified to do so? Of all the great ones who have influenced my life I would say that no one has helped me more in so short a time as Sir Francis Dillon Bell. I at once recognized in him a born leader. I found a challenge in his very first words of greeting: 'You have come at an inopportune moment. There has been a crash in Wall Street and there is no money for forestry. They are going to close the Department.'" Baker protested that the Forest Service must not be closed, saying that he had just been all over America telling the foresters and others that New Zealand was the world leader in forestry and they would soon come in droves to see for themselves!

> From Sir Francis I soon learnt the power of the press in a crisis. He replied: "I wish you could tell that to the press," and he immediately invited the editors of the two leading papers to lunch with us. While Sir Francis was feeding them I was giving them the story which would alert the Government to the destiny of New Zealand's forests. I was in no mood to wait until the meal was finished and coffee served. I talked through every course and held forth on the foolishness of cutting the one service which would pay for itself. I dragged in every argument I could conjure up, including a slightly romanticized story that America was ready and eager to learn from New Zealand in intelligent forestry. The editors must have forgiven me their restless lunch for the next day my words made the front page. Within twenty-four hours I received a message asking me to meet the head of the Treasury Department!

Once more Baker laid on the facts and figures, producing every argument he could muster. He secured a reprieve. The department would stay pending a more complete investigation. The crisis had passed. Farmers who were getting only three pence a pound for their wool were taken on by the Forest Service at Kaingaroa Forest plantation on the North Island and given rations and ten schillings a week pocket money; they planted twenty-two thousand acres the first year.

In the meantime there was the question of money—for himself. He had arrived in New Zealand with his customary five-pound note. Fortunately, his publicity led to some private consulting for a lumber company that had acquired a large piece of land that was deficient and unsuitable for farming; they wanted to know if it had potential for forestry. They asked him what he would find a reasonable fee for his consultation; he said that he would leave that entirely up to them—but did mention that in his last position he supervised a forestry area the size of France and had a uniformed staff of 132 rangers and foresters!

He did a survey of the area and recommended the use of the Californian Monterey pine, which responded in a remarkable way to the local soil type. A few of these trees had been transplanted there by early settlers, and about all Baker had to do to prepare a report was look around and see which species responded best to the local environment. The week's work netted him £50, but on its strength the company sold £4 million of forestry bonds and began planting twenty thousand acres annually. "And so as a result of my first visit to New Zealand, 44,000 acres were being planted a year."

His other campaign was aimed at saving natural forests. Above all the trees of New Zealand towered the giant kauris, which had enjoyed lives of a thousand years. One of the last stands of kauri trees in the Waipoua forest was threatened and he lent the support of the Men of the Trees to the committee trying to save it. Thousands of signatures were collected in many countries to add weight to their argument for preservation.

For the rest of his stay in New Zealand, Baker spoke widely to sympathetic audiences. In a farewell broadcast from Auckland, he made a final appeal for widespread cooperation to preserve the remaining 3.5 million acres of natural forest. Soon, New Zealand renewed its national forest policy, with conservation as its principal objective.

THE BATTLE DRILL

While still in New Zealand, Baker had heard that the Depression had also had a serious impact on Australian forest services: the Canberra Forestry School was to be closed down. He prepared his plan of action en route: "By now I was beginning to evolve a battle drill...close with the enemy, blind him with science and bombard him with newsprint."

He was unprepared for the enthusiastic and generous reception that awaited him in Sydney: it seemed the two countries shared more media contact than he realized. He was warmly welcomed at a luncheon hosted by the Lord Mayor and 250 tree lovers and conservationists.

Baker's visit coincided with emerging public awareness of the effects of Australia's land practice. The Sydney *Morning Herald* and other papers had taken up the story. The wheat lands of New South Wales in particular were in jeopardy, having been established on sloping forestland; with heavy summer thunderstorms, the climatic conditions there were more conducive to erosion than in other states. What was more, the fire hazard was increasing, wind erosion was a problem, droughts were common, and rabbits caused a lot of damage. A conservation policy was long overdue.

Australia once had extensive forests, but these had been subjected to the unprecedented level of destruction that accompanied European settlement. St. Barbe describes something of this in *Dance of the Trees*:

> *What has happened to the great eucalyptus forests of Australia? Those virgin domains were protected for countless generations by the inoffensive Aborigines who, like the redskins of the North American continent, had been content with a few dried sticks to cook their food. Their only recourse to felling was for wood for their wigwams or tent poles.*
>
> *Into this forest paradise, with its two hundred and thirty-five species of eucalyptus, colonists came. The rhythm of growth was broken by wholesale felling, when wide stretches of forest were laid bare to grow crops.*

The discovery of gold brought more men to drive back the forest folk and speed up the destruction of the trees. The newcomers knew nothing of the vital functions of the living trees or the dependence of man upon them. To them the bush was there only to be attacked with axe and fire. They found, after a very short time, that the ash from the burned trees formed a hot-bed for their seed and more and more of the forest was laid low.

Not content with the felling of single trees, they invented an ingenious and infamous method by which they could clear an acre in less time than it took to fell one tree. The axe man lays into the trees in such manner that each falls upon its neighbour and takes it with it. This saves labour, especially in hilly country. When they are set off by felling of the big drive trees—those high up on the hill—the trees below the "drive" fall like ninepins until the mountainside looks like the aftermath of a tornado. Trees are shattered and scattered in all directions. Timber that would have made thousands of homes and provided shelter for generations is torn to splinters, while the mountains echo with the explosions like an artillery bombardment, as the stricken trunks fall to the earth.

Tall timber which has clothed the mountains for centuries is laid low and left in a tangled mass. By the end of the day the ground is covered to a depth of twenty or thirty feet with the debris of splintered trees and branches. All this lies on the forest floor with its deep rich life-giving humus which has accumulated through the ages. It is left until it becomes as dry as tinder. Then oil soaked sacks are laid on the dense dry branches and lit. Flames roar up the mountainsides. Black clouds of smoke rise over the area and then go higher with the fierce heat that is generated. The inflammable oils from the eucalyptus produce highly combustible gases. Furnace heat is generated and soon the whole valley ignites, with deafening explosions, blowing burning trees into the air and hurling them like fiery javelins across the valley to spread the conflagration. The stored up wealth of millions of years in humus and timber has gone into the inferno. Rocks explode with the heat like land mines in some awful air raid. The burning travels faster and faster as this fiery, man-made hurricane is whipped up by the growing intensity of heat, flaming logs and tree trunks are driven before its force like leaves in an autumn gale.

The speed of destruction is like that of an express train. When the fire dies down, the seed is quickly planted, even while the earth is hot and sometimes still smoldering. Many planters have been badly burned through working while the ground was still alight. This gigantic hot-bed produces incredibly quick crops of wheat. The process starts all over again the next year.

So went the Australian war on nature. Baker knew that humanity would have to pay for its destruction and envisioned a second wave of settlers—conservation pioneers—to help make right the mess.

The role of public educator opened rather nicely for him in Australia. After his initial meeting with the mayor and townspeople, he made his first broadcast to Australia, toured the national park

Getting to know—and love—the big trees of Australia.

near Sydney, where a small area of primeval forest had been conserved, and lunched at Government House with the governor general and his wife. She was interested in promoting Arbor Day and was encouraging the Girl Guides to plant native trees.

A LONE FIVER

With just a "lone fiver" in his wallet, again, Baker proceeded to Melbourne. On the bright side, 350 tree enthusiasts welcomed him, with the chief forest officer presiding at the reception. "This was the opening day of some weeks of activity. Little did I realize what a big programme had been arranged for me." Visitors and telephone calls poured into his hotel room, and with the entertaining required he ran up a twenty-pound bill in less than a week, four times the amount he had in his pocket when blithely setting out on his first world tour.

Off he went to the largest Melbourne paper with a plan to sell some stories. On his way he quietly affirmed, "God suffices all things above all things." Overcoming his trepidation, he described his plan to the editor who, once Baker had agreed to throw in the illustrations, agreed to the payment of twenty pounds. He quickly wrote the articles, received the cheque, and paid the hotel.

Nonetheless, his situation remained precarious. Though treated as a distinguished guest and world tree expert, he was again penniless, caught in the Great Depression's squeeze. But once again, fortune intervened and arranged an encounter with Sir Harold Clapp of the Australian Railways, who arranged a free rail pass for Baker. He also introduced him to the Fruit Growers' Association and directed him to the famous orange-growing district of Mildura, where a project to provide farming opportunities for returned servicemen was underway. Baker calculated that if the English could be encouraged to eat two more oranges each, and if those were Mildura oranges, the industry there would prosper. Out came the camera and footage was shot to incorporate into his film on oranges. Sir Harold arranged for a load of oranges to be sent back to Britain, with Baker as chief agent and salesman. The oranges were well received in London and grew in popularity year after year. Mission accomplished.

I NEED BOTH LEGS

Baker now set off for the next leg of his trip, to Ceylon, with half a ship-load of oranges in tow. While filming the efforts of the crew to secure the cargo in a rough sea, Baker fell down a stairwell. He managed to hold onto the camera but his leg had been ripped open, exposing the bone. When he regained consciousness his first concern was to save the film. He hobbled back to his cabin, made an impromptu darkroom under the bedcovers, wound the film back, canned it, and then made his way to the surgery. Finding it busy, Baker tried his own remedy, soaking the wound in salt water—a big mistake.

By the time he received first aid the leg was badly inflamed, not to mention broken in three places. He became delirious and developed lockjaw and tetanus poisoning. He was carried ashore in Colombo to have his leg amputated.

As luck would have it, he was able to acquire the service of a Singhalese boy, who made arrangements to take Baker by train out of the heat of Colombo to the cooler mountains at Kandy. A surgeon was called to examine the leg. Amputation was required. Unable to speak, Baker wrote, "I am a forester. I need both legs," underlining both twice. The doctor said it was necessary to amputate without delay. Baker wrote, "Tomorrow."

Tomorrow came and Baker again wrote, "I am a forester. I need both legs," underlining "forester" twice and "both" four times. He was on fire with fever and could no longer sleep. Still, he was so ada-mant that the surgeon gave up, concentrating on those who would accept treatment. Meanwhile his Singhalese helper kept treating the wound with a concoction made, appropriately, of tree leaves.

On July 13, 1931, Baker wrote a last will and testament in the form of a letter to his dear Bahá'í friend and trusted member of the council of the Men of the Trees, Claudia Coles. (Unbeknownst to Baker, she had died a few days earlier.) When it was completed, he passed out. For three days his spirit wandered in the redwoods, basking in glori-ous shafts of light, before coming back. It would not be the last time his health was restored by redwood trees, if only in the dream world. After three weeks he was up, seeing something of the country.

A LIFE NOT HIS OWN

Since their first meeting, when she had introduced Baker to the Bahá'í faith, Claudia Coles had been his mentor. Upon arriving back in London in the fall of 1931, he was informed of her death. He went immediately to her daughter to see if there had been any final messages; along with her mother's last words of encouragement, she handed back the letter he had sent from Ceylon, which had arrived two months after her death.

I had been spared to fulfill the mission which in extremity I had entrusted to another....That letter remained with me during the following weeks as a stimulus to fresh endeavour. I must at all costs return to the redwoods and fulfill my mission to them. Their immediate preservation had become the chief object of my life. I had pledged myself to the task of saving them when my life was hanging in the balance. My life was no longer my own. It seemed to me that I had been spared for this express purpose.

On his return, Baker had joined a lecture agency, which had booked him into a test venue—Picton Hall, Liverpool—to check out its new man. It was a success. A nationwide tour was launched. The subject was the California redwoods, with Baker's illustrated lecture titled, "Wonder Trees of the World."

The first event was in Manchester. As he worked northern Britain, he caught cold and contracted laryngitis; but he never missed a lecture, making use of pinch-hitters to add a comic touch to the occasion—he would stand by and whisper his comments to the voice, liberally spicing the talk with jokes about laryngitis. When he arrived back in London for his major lecture to the Royal Geographical Society he was completely without his voice.

However, that night fortune had it that he was able to talk freely. He told the audience about the wonder cure he had received—and how appropriate it was for a Man of the Trees. The treatment was pine and camphor, from two forest trees, and who should administer it but a "charming little woman by the name of Sister Squirrel."

The audience enjoyed the anecdote and were now nicely primed for his talk.

This lecture was a rally for the redwoods. Some of the most important conservationists in Britain were in attendance, providing the great opportunity Baker needed to spearhead an international campaign.

The response to the lecture tour was encouraging and generous. He now had some steady money coming in, much of which he sent to Palestine to support the planting there. He also started a British Save the Redwoods Fund, which was well supported.

HE'LL MARRY A TREE ONE DAY

Baker was able to return to the United States in 1932 to undertake another lengthy tour. His first stop, in New York, was a broadcast with Lowell Thomas on *World News*.

> *He introduced me in his usual lively fashion: "Hello everybody! Who do you think is with me on the air tonight? The Man of the Trees. He's been planting trees in Palestine, he's visited the groves of the oldest living trees in California, he's seen the Kauris in New Zealand, the giant eucalyptus trees in Australia, he's met the tree worshipers in Ceylon and no doubt worshipped with them, and now he is here, back again, just as much in love with trees as ever. I believe he'll marry a tree one of these days! Where are you off to this time, Man of the Trees?"*
>
> *I'm off to California, to the Redwoods—the wonder trees of the world. Tree lovers in England have given their money to help save these groves, and now I'm on my way to the Redwoods to form a Grove of Understanding, a mecca for tree lovers from all over the world. These trees are your heritage from the past—what are you doing for the future?*

At the end of the broadcast, Baker's first big break in the fundraising campaign came when a very wealthy man called the station. They got together over lunch and Baker, amazed that a wealthy American hadn't taken time to see the redwoods, went immediately to the tele-phone and called the secretary of the Save the Redwood League, arranging a guided tour of the giants. After the man returned, he donated a half million dollars to the redwood conservation fund, adding to gifts of $3.5 million from the Rockefeller family, which went into saving the redwoods at Bull Creek Flats and other areas. The great majority of donations, however, were small, starting at ten cents.

Baker now set off across the United States. On the Californian wing of the excursion, Baker again visited his tree mecca. His friends Sheriff Breen and Fred Endert, activists from Crescent City, informed him that the groves he had chosen as the finest trees in the world—and had taken on as a personal mission to safeguard—were threatened because eighteen million board feet of timber were needed for forms to use in the building the Golden Gate Bridge.

They decided to bring together all concerned, conservationists and lumbermen, for a meeting in the Mill Creek grove. On a Thursday

Baker made twenty 'pilgrimages' to the redwoods, in whose presence he often found healing.

they spent the day contacting the California press and then held a press luncheon. The meeting took place on the Sunday.

I shall always look back on that gathering as one of the momentous events in my life. Foresters, lumbermen, old time prospectors, gold-seekers, mingled among the local residents, who were supporting me in a fervent appeal I was making to save what I regarded as the finest forest in the whole world. As I spoke the sun lit up the ground mists and made patterns on the fern covered floor. Myriads of tiny sparkling drops glistened like diamonds on the leaves, and the colours of the rainbow were reflected in a short arc of the visible sky, where the canopy was broken along the creek.

Inspired by the pristine beauty, he shared his thoughts and feelings for these trees. The trees, he claimed, would be much more valuable if protected than if exploited. He reported that the Men of the Trees and common folk in England had sent gifts to save the redwoods as a thank-you to America for its war aid. He appealed to the lumbermen to give him a chance to buy back the trees at the timber cruiser's valuation.

Three days later I had the deep satisfaction of hearing that the immediate threat to supply eighteen million feet of timber for the Golden Gate Bridge from those groves had been lifted. Great financial resources were involved. It would mean that huge sawmills were idle, lumberjacks would have to seek work elsewhere, dividends would not be paid, shareholders would have to go short. But it was a triumph of the imagination. They had seen a vision and dreamed a dream.

It was a dream that would take nine years to fully realize, but round one of the struggle had been won.

CHAPTER SIX

The Civilian Conservation Corps

FDR AND MORGENTHAU

As Baker continued his journey through America, his progress was assisted by both his connections in the Society of American Foresters, which were reinforced when he spoke at their congress in Washington that year, and his letter of introduction from President Hoover. Through broad consultation and his own observations, he was able to form a general appraisal of the American forestry situation. His intention was to develop an overall forestry plan for the American authorities.

Undertaking a seventeen-thousand-mile journey through the forested areas of the country helped him complete the forestry plan. He described this trip, which included a jaunt into Canada, in his 1949 book, *Green Glory*:

> *It was evident that the situation [in America] called for imme-*
> *diate action, the rate of timber consumption, including loss by*
> *fire and other destructive agencies, being four times as great*

as the rate of timber growth. The country's requirements amounted to about 25 billion cubic feet each year, while but approximately 6 billion cubic feet was being grown. I recalled that in 1909 the United States produced its entire newsprint supply, but at the time of my survey I found that the country was dependent upon foreign resources for at least two-thirds of it. One Sunday edition of a metropolitan newspaper was using 24 acres of forest a day, while a Chicago paper required 100 acres of Canadian forest every week. The United States... was already using more wood per head of population than any other country in the world.

I visited cut over areas and witnessed the destruction caused by forest fires. I saw the dreaded scourge, hurricane-driven, death-dealing flames; at times I fought forest fires alongside of foresters, and heard many stories of the destruction of human life and property.

While camping with an old Indian in the redwoods in Northern California, where I had been in search of the finest groves, many of them being threatened by the axe, suddenly over the campfire one night, almost out of the blue, the old Indian remarked, "Plenty men no get work; there'll be plenty forest fires this summer." He was a man of few words; in fact, for the previous three weeks we had spoken little, most of our intercourse being carried on by signs. This remark therefore caused me to think very deeply. Under the existing regime in those days men were employed at a rate of five dollars a day to put out forest fires, casual gangs were taken on, and no sooner was one fire under control than another would spring up, so that such men would have almost continual employment throughout the summer months. Did the old Indian mean to imply that persons needing employment would set fires going to keep the gangs employed?

Baker returned to New York, where he met two young men who were supporters of Norman Thomas, the socialist candidate for that year's presidential election. They introduced Thomas to Baker, who described his conservation plan for America. Thomas immediately said: "Roosevelt is your man; he is going to be the next president."

Baker wired Roosevelt for an appointment. He was well aware of the tree-planting governor of New York and already had an introduction through his daughter, Anna Roosevelt. Months earlier, she had taken an interest in his work and suggested that he meet her father, who was a strong advocate of forestry. Baker describes the meeting in *Green Glory*:

Driving up through the night from New York, I arrived in Albany about six the next morning, and just before ten o'clock I was awaiting my appointment at the Capitol. I was greeted warmly by Franklin D. Roosevelt, who exclaimed, "I have been wanting to meet you for a long time." And I replied, "Me, too, you. Do tell me how it was that you first became interested in forestry?"

"I was staying in your country," he said, "back in 1905, with the Novars in Scotland, Lord Novar...my wife is a kinsman of his. He took me around his woodlands, 20,000 acres, and showed me how he had been able to stem years of agricultural depression by falling back on his woods. He was able to give employment to his dependents in his forests when there was no work for them on the farms."

FDR told me that when he got back to New York he sought out Gifford Pinchot, who pulled out of his pocket two pictures: one was of a painting made in China 300 years ago, and the other was a photograph of the same site that very year. In the first the hills were covered with an evergreen forest. At the base of the hills there was a populous city, settled in a fertile valley with a river running through it. The only indication of logging to be seen in the painting was a little water chute with some logs coming down the slipway. The photograph taken 300 years later showed the same contour of the hills, but they were bleak and bare. Not a vestige of their former glory remained. The one-time fertile valley was strewn with great boulders, the cover gone, and the dried up soil with its fertility lost forever. All that remained of that flourishing city was a few derelict huts. Mr. Roosevelt said that that had made such an impression on him that he asked Gifford Pinchot to come and talk to the businessmen of New York.

Mr. Roosevelt said, "From that time I have never looked back. You know what I have done by way of planting on my own place at Hyde Park, and you know what I have done for the state of New York." I said, "Yes, indeed. I know that here you have planted sixty percent of all the trees planted this year in the whole United States and now you are going to do for the whole country what you have done for the State of New York."

He looked right at me and said, "What do you mean?" I replied, "But you are going to be the next President." "What makes you think that?" he retorted. "Well," said I, "I have just done 17,000 miles in your country, preparing a forestry plan, and don't you think an outsider often has a better perspective than the man on the spot? Besides, yesterday I was discussing my plan with Norman Thomas, and he said, 'Roosevelt is your man; he's going to be the next President.'" "Did he say that?" "Yes, he believes you will bring relief to millions of unemployed as he would like to have done if he had a ghost of a chance of the Presidency." The Governor's eyes twinkled as he said, "All right, Baker, go ahead and say what you want me to do."

Baker needed no second invitation. He told Roosevelt that America must have an overall forestation scheme and described what he had seen in his travels; the scheme must be conceived and carried out on a gigantic scale and provide a new frontier for ambitious young Americans, giving direct and immediate employment to 250,000 men. He talked incessantly in an unbroken flow, but at the mention of 250,000 men Roosevelt snapped back with a question: "Could that number be 300,000?" Baker said it could be 500,000 if need be.

They discussed the enormous rate of unemployment: there were already eighteen million unemployed and projections of thirty million were being made; they discussed the scourge of forest fires, what Baker's Native American friend had told him about the unemployed setting fires, and that in Canada when they stopped paying casual labour for firefighting, fires had declined 50 percent.

"At that moment like a flash," Baker said, "Mr. Roosevelt caught the idea which later brought the Civilian Conservation Corps into being."

"Very well, Baker," Roosevelt said. "Your work is dear to me and I should like to help you. Leave your papers for me to study. I might be able to do something about it—if I am elected. I want you to meet Henry Morgenthau, Jr." Morgenthau was the governor's right-hand man in matters of forestry and conservation. He later became secretary of the treasury and designed the New Deal.

A NEW KIND OF ARMY

Leaving America for England, Baker continued to read about the American political scene with great interest. On hearing the results of the election he cabled congratulations to the president-elect. When FDR assumed office, with the country apparently headed for economic disaster, the theme of his acceptance speech was "back to the land with forestry—without vision a people perish."

"I received a charming letter from him from Warm Springs, which prompted me to take the next boat out," Baker wrote. On reaching New York, Baker wasted no time in contacting Henry Morgenthau, Jr. At that time Morgenthau was chairman of the Federal Farm Board, which was actively bringing marginal land into use for forestry. These lands had once been pine forests that had been cut and farmed, with poor results. Considerable success was achieved by the Roosevelt administration in New York, to the extent that of the one hundred thousand acres re-treed in the United States, sixty thousand had been planted in that state.

In conference with Morgenthau Baker recounted briefly his meeting with the president, adding, "What you and the President have done for New York you can do for the whole country. You can plant trees and grow gold for the nation and by so doing can serve the land, assist agriculture, and help to stem the oncoming timber famine." He pointed out that he had written a report on which the largest reforestation corporation in the world had been launched. He presented facts and figures.

Morgenthau played devil's advocate, though Baker instinctively felt that he was on his side, that he had felt the emotion of the ideal. Baker had to prove the economic aspects of the proposal; while he thought in millions of acres, Morgenthau thought in billions of dollars.

> *Quickly he grasped the significance of my figures—figures laboriously collected over many years of practical experience in many lands. He swiftly absorbed them and, instead of crabbing the scheme, wanted to make it even bigger...in his mind the project quickly evolved into a nationwide scheme. The child of my idea had grown into a giant before my very eyes. Working in close collaboration with Morgenthau, the President requested $3,000,000,000 for work relief as his first measure when he was installed in the White House. The second measure was to establish the Civilian Conservation Corps.*

Things moved quickly. On March 22, 1933, the president sent his bill to bring employment and conservation together to Congress. On April 5, he appointed Robert Fechner the Civilian Conservation Corps' (CCC) director. The next day the president sent for him and asked how long it would take to get the first camp going. Fechner thought it would take some time, but the president wanted the first camp in place in three weeks. It was.

Baker spent these months watching the program come into being, conferring with the authorities, joining the men in the camps, sharing his experience, and giving many talks and broadcasts in support of conservation. Soon 250,000 men were in the field, planting new forests, starting nurseries, preventing forest fires, and managing woodlands to increase productivity. By the second year there were 300,000 workers and by the fifth, 4,500 camps with 200 men each.

Their most spectacular success was in reducing forest fires by 75 percent. To control wind erosion, they built a wall of trees from the Canadian border down to the panhandle of Texas. By 1942, 220 million trees would be planted, stretching across 18,600 miles in a 100-mile-wide band from Canada to the Brazos River. Even today, the federal response to the Dust Bowl, including the Prairie States

Forestry Program, which planted the Great Plains Shelterbelt, and the creation of the Soil Erosion Service, represents the largest and most focused effort by the US government to address an environmental problem. After only eight years, six million men had passed through the greatest conservation movement the world had ever seen. Roosevelt had created a new kind of army in a new kind of war: an army of peace for greening the earth.

What was St. Barbe's part in all this, really? To what extent did he influence Roosevelt's massive conservation scheme?

Douglas Brinkley's 2016 account of Roosevelt's conservation activities, *Rightful Heritage: Franklin D. Roosevelt and the Land of America*, discusses many individuals who influenced the president, but makes no reference to Baker. However, in *Franklin D. Roosevelt and Conservation, 1911–1945, Vol. One, 1911–1937*, a collection of Roosevelt's documents compiled by Edgar B. Nixon of the Franklin D. Roosevelt Library in 1957, Baker does get a mention. The documents indicate that a large number of individuals claimed to have inspired the CCC. In a memorandum dated October 10, 1933, Roosevelt comments on one such claim, generously conceding "there were probably a great many...people in various parts of the country who had the same general idea at an equally early period....It seems to me that there is plenty of credit due everybody who saw the importance of this fine project." Edgar Nixon notes that "Richard St. Barbe Baker, a British forester, says he suggested the idea to Roosevelt at a meeting with him in Albany just before the 1932 election," referring to the story in Baker's book *Green Glory*, quoted above. In fact, the ideas presented to Roosevelt by Baker and others were not new. Roosevelt himself comments that "I myself as early as the autumn of 1929 decided to ask the Legislature of New York State for additional funds for conservation work, with the idea that these funds would be used primarily to employ people out of work." Roosevelt came to the presidency with well-established conservation-employment plans.

Still, there are other hints supporting some connection with the Man of the Trees, such as Baker's photograph of the president with the written dedication, "To my friend Richard St. Barbe Baker from his fellow 'Man of the Trees'," signed by Roosevelt. Baker was moving in circles that provided opportunities to connect with figures like Anna Roosevelt or Henry Morgenthau. In 1931, for instance, newspaper notices place Captain Richard St. Barbe Baker lecturing on the same New York City stage as Henry Morgenthau's father, the former United States ambassador to Turkey.

Baker's CCC story may provide some insight into the nature of his autobiographical narrative. While his stories of serendipitous involvement in conservation history are not fabricated, they are at times inflated. The impact of his involvement with redwoods conservation also may have been overstated. As a biographer, my confidence in the accuracy of these and several other stories was shaky, but, as we will see, at other times seemingly incredible stories are verified. At any rate, the success of the CCC project gave Baker another, bigger, global idea which would emerge in the 1940s and '50s to become his major life work.

MEN—AND WOMEN—OF THE TREES

Richard Baker loved big ideas. The very idea of a vast, national conservation scheme, including forestry and employment relief for the army of the Depression's unemployed, appealed to him at his core. The idea that this vision could be implemented, not only in America but everywhere, especially Britain, inspired Baker to work harder and longer for a global conservation ethic.

Conservation of the redwoods, the oldest and largest of living things, as the symbolic—perhaps actual—nature mecca of the planet, remained a constant concern that he pursued with messianic intent.

Thus, the remainder of the thirties was spent alternating between Europe and America. In Britain, Baker assisted in building the Men of the Trees Society, working in the head office, visiting the local chapters, editing its *Trees* journal and the annual *Tree Lovers' Calendar*, while continuing with his writing, lectures, and at times, forestry consulting.

Despite being the "Men" of the Trees, the nuts and bolts tasks of the organization typically fell to women. In Baker's absence, editorship of the journal was handled by Diana Buist, who also assisted the honorary secretary, Marjorie Mumm, who was often overwhelmed by the correspondence that flooded the office. Buist was also active in the society's collaboration with the Forestry Commission, the government's forest agency.

Nineteen thirty-eight was a banner year for the Men of the Trees, which, with some five thousand members in 108 countries, had arguably become the world's first and largest international environmental non-governmental organization.

That year the first summer school of the Men of the Trees was convened at Oxford, the site of the Imperial Forestry Institute. Some 150 members were in residence for ten days. Four papers were read each weekday morning, field trips to forested estates were arranged each afternoon, and illustrated lectures were given each evening, including one open to the public. This represented a new departure: a more serious and formal approach to member education and an opportunity for intensified networking of tree enthusiasts, professional foresters, practitioners, and nurserymen.

The membership of the Men of the Trees always included its fair share of eccentrics—Richard St. Barbe Baker arguably being one of them. It was always a headache, but also great fun, to sort out

The first summer school of the Men of the Trees, Oxford, July 18–21, 1938, Baker front and centre, in black tie.

the various peculiar needs of the attendees: for instance, the convener, Margaret Tennent, might be found searching the rooms with a compass to find beds with the proper magnetic orientation for some 'scientific' member.

LIKE A RAVEN

How did Baker keep body and soul together, and manage to travel extensively worldwide, without steady work, over several decades?

Baker's close friend and sometime publisher, David Hofman, who became a prominent member of the international Bahá'í community, shared a flat with Baker for several years at Jay Mews near the Albert Hall. Hofman recalled that Baker never had much money. An iconoclast, he was not always popular with people in a position to employ him, such as the Colonial Office. Similarly, he was often at odds with the British Forestry Commission because of his radical ideas, in particular his advocacy of mixed broadleaf tree plantings, as opposed to strictly commercial conifer plantings.

Consequently, he never had a steady and reliable income. He worked constantly as a volunteer or in fee-for-service engagements. Hofman recalls that during the Second World War Baker would work late into the night and stumble in, exhausted, around midnight, having spent the evening on civilian mounted patrol. Hofman would pour him a bath and sit by the tub reciting prayers for his friend, who seemed on the verge of collapse. At five in the morning, however, he would be up, writing ten letters before breakfast.

Baker himself said he lived like a raven, a scavenger. Intermittently, he had royalties from his books, but these did not amount to a reliable income. From time to time he had a considerable consulting business, being quite popular among the British landed nobles who would call him in to make a forestry plan for their estates. Baker would visit for a week—a week of free rent in a fine house—make use of a fine horse to ride the land, write up an overall forestry plan, and receive his fee.

From these sources he eked out a living, but he also required, and received, a great deal of support from his friends, many of whom were deeply devoted to his work and the causes he espoused. Hofman said that although Baker was never a burden and certainly did his share of the cooking and other work, at the end of the month Hofman was usually left with the rent and the bills to pay. Said Hofman, "I never minded...much."

Baker had a way with people, said Hofman, and many people willingly offered to help him with his work and projects. He might have an idea—using trees to guide aircraft flying south from Scotland to London, for instance—and he could muster Boy Scouts or some other group to plant them according to some grand scheme. He could commandeer an office of secretaries and assistants, perhaps the office of a university president or a cabinet minister, to type and mail his letters or prepare a manuscript—without their realizing what had happened until it was over. Hofman recalled that a very wealthy woman worked full time as Baker's secretary, for free. People might share their homes with him. During periods of convalescence from an illness, his friends gladly took him in and cared for him for long periods with no thought of repayment.

Though Baker rarely had money, he could always come up with trees; if a thousand trees were needed for a project, he would have them donated, or obtain them from his family's nursery for free.

One day, Hofman recalled, he had arrived at work at his publishing company, George Ronald, and was going through the mail, when Baker called, asking to borrow ten pounds. Hofman was able to say, "I'm just about to send you £200 pounds." Hofman had just received £400 in royalties from the Norwegian edition of *Africa Drums*.

As mentioned earlier, Baker had a propensity for 'embellishing' some of his achievements. Mr. Hofman was able to shed some light on this characteristic. Among other occupations, in the 1930s Hofman was a television announcer for the BBC, which operated the only public television station in the world at the time. He recalled an interview program in 1937 called *Picture Page* that featured various VIPs who were living in or visiting London and that he hosted. He once had Baker on the show, discussing the same book, *Africa Drums*. Baker brought in his own drum collection, played African music, and demonstrated how the drums were used to communicate.

He also brought in an African rain stick. It so happened that London was experiencing a rare period of drought. Hofman jokingly told Baker to use the rain stick to make it rain. Baker took him up on it and before he left the studio it was raining!

Hofman recalls that Baker claimed to be the first white man initiated into the Kiama, the elders society of the Kikuyu tribe. Indeed, he was able to sense intuitively what was happening to his African friends, who seemed able to communicate with him and send messages through drums. He recalled that on one occasion Baker grew restless, saying that there was something wrong in Kenya and the Colonial Office was part of the problem. Hofman asked, "How do you know?" He just felt it. He went down to the Colonial Office but was sent home—there was no problem. The next day, however, he was called in to advise the office on some problem that had erupted in Kenya.

Hofman often wondered if Baker's claims to association with the famous and powerful were believable. But often, such stories were verified. For example, Hofman noted that one of Baker's close friends was Jomo Kenyatta, who was a student in London and later the first president of an independent Kenya. Baker had introduced Kenyatta to the prominent Bahá'í scholar, Hasan Balyuzi, and taken him to a Bahá'í summer school. Hofman recalled that much later, when Kenyatta was president, a messenger arrived from Kenya with gifts from Kenyatta for Baker, including a vessel filled with huge dates, as well as a sacred stick.

THE ROYALS AND THE REDWOODS

In 1938, Baker was asked by Sir Edward Grigg to address selected members of the House of Commons concerning the Civilian Conservation Corps and a possible comparable project for England. This meeting was followed by a public forum at Kensington Town Hall, which in turn led to an invitation from King George VI for Baker to visit the Buckingham Palace and show his pictures of the CCC camps. The future king had attended Cambridge with Baker after the First World War.

The king later decided to visit the CCC camp at Fort Hunt near Washington on his American tour, and Baker was able to help with the arrangements. In turn, it was his hope that the king would in some way encourage the British government to enact a similar program in England. Baker was in the United States in 1939 during the royal tour and was able to help rehearse the camp the day before the royal visit and join the tour itself.

Baker's conservation efforts in the United States climaxed that year when he took a seven-man delegation of the Men of the Trees to the redwoods. The group made an eighteen-thousand-mile tour of the United States, building bonds between the two countries around the issue of trees.

For eight years, Baker had travelled back and forth between Britain and the redwoods, lecturing, building networks, arousing the press, and collecting funds, all with the objective of saving the grove at Mill Creek. He describes the culmination of the campaign in *Dance of the Trees*:

> *In the summer of 1939, when I visited the redwoods of Northern California with members of the Men of the Trees from Great Britain, the Mill Creek Redwoods Park, about which I had been so greatly concerned, was still but a project. Funds collected and distributed through the Save the Redwoods League had purchased threatened areas further south. The world's tallest tree—the Founder's Tree, near Dyerville on the Bull Creek Flats—had been saved. Many beautiful redwoods had been rescued from the great lumber mills, but the greatest trees in the world in an area of 12,000 acres, close to the boundary line between Oregon and California, were still at the mercy of the axe.*
>
> *I had been under the impression that further progress had been made, and that the area for which I had pleaded and raised funds had passed the project stage. It was therefore a great shock to me and my fellow members of the Men of the Trees, when we learnt that negotiations for the acquisition of this area had not been finally completed. We lost no time*

in making strong representations of behalf of the Mill Creek area—the Grove of Understanding, the Mecca of my dreams.

Hard by these groves we were negotiating for land in which to establish a world centre, where plays might be performed and where people might come for all time to enjoy the redwoods.

Once again our friends of the Press rendered valuable help and those who for so long had devoted themselves to saving these groves redoubled their earnest efforts. Throughout all, one of the most tireless workers for these redwoods was Fred Endert, Honorary Treasurer of the Men of the Trees at Crescent City. On 13 August, 1939, he wrote, "It is possible that your Mill Creek 'baby' will be saved, providing enough pressure is put on the California State Park Commission and the Save the Redwoods League. It is within the power of the State of California to take over a proposed park of 12,000 acres, the cream of the redwoods, in the Mill Creek tract.

"Now I am asking you to write to the Chairman of the California State Park Commission and ask that they take over this body of timber. They want encouragement, so ask your friends, wherever they might be, to do likewise and lose no time in doing so. Our National Government is interested, but acts slowly."

In response to this pressing appeal, I cabled and wrote urging the formation of a State Park, and was greatly encouraged to get a letter by airmail from Fred Endert, dated 26 October 1939:

"At last the Mill Creek Park has been definitely established. Nine thousand acres of the best redwoods in the world—your 'baby' has been saved. This should be of some consolation in these troubled times. I have been quite active in following this through and helping wherever I could. I feel that we have done a great thing for all people for many generations to come."

Cabling my congratulations, I urged that the balance of three thousand acres be declared a nature reserve.

The vision of a still larger conservation area was held by the Forest Service, who wished eventually to expand to sixteen thousand acres. Baker was aware that it was necessary not only to preserve a large mass of trees but also the local climate and watershed that support the trees, both of which were threatened if the area around the reserve were too extensively logged.

After the Second World War, the reserve was brought up to seventeen thousand acres when the Patriotic Women's Clubs of America collected funds to purchase another five thousand acres as a National Tribute Grove to the men who died in the war effort.

Still, the battle for the redwoods was not over.

THE SCANDINAVIAN FRONT

Activities during the 1930s went beyond the British and American fronts. Baker established some strong ties in Scandinavian countries, where forestry policies tended to be much in advance of the rest of the world. On at least one occasion, Baker was able to combine forestry and faith, in collaboration with one of the most prominent international representatives of the Bahá'í community.

I had the honour of being Shoghi Effendi's emissary to the King of Sweden. I was giving a lecture to the Royal Norwegian Geographical Society on African drums. The lecture was by Royal Command, and my traveling expenses were covered by Norway. It was reported the following day in the national press. Martha Root, who had been sent by Shoghi Effendi to take the Faith to the Kings of Norway and Sweden, was seriously ill. She saw the report of my lecture before the Royal Family in the Oslo papers the next morning, and got one of her nurses to ring me up and ask me to come to her bedside.

Martha Root explained that she had already had an audience with the King of Norway, and had given His Majesty the Bahá'í Writings, according to the instructions of Shoghi Effendi. Before she could set out to Sweden she had been laid low. She had a night and a day nurse, and was unable to complete the mission entrusted to her. Would I visit the King of Sweden to present His Majesty with a copy of [the book] Bahá'u'lláh and the New Era? I agreed to take a train early the next day and to do my best to have an audience with His Majesty.

In the meantime, Baker had an appointment with the Afforestation Society of Norway and its founders. While lecturing in Jerusalem, he had suggested that armies be used in reforestation, as this would provide excellent initial training—and get a few trees planted in the bargain. This idea had been reported in the Norwegian press and had in fact been implemented.

Arriving in Stockholm I went straight to the Prime Minister. After talking about Sweden's "white coal", meaning water power, and the interesting fact that Sweden had no unemployment problem while Great Britain at that time had over 3 million unemployed, I explained my mission and asked the Prime Minister's advice as to the best way of fulfilling it. Mr. [Hansson], the Prime Minister, explained that he was shortly expecting a visit from the King, and if I walked in the park I would meet him and his family; it would be an easy matter to explain my mission and present the book to His Majesty in person. Ten minutes later this had been done and I had been invited to walk with the King to the office of the Prime Minister. His Majesty expressed his gratitude to Shoghi Effendi and assured me that he would read the book with interest. I returned to Oslo to report to Martha Root, and we had prayers of thanksgiving and for healing before I continued with my lectures for the Handelstag Forening and the Norsk British Forening. I even went up to Bergen to give a lecture there.

Baker often remarked that when he made efforts to support the Bahá'í movement, his conservation efforts were invariably strengthened. That Baker would be attracted to the Bahá'í faith is not surprising, as it honours and embraces all faiths, including the Indigenous religions to which Baker felt an affinity. As a Bahá'í, one does not reject one's former faith, rather one finds it fulfilled in the Bahá'í teachings. Raised in millennial Christianity, Baker saw this new religion as fulfilling his hope for the return of Christ and the coming of the kingdom of God on earth. Beyond that, the Bahá'í writings are positively alive with extraordinary tree imagery.

THE WAR EFFORT

By the late 1930s Baker was aware that war was imminent and decided to offer his services in ways befitting his age and abilities. He was instrumental in helping to mobilize the average citizen in the war effort in a manner typical of his *modus operandi*: Keep making suggestions. Go to the top. Occasionally it clicks.

On a bus he chanced, for instance, to run into the portrait photographer Howard Coster, who made the suggestion that Baker contact the King's private secretary on behalf of the thousands of working citizens who were willing to give their spare time to the war effort as members of the Home Guard. Baker called the secretary, who in turn passed the idea on to Anthony Eden, whose broadcast to the nation that night resulted in thousands volunteering within twenty-four hours.

For his part, Baker joined the Metropolitan Mounted Branch and was on duty, on horseback, at the House of Commons on September 1, 1939, the night war was declared. With the older men and veterans of the Mounted Branch taking on much of the local policing work, many police officers were able to enlist in the services.

Throughout the war, Baker made good use of his old NAVARAC caravan. Fitted with blackout curtains, it became the mobile headquarters for his fellow home guard officers, as well as his personal office for both his writing and for the Men of the Trees. From here, he composed his cables and letters in the battle for the redwoods.

At this point, Baker was fifty years of age. As the oldest man and most experienced rider in the force, he was given an excellent but dangerous horse. After ten days of good riding, Baker was stabling the horse when it crushed him against the wall, breaking three ribs. He drove himself to the doctor, was put in a cast, and returned to saddle the horse and do a patrol of eighteen miles, returning to the stall without mishap.

He did, however, take sick leave and used the time to begin what would be his major war service, marking timber for the Ministry of Supply. This took up to five days each week. Britain was in great need of timber for the war effort and it was Baker's objective to see to it that supplies were cut carefully and replacement plantings made.

He had never considered himself a preservationist. Rather, as a conservationist he advocated use—but wise use—of the forests, in order that they could provide a perpetual supply of products. Aside from certain special areas, such as the fine redwood groves, one conserved forests so that they could be used sustainably. As far as possible, given the fact of total war, Baker saw to it that all cuts were "improvement fellings" and in all lands under his supervision, clear felling was ruled out completely.

I felt that it was essential to retain tree cover, especially on hill-sides, and not allow the tree beauty to be sacrificed as a panic measure. Looking back on the war years perhaps my greatest contribution was the saving of these woodlands from complete destruction by Military Forest Corps from New Zealand, Australia, and Canada.

A STRANGE LIKENESS OF SHAW

The Million Shilling Fund started by the Men of the Trees during the war to support reforestation not only assisted planting, but also served to attract many new members to the Men of the Trees, not the least of whom was George Bernard Shaw. St Barbe had met him at a party for authors and had, of course, cornered him on the subject of trees. Shaw said, "I'm only interested in cutting them down." St. Barbe, recalling this, wrote Shaw:

Dear Mr. Shaw,
The last time I spoke to you about trees, you said you were only interested in cutting them down. Perhaps the war is now doing

this extensively enough to satisfy even you. I know you may not be interested in what I am doing in trying to plant trees which will in time take the place of those now being felled, but a note of encouragement from you would, no doubt, help the cause very considerably. We would welcome you as a member of the Society.

The following letter was received in reply:

Dear Mr. Baker,
Upon the roof of the summerhouse where I write my plays, thousands of acorns shower themselves down. For the past thirty years I have collected them and, like Nelson's admiral, dibbled them in with my stick, but they will not grow for me. During the past five years, I have sent the acorns to Lord ——'s forester and now you can see row upon row of saplings raised from acorns of my collection. Is my hand accursed? You are doing a good job of work. I would like to become a life member and enclose my subscription. As I am an old man, I will not burden you very long. Good luck and success with your planting.

To which Baker replied:

Dear Mr. Shaw,
We are glad to welcome you as a Life Member of the Men of the Trees. Now that you have become one of us, the curse, if any, will be removed and all the little acorns will grow for you. We wish you the health of a pine, the strength of an oak, and the endurance of a redwood tree.

In gratitude for Shaw's support, Baker presented him with a copy of his book *Among the Trees,* with its picture of a giant sequoia in whose bark was a strange likeness of Bernard Shaw. Baker claimed that this was one of Shaw's most prized possessions, which he kept by his bedside and showed to all his visitors.

During the war, the *Trees* journal and the *Tree Lovers' Calendar* were published, though in modified form. Saving the extensive mailing lists for these publications from their secretary Clayton Davis's flat in Kensington was the cause of some excitement and bravado.

A stick of bombs had been dropped across the square and the area was cordoned off. Only one of the five bombs had exploded. There was no one around when I arrived in my car, so I moved the barrier far enough to let my car through and drove up to Clayton's house. On entering the basement I found an Irish maid crouching beneath the kitchen table, waiting for the next explosion. I asked her if she was all right and had enough food, seized the Calendar files and bolted back in triumph to my car. When I presented Clayton with the files, however, he exclaimed, "But you've left out the drawer of the S's—and it has the largest number of subscribers!" Early the next morning I ran the gauntlet again. Two more bombs had exploded in the meantime, and the last remaining inhabitant of the square, the Irish maid, was still hiding under the kitchen table! When I had found the drawer of the S's I tried to persuade the girl to leave the house and come with me to safety. She remained adamant, convinced that she would be safer in the house than anywhere else. I and the missing drawer of files escaped unscathed: but I often wonder what happened to my lone Irish maid.

Baker's own London flat did not fare well. It was destroyed by a bomb with the loss of most of his personal papers, clothing, and possessions, including his staff of office of the Kiama.

WORLD FORESTRY CHARTER GATHERINGS

War or not, the work of the Men of the Trees continued, which meant numerous lectures, film showings, and exhibitions to schools and organizations of all kinds. The Million Shilling Fund allowed for the replanting of extensive areas that had been felled for the war effort.

July 22, 1943, marked the 'coming of age' of the Men of the Trees. A celebration was held at Puncknolle, Dorset. One week later, on July 29, the society made a significant move onto the global stage by hosting the first of its World Forestry Charter Gatherings. Recognizing the global interdependence of people and forests and anticipating the establishment of the United Nations, Baker called together the ambassadors of many nations to discuss a World Forestry Charter that might be put in place after the end of the war. In the name of those present he sent the following message to the King:

The representatives of the United Nations and members of the Men of the Trees meeting in London today tender their loyal greetings to His Majesty on the occasion of their gathering to discuss the place of forestry in a World Charter after the war. They believe the work of reclaiming the waste land and stemming the oncoming tide of destruction provides a task so great that it will need a concerted action of all the nations. They also

Diplomats from eleven nations join Baker to discuss a World Forestry Charter.

believe that it will be the means not only of healing the scars of
the earth but those in the hearts of men everywhere.

His Majesty replied: "Please convey to the Men of the Trees and
their distinguished guests together today the King's sincere thanks
for their kind message and his best wishes for the success of their
meeting."

It would be the first of a series of international meetings to take
place over many years.

During the war Baker dictated a largely autobiographical book,
I Planted Trees, during a ten-day bout of influenza. First published
in 1944, it was reprinted a number of times in succeeding years and
attracted many readers and many young men to a career in forestry.
"Some years later I was complaining to my publisher that I had
never succeeded in writing a bestseller. He thought for a minute and
then replied, 'I wouldn't say that because we sold 32,000 copies of *I
Planted Trees*.'"

This was followed by *Africa Drums*, published in many editions
in Britain and the United States, as well as in French and Norwegian.
The Norwegian royalties padded the 'thin wallet' for a time.

CHAPTER SEVEN

A New Earth

AN EMERGING GLOBAL CONSCIOUSNESS

A new consciousness had emerged in the First World War: on the one hand, there had been a stark realization of the danger inherent in unbridled nationalism; on the other, a new understanding that international cooperation and peace was a possible and perhaps necessary alternative. This manifested itself in the League of Nations, humanity's first attempt to actualize its global identity.

With the Second World War, the stark alternatives—annihilation or peace—became clearer. Many people began to realize that peace was associated not only with the elimination of negatives—racial, ethnic, national, religious, and class prejudices—but also with building positives: a sense of humanity's oneness; promoting the principles of justice and equity; and enhancing communication, education, literacy, and socio-economic development. Humanity began to feel its identity as one diverse yet global reality, above traditional, divisive barriers. More and more, it seemed we would accept the unity of humanity, of one world, or face horrific consequences.

It is no surprise to see Richard St. Barbe Baker active in the movement to establish the United Nations. As a Bahá'í, he was by definition a globalist, though his evident patriotism was never compromised by his broader identity as a world citizen. It was his conviction that a global commonwealth would serve the interests of its member nations better than nationalism alone.

Baker had an inherent sense of world citizenship, feeling equally at home in Africa, the Middle East, the Americas, the Antipodes, Asia, and Europe, through all of which he had travelled and many parts of which he knew intimately. To this universalism was added his powerful sense of the oneness of life, a natural understanding of the interrelationships and interdependence of a global ecosphere.

He knew instinctively that peace and unity were linked to a right relationship to the earth, to the land and its forests. Fed by his biblical background, his adopted Bahá'í faith, and his training in forest ecology, a vision took shape, a prophetic vision of a great, global enterprise to restore the damaged earth as a vehicle for the unification of humankind. The biblical vision of the end times, of peace and harmony in an agrarian society, of the desert blooming, of spears beat into pruning hooks, loomed large in his mind.

Baker had a particular attraction to an all-encompassing vision, to the big project, the 'One World Purpose'. At the same time, no element of the great plan would be too small to merit attention. He would battle to save a single tree or an entire forest with the same vigour. He relished his encounters with the wealthy, powerful, and famous, but gave his time and attention equally to the tribesman and the rank-and-file members of the Men of the Trees. He would speak to meetings of the influential, to members of Parliament, or associations of foresters, or stroll down to London's Speaker's Corner and harangue passers-by. He knew that it was both the powerful and the humble who shaped and transformed the world.

The global consciousness behind the United Nations movement began to manifest during the Second World War. Baker and the Men of the Trees had decided to take advantage of this movement and move boldly to promote a substantive role for forestry in a world charter. To this end, invitations were sent to all of the national ambassadors in London to attend the World Forestry Charter Gatherings from 1943 to 1958.

At the first gathering Baker had presented his analysis of the world forestry situation.

I pointed out that in spite of the fact that this is an age of coal, iron, steam and electricity, wood still plays a vital part in everyday life; it is the basis, in fact, of modern civilization. I went on to explain to the diplomats the global details of the forestry consumption problem which had affected every man, woman, and child in the world and generations as yet unborn. That speech was a testimony; it expressed the driving force behind my career.

In reviewing the words of the speech Baker made to the diplomats from some forty nations, we can see quite clearly the prophetic character of Baker's observations. Since his time in Africa in the early 1920s he had recognized the great danger of environmental destruction, that humankind was destroying the earth, thus threatening its future. He saw and described the future of Africa blighted by desertification and drought; envisioned the need for sustainable development far in advance of the spirit of the 1987 Brundtland Report; foresaw the Third World fuel wood crisis; grasped the global character of environment and development and the need for concerted action at the international level; understood the effect of forests on climate, thought at the time to be nonsense; foregrounded the issue of conserving biodiversity; and promoted the intrinsic value of trees and forests above and beyond any economic consideration.

Baker addressed the initial gathering with this insightful assessment of contemporary world forestry:

The picture is a gloomy one. The tremendous material strides that have been made by our modern civilization have eaten into the natural resources of our earth. The impact of modern industrialism with its insatiable appetite for raw materials has caught the forests of the world before man has become aware of his eternal dependence on them. To the trees he owes the stored up wealth of the coal-beds, the fertile earth for the production of food, water for irrigation, and the purity of the very air he breathes. The rise and fall of civilizations waxed and waned as man exploited and devastated the forests. A demon of destruction is at large in the world today and deserts are on the increase.

The tasks confronting us are gigantic and the time at our disposal limited. There is no need to wait, indeed it would be disastrous to do so. Let us begin today, realizing the vital importance of trees and forests throughout the world. Further, the work of reclaiming wastelands and stemming the oncoming tide of destruction and the growing deserts of the world by large scale reafforestation is a task so great that this will provide a common meeting ground for all people everywhere.

With this end in view, Baker proposed that the representatives assembled, together with those of all other countries, form a World Forestry Committee.

At the second charter gathering, with forty-four national representatives attending, Baker used the opportunity to present each of the ambassadors in attendance with a questionnaire relating to their forest resources and the planting efforts in their respective countries. Their replies helped him in writing his book, *Green Glory, The Forests of the World*, which he completed two years later. The book was published in Britain, the United States, and Germany. The German edition won him an honorary life fellowship in an unusual organization of eccentric intellectuals known as the Institute of Arts and Letters (London). Baker later made the dubious claim that *Green Glory* had "become a textbook in the U.S.S.R., prompting the Russians to treble the Roosevelt shelter belt planting programme and achieve it in the same time." Hyperbole aside, it was ahead of its time in proposing that forests play a key role in global ecology.

MARRIAGE, CHILDREN...AND TREES

While on a lecture assignment in Worcester, Baker met Doreen Long, who became his secretary. Two years later, on January 23, 1946, they were married at the Church of St. Mary's, Puncknowle, by his old friend, Bill Anderson, the bishop of Portsmouth. As they left the church, they passed under an arch of spades and axes, the novel idea of his friends in the Home Guard.

Richard Baker was fifty-six at the time of the wedding, his wife twenty-six.

The staff held the fort at the Men of the Trees headquarters while the Baker's enjoyed a honeymoon in Jersey, taking time to meet the many Jersey members of the society. Following the honeymoon, the couple returned to Puncknowle and he completed *Green Glory* at about the same time that their first child, Angela, was born on November 4, 1946. The next year, they moved to Gate Farm, a run-down place Baker decided to work himself. Their second child, Paul, was born at their new home on November 7, 1949.

Baker was now intent on earning a stable income for his family:

While at the Gate I launched Tree Services for the care and repair of ornamental trees. I acquired two Red Cross vans to accommodate the two teams of three lads I trained. One stretcher was taken out of each van to allow room for the equipment necessary for climbing the tallest trees. One of the sights of London, in those days, was to see our teams working on branches near the tops of the great plane trees. The training included an appreciation of the artistic anatomy of trees and the art of lightening the heads of trees without lopping them. There were members in our teams who could walk up trees as I could walk up stairs and their exploits attracted crowds of London sightseers. Many valuable trees that had been threatened were saved in this way and are still enjoyed by Londoners. The same was true in other cities, including Bath where the great planes of the Circle were saved by the Men of the Trees and our Tree Services.

It 1947, Baker presented his New Earth Charter to the general meeting of the Men of the Trees at the Chelsea Physic Garden. The charter, a broad and progressive ecological manifesto, was translated into many languages with the help of the Esperantist organization. For three years Baker invited suggestions for modifications or additions, but it remained unaltered, and he continued to present it to audiences throughout the world for several decades.

A HECTIC SCHEDULE

With the financial pressure of a young family upon him, Baker visited the Colonial Office to remind them that he still worked for them— and that he had never received a pension for his African service.

The Colonial Office introduced me to the Central Office of Information who invited me to join their headquarters lecture staff, for they were needing people with African experience to meet the growing demand for lectures throughout the country. The work occupied about five days a week and I would fill as many as three or four engagements a day. I was able to get back to the farm on Fridays and tackle the Men of the Trees' correspondence. As far as possible I fitted my forest advisory work in with my lecture programme. In the course of three years I had addressed all the principal Rotary Clubs in the United Kingdom, Co-operative Societies, Women's Luncheon Clubs, and a wide cross section of principal schools and universities. On one occasion a sedate chairman introduced me to a large audience as the "Founder of a Society of Free Lovers"! It was not the first or the last time that this amusing, if slightly embarrassing, slip was made.

The hectic nature of Baker's life at this time can be seen in his appointment books and diaries. They are largely illegible, but a listing of the legible dates in 1948 alone is mind-boggling, especially when one remembers that these are in addition to up to four lectures a day for the Central Office of Information. Limited international travel also continued. Of a trip to Ireland in 1948, he wrote:

Our visit to Ireland...will always be remembered by the huge gathering at Phoenix Park, when the President entertained the Men of the Trees not only from England but from Northern Ireland and Eire. Seven hundred and fifty guests were welcomed to a wonderful strawberry tea party after a ceremonial planting of nine Atlas cedars in the Park.

During the tea party I asked the President what percentage of Eire was tree-covered and ventured to suggest that it might be two-and-a-half percent. Turning to the Minister of Lands, the President queried, "Is that so?"

"No, Sir, I'm afraid it's not as much as that. Perhaps not more than two percent." The President turned again to the Minister of Lands and said, "I want you to double the planting program next year." I ventured to suggest that he might have some difficulty doing this as many of the trained planters were coming over to help with forestry in England because they were getting such poor wages at home. "Double their wages," said the President. From then on a progressive forestry policy was adopted and the forestry situation in Eire was thus saved.

In 1950, Baker again visited the United States and in May met with the executive of the Garden Clubs of America in New York. They were often a source of lecture contacts that helped to finance his travels.

His book *Green Glory* began to receive acclaim and a number of individuals took up its promotion. One of these was a German forester, Dr. Carl Schenck, who wrote on October 19, 1950, describing Baker as his foremost friend, "wielding the most lucid and eloquent pen among all foresters...the most sympathetic of all tree-writers." Schenck invited Baker and the Men of the Trees on a tour of German and Swiss forests, which he would guide. On another front, a Mr. E. Roth of the Israel Literary Guild, wrote Baker on December 7, stating his intention "...to make of *Green Glory* our New Testament here in Israel" and that he would make special representation to Prime Minister Ben-Gurion, who was a keen advocate of reforestation.

THE GREEN FRONT AGAINST THE DESERT

In 1951, the Seventh World Forestry Charter Gathering, held on March 21 with thirty-two nations represented, acclaimed the proclamation of a Green Front Against the Desert. This launched Baker's major life project: his efforts to lead the reclamation of the Sahara desert as a "One World Purpose, Uniting East and West."

Since his days in Africa, when he had witnessed the effects of the encroaching desert on the people of Kenya and northern Nigeria, Baker had come to a realization that the choice before humanity was either to live in harmony with nature, to embrace an ecologically sound land ethic and policy, to protect the soil, water, and forests, or to live and perhaps die out in a desert world. He would do what he could on behalf of the former. Through his work with the Kikuyu and Nigerian tribesmen, he had seen that it was possible to mobilize Indigenous people in a new land ethic. Could people everywhere be mobilized?

Throughout his world travels, he had seen the universality of the ecological battle, that the world was being destroyed, slowly but surely, by industrial 'progress,' but also that alternative policies were available and did work, that they even enriched human beings' choices and ways of life.

With his firsthand experience of war, Baker hungered for peace and imagined alternate constructive uses for this warped expression of human ambition. He was familiar with unemployment and the need to find a useful role for the millions condemned to a wasted existence. His experience on the American plains and prairies, the devastation of the dust bowl, and the huge response via the Civilian Conservation Corps—which tapped what would otherwise have been wasted human resources to tackle environmental destruction for the largest conservation project in human history and which ultimately employed six million people—had shown the way.

His many efforts to garner support for nature conservation convinced him that people, once educated about environmental problems, were willing to respond and do their part to support conservation. Added to this conviction was his visionary side, his millennial zeal, his sense of the timeliness of efforts to build the 'Kingdom of God on Earth' and usher in a 'Golden Age of Humanity.'

Combining these varied streams of thought, he devised a plan to unite all the world's governments in a single purpose that would serve as an alternative to war by harnessing and repurposing humanity's warlike spirit. It was a colossal vision: nothing less that the reclamation of the entire Sahara Desert through the planting of trees. By uniting in a peaceful accord humanity could reclaim the world's largest desert, the worst example of human environmental devastation. The project would restore an area larger than the continent of Australia, adding millions of acres of agricultural and forest land to a resource- and food-hungry world with a mushrooming population; halt the desiccation and erosion of the continent of Africa; tap all of the excess labour force that could be assembled, employing a force equivalent to all of the standing armies of the world, some twenty million strong; and give new purpose to the powerful military-industrial complex, which could handle the project like a military campaign of conquest.

From this point, the Sahara project would dominate Baker's life.

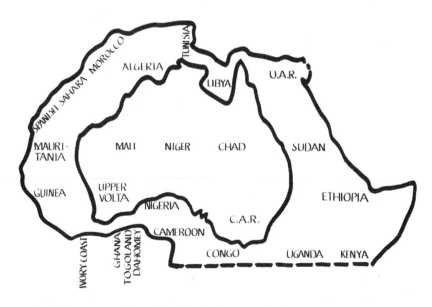

Baker's drawing reinforces the case for desert reclamation.

ON THE CONTINENT

Early in 1952 he took up Dr. Schenck's invitation and in the early spring toured the Continent, addressing biological conferences in Germany and Austria. Simultaneously, he mustered support to establish the Green Front Against the Desert and made many broadcasts in support of reclamation efforts.

When discussing forestry issues with the responsible Austrian government minister, Baker learned that the exploitation of the forests was necessitated by the need to repay American aid loans. With the Iron Curtain rising on one side and the Allied forces putting pressure on the other, the Austrians faced a perilous situation. Baker observed that "The tendency was for them to live for the moment and drown their distress with cocktail parties."

Baker realized the importance of these political questions in the environmental equation. He began to stress peaceful coexistence and environmental restoration as an alternative to national animosity. In speaking to an audience of six hundred university graduates in Vienna on the topic *Trees of the World*, he concluded his impassioned plea for international understanding by saying, "Is it too much to hope that the Iron Curtains of the world will give place to the Green Front and the scars in the earth as well as the scars in peoples hearts may be healed by tree planting? As the Persian seer declared, 'This is the hour of the coming together of the sons of men. The earth will indeed become as a Garden and a Paradise.' I truly believe that 'the leaves of the trees will be for the healing of the Nations.'"

The European contacts made through this tour proved significant for Baker's Sahara project, one component of which was to be the establishment of a University of the Sahara. Baker was ever open to opportunities that came his way: when at one of his talks he was congratulated by an Austrian count and invited to dinner, Baker brought along seventeen supporters and Austrian members of the Men of the Trees. The count turned out to be one of the largest forest landowners in the country.

His only child, a daughter, was married to a forest engineer who was supervising his woodlands and he was paying an Austrian forestry professor a retaining fee to prepare and supervise forest working plans. The Count invited me to stay with him. After a few days there, I decided that this would be the ideal training ground for students from the University of the Sahara and the Count agreed to take up to thirty for six months a year. The following day I was continuing my journey in the mountains of Austria when I met a professor who had been deploring the establishment of destructive paper mills and had warned the authorities of the risk entailed. He had become a thorn in the side of the ruthless supporters; to get rid of him they had offered him a professorship in the U.S.A. This he had politely declined as he felt his duty was to educate his own people. He seemed to be just the man I needed to train my Sahara students. He willingly consented to be the first Dean of the University of the Sahara, unpaid, and to take charge of thirty students for six months in the year.

So, by coincidence, in a couple of days he had two new active supporters eminently qualified to provide material and intellectual resources to the great project.

Baker returned from the Continent in time for the World Forestry Charter Gathering on March 21, this time with the ambassadors of some forty countries in attendance. He renewed his appeal for the Green Front, and with the blessing of the ambassadors was able to approach the universities of the Sorbonne, Oxford, and Cambridge to provide support for an intensive reclamation plan for Sahara lands and for the idea of the university. Baker proposed to launch the effort himself by conducting, under his own leadership, an ecological survey of the Sahara. This he planned for the fall of 1952.

SKINNED ALIVE

The earth was being skinned alive; already one quarter of its surface was desert. The fact that much or most of this desert is man-made, or at least assisted by humanity in its advance, was slowly dawning on the conscience of humanity. "Wherever man walks, he leaves a desert in his footsteps," went one aphorism; it was sadly true, at least in the regions of the globe that were arid or semi-arid by nature.

The oldest civilizations, in the Middle East and North Africa, contained the greatest expanse of desert, but conditions favourable to desertification were taking effect much more rapidly in the newly farmed and forested lands of the Americas and Australia, where erosion was undoing in decades what nature had created over millennia. Reports were coming in from conferences sponsored by the Food and Agriculture Organization (FAO) and United Nations Educational, Scientific and Cultural Organization (UNESCO), newly formed agencies of the United Nations, indicating the terrifying speed at which the deserts of the world were advancing.

A cold war was heating up the world once again, dividing East and West into two armed camps, squandering the resources of mind and earth in a madly escalating struggle for weapon supremacy as the nuclear nations stockpiled weapons of mass destruction. The first skirmish was being fought in Korea.

But what and where were the real enemies of humanity? Was it the imagined enemies of communism or capitalism, or Soviet or American imperialism? Or were these animosities merely obsolete expression of a moribund world order? Was not the greatest threat to humanity the destruction of the surface of the planet, which we chose to ignore, our collective energies and capacities wasted in the battle for supremacy on a plundered, drying, dying planet?

Baker's vision of a world healed through the planting of trees, the restoration of the soil and watersheds, the reclamation of deserts and wastelands, seemed—still seems today—an impossibly utopian dream. But to him it was entirely practicable. He had been a forester in equatorial Africa for a decade and had seen the potential for good management to reverse the pattern of destruction. Why, you simply had to convince all national governments to use their armies, twenty-million strong, to attack the desert, armed with shovels and trees, and together put an end to war and erosion in one bold stroke!

He had no doubt that entrenched centuries-old practices and cultural patterns could be overturned and a new culture, a new order established. He foresaw a new human race that loved the land and forests as he did. He was convinced that that capacity was there, in each person—just scratch the surface. He set about to do his part. Like the prophets of old, he was largely ignored, but also had small successes that would, in the fullness of time, bear fruit. He had no doubts. But he had to convince others:

> To convince others I knew that I must have detailed information, both with regard to the speed of the desert's advance and to the means of stopping this encroachment, and to the possibilities of reclamation. I decided that an ecological survey must be made and that I should head it.

THE SAHARA EXPEDITION

To begin the expedition he needed several things: public and institutional support, money, and companions. Support came from a number of sources: moral support from his coalition of national ambassadors, assembled annually for the World Forestry Charter Gathering, and from the Men of the Trees at their annual general meeting, as well as the organization's Green Front Summer School held at Harrogate. A number of commercial firms wishing to have their products tested under tough conditions—and to receive the associated publicity—donated materials such as tires, oil filters, and food. *The Daily Telegraph* supported the expedition and provided extensive press coverage. Several major universities gave their blessing.

As well, there was a good deal of popular support, both from the Men of the Trees and from the general public. Shortly before his departure for Africa in September of 1952, Baker went on the program *In Town Tonight* and invited listeners to donate their peach pits to the expedition. He would plant them in the Sahara, a gift from the heart of London to the heart of Africa. After a dedication ceremony in the chapel of St. Martin-in-the-Fields, "thousands of people came to see us off and most of them brought peach stones. Barrow boys did a brisk trade and many were the peaches we ate that day instead of lunch. The newsreel cameras were busy and soon the world had the story."

Many individuals provided financial support, not the least of which was Baker himself. To finance the project, he wrote *Famous Trees* for Lord Kemsley's Dropmore Press, which was handsomely produced, with a special "sumptuous" edition of fifty produced at an equally sumptuous price. "It was given the National Book Societies Award for one of the twelve best books of the year, and the advance payment I received was invaluable in financing the Expedition."

The expedition team was made up of Baker, leader and expert on 'biosylvics'; Ray Perry, forester, artist, and dowser, who had worked for the Forestry Commission and dedicated his life to desert reclamation; Audley Money-Kyrle, botanist and ecologist, who had just taken a degree in ecology; and Major Bob Harrison, who had been a transport officer in Palestine, familiar with desert travel. The team met together for the first time at the annual summer school.

Social marketing, 1950s-style. Collecting peach pits in Trafalgar Square to plant in the Sahara alerts thousands to the need for desert reclamation.

Baker purchased a second-hand desert Humber from the Government Disposal Board. It had a reconditioned engine and cost £350.

My friends protested about using an old war vehicle: "Its all very well for you," they said, "if you want to commit suicide that way, but its not fair to take these young people with you." However they had made the decision themselves and were keen to set out as soon as possible. None of us had that much to lose, least of all myself. My home had become unhappy and my marriage was in the process of becoming legally dissolved. One other member of my team was also broken-hearted and a third had been threatened by loss of sight.

Apparently, Baker's wife had had enough of his single-minded focus on trees. Essentially, the problem was that he was rarely at home and she was left to raise the children on her own in a rural area.

Broken-hearted or not, his life mission apparently trumped marriage. He would drown his personal sorrows in the desert.

On the morning of September 3, 1952, Baker awoke with excited expectation and rang up Field Marshall Viscount Alexander of Tunis, former governor general of Canada, then British minister of defense, and vice-president of the Men of the Trees.

With all his desert campaigning, I felt that we needed a message from him and some last words of instruction. We would like to have his strategic skill as our Commander-in-Chief of the Green Front against the deserts of the world. I said as much and his farewell message was: "I only wish I were coming with you." We had occasion to be extremely grateful to him later.

That day they set off for Dover, first stopping at the French consulate to ask permission for the expedition to cross the French territories in the Sahara. It was flatly refused! Only recently, three scientists had set off on an expedition and not come back; then the search party was lost, an aircraft search failed, and finally a party was sent out on camels. The French were tired of searching for lost explorers!

Undeterred, they decided to seek out higher-ups in Paris. Arriving in France, they found that their expedition had hit the news. They made the rounds of the French colonial office and various government departments, seeking permission for the journey, but got nowhere. Finally, they called on the agent general for Algeria, who with a wink suggested, "Do you need permission?"

That was sufficient, and off they went, travelling through France and Spain to Gibraltar and on to Morocco.

CHAPTER EIGHT

The Desert Shall Bloom

Stop on the fringe of the desert and light a cigarette: before you are ready to grind the butt under your shoe, the driving sand has advanced several feet beyond you. The Sahara is the largest desert in the world. It covers an area bigger than the United States of America and it is relentlessly advancing, year-by-year, month-by-month, hour-by-hour. It is a hungry pitiless monster threatening our very existence.

THE MOST INHOSPITABLE ROUTE

The team of four had more than four thousand miles ahead of them. Next to a polar expedition, this was the most bleak and inhospitable route in the world: at least polar travellers were assured of water. They would pass through Algeria and what was then French West Africa (now Niger), past Lake Chad and the northeast border of Nigeria into French Equatorial Africa, through the Belgian Congo into Uganda, Kenya, and on to their ultimate destination, Mount Kilimanjaro in Tanganyika. The trip would take the better part of four months. On actual travel days they would average one hundred miles a day, but there would be multiple layovers.

Before the journey had properly begun, however, the crew was reduced to three when Major Harrison was repatriated from Algiers due to illness. On top of that, their truck broke a half-shaft and temporarily lost a wheel. They had to settle down in Algiers to wait until spares were flown in.

Meanwhile, the team had an opportunity to inspect the forestry efforts of the French in Algeria. Their system of land restoration was adapted to accommodate social concerns and consisted of the use of terracing and, notably, banquettes running at right angles to slope and an intricate series of small canals to channel water during periods of rainfall. Horizontal lines of binding plants, such as thornless cactus, and the use of twenty-yard-wide green belts of tenacious vegetation were part of the system of defense against soil erosion. Fruit and nut trees were included in the green belts to provide food and income. The low parts of the watershed were given to grains sown

Four thousand miles across the Sahara in the desert Humber.

in contour strips. Thus, people continued to inhabit the land and benefited from the restoration rather quickly given the rapid growth of plants in the North African climate. Here was proof that careful husbandry could reclaim the desert when political will is present.

As interesting and valuable as this Algerian layover was, the team was rapidly depleting its small allotment of French currency, needed to purchase gasoline. Through the intercession of Viscount Alexander they were able to replenish their money supply and on November 6 were underway again.

"We set out with a heavy load; in addition to cans of pineapple juice, soup powders, hard biscuits, fig preserves, lots of fresh citrus fruit, and dry tablets of Horlicks malted milk, we had taken on seven jerry-cans of petrol given to us by the Shell Company who were interested in our expedition. We were to be the first car to attempt the crossing at the opening of the season that year." The authorities had closed the desert earlier that spring when several parties were lost. At Blida market, the little team of surveyors took on a supply of fruits and vegetables.

Sunglasses were a must when driving across the expanse of blinding sands. Early in the trip, Baker lost his while releasing tire pressure. This was a regular chore since the heat of the sun would cause the tires to explode if overinflated. On top of this, the pressure had to be adjusted according to the density of the sand. Even a pound of pressure could reduce the risk of sinking into the soft surface.

While the party wore hats of various kinds, Baker adopted the traditional Arab headgear after losing his pith helmet. The Arab gear protected against the glare and also the dust as it could be drawn over the nose and mouth.

As they entered the perfect air of the Atlas Mountains, they saw their last of running water for two thousand miles. On their descent, before them for the first time was the great Sahara. "There were badly eroded hills behind us to the north," wrote Baker, "and in all the great expanse not a tree was to be seen. As we came down we had our first experience of sunset over the Sahara, it was an experience which for me recalled sunsets on the Saskatchewan prairies when life was new and romantic."

At Djelfa, in Algeria, the railway and road ended. Here the real desert begins with its stony wastes and dried out riverbeds. The surface of the Sahara, they soon realized, was quite varied. Contrary to the popular image of shifting sand dunes, only 15 percent of the desert is sand.

Once we were in the desert we were to understand why the authorities had not encouraged us. We were to come upon the wrecks of many second-hand cars....The abandoned cars were not the only sign of abandoned hope. For sometimes, by such a wreck, we would find a human shinbone, sticking out of an old boot...

The tracks were corrugated and they found that, given the weight of the vehicle, if they travelled fast the ride was smooth, saving the springs as well as their backs. Travel at night conserved fuel, so they took to driving fast, after dark.

One morning they arrived at Laghouat and entered as it was waking. "There we visited an Arab bake house and indulged in a sort of doughnut made in rings, freshly fried in oil, crisp and delicious." They took on more petrol. Laghouat is in a sparsely populated area, but had a market and a mosque. It was a junction of the trans-desert trade "and there may be seen the dignified Arabs with their camels loaded with salt and other merchandise."

The mornings could be cool, with an icy wind blowing. As they continued on their journey they came upon sparse vegetation checked by constant grazing. They passed old thorn trees tortured into fantastic shapes by grazing, but still alive. Soon they came to their first oasis and were astonished by its richness:

Never before had we seen such palms or dates, which are described by the Arabs as the "Fruit of the Gods". They are larger in size than any shipped to England....One is enough for a meal, being 2.5 inches long, light brown in colour, perfectly dry, with no suspicion of stickiness. The flavour is delicious and there is an aromatic scent which heightens the enjoyment. The growing of dates is a skilled art and the propagator is known as a "fundi", which implies skill. The male flower is taken to the female palm and scattered by hand to fertilize the female blossom. In the desert it is possible to leave the crop of several years on the palm, for they never fall off unless cut as the stems are very persistent and do not rot; neither is there a fall of the leaf. In the oasis the water from the natural springs is carefully dispensed in the most primitive way by placing mud in the channels and stopping or turning on the water as required, thereby regulating the flow with precision. The continual sun, and the constant moisture regulated at will by the owners who turn on the water, produced this surprising luxuriance and richness of growth....It is always intriguing to speculate where such water comes from...here in the arid desert one suddenly encounters quantities of water, produced from ancient wells which lie along a line at regular intervals.

Fossilized evidence of forests in the Sahara.

They rested briefly in the oasis town and ate a meal at a small cafe before setting off again across sand and pebble, checking their bearings against the stars, grateful of the guidance. They could not follow tracks, for the old tracks became treacherous with loose sand so deep that it could halt all progress. At El Golea they reported to the desert commandant and were astounded to find that their story of the peach pits had travelled before them in the French papers. Their host was anxious to try planting peaches in his irrigated garden. They traded potatoes, there a rare luxury, for dates and enjoyed a fine meal. Here, hundreds of miles from the nearest forest, they were shown huge fossilized tree stumps. They wondered how long ago these trees had grown, and what was the size of the forest?

MIRAGES AND FOSSILS

Travel was incredibly tense, due to ground conditions—either rough corrugated stone, which had to be traversed at high speed otherwise the vibrations would smash the springs and shake the vehicle to pieces, or dangerously soft sand.

At Forte Mirible, an outpost of the Camel Corps, they learned from the long-time residents that the desert was getting drier and treks for water—even camels must drink once a week—were growing longer. A number of the old wells were now marked dry.

They next came down from highlands to the Plateau of Tademait, where Baker reported "there was absolute flatness, a vast sea of pebbles and sandy grit, with here and there sparse vegetation which had come as the result of recent rain, green patches in a dark brown interminable waste."

Next was a region of hills worn by wind into a land of mirages. At first they saw, with wonder, a lagoon with African sailing boats, or *dhows*, upon it. Then a palm-lined lake. Soon these fantastic scenes became commonplace and they ceased to wonder or attempt explanations.

Along some dry riverbeds they found real trees growing. Assuming that the water had gone underground and the roots were able to reach it, this suggested that underground waters could be utilized in reforestation efforts.

Now they came into lands of drifting sands and dunes. In the distance they saw another mirage, which turned out to be the real town of In Salah, located in central Algeria. As they traveled toward it, across constantly shifting, living sands, they realized it was in fact a calm day and only the slightest of winds was moving the land, endlessly.

In Salah was a large oasis, several thousand acres irrigated from one central well. Here they discovered more fossilized remains of great trees. The town consisted largely of buildings constructed of bricks made from violet and red sand. They settled into a grove of palms to pass the worst heat of midday and found themselves at the heart of this thriving and cosmopolitan town, a curiosity for the youth of the community.

Here was a place of agricultural plenty. All kinds of crops were grown. Hedges reinforced with thorn bushes surrounded the town, which kept out the shifting sands. But the insistent *sirocco*, the drying, dust-laden wind of the Sahara, was inescapable. Baker observed:

As I looked at this extensive and fertile area with its throng of people and their donkeys passing by, I wondered if this was a remnant of a great fertile valley; and I conjured up the possibility of large-scale reclamation by tree planting, sufficient in area to create a micro-climate for more extensive food production, with shelterbelts to reduce the force of the winds and the drying sirocco.

On they went, into the black gorge of Arak. The air became stifling, the battle one of staying awake. They slept and woke to the sun shining on the high cliffs about them, below were reeds and rushes growing out of a water hole. Unexpectedly, they found a well-arranged guesthouse, with water and a petrol pump to boot. But the tanks were empty; gas was to be conserved if they hoped to reach the next town, Tamanrasset.

They plunged on. The land became entirely black, unlike anything Baker had ever seen or imagined. The sun glinting off the wind-polished, blackened stones burned the eyes. His first thought was that it had been burned in an oil-fed fire. When they next stopped to deflate the tires, they turned over the stones to find them a natural colour—the sun had blackened only the tops. "Such is its fierceness," noted Baker, "that it even causes the stone to change its pigment."

As they continued, the land resembled a mining area of great pit mounds, all shimmering in the heat. Occasionally, they dropped into dry riverbeds, which became damp as they moved on, indicating some recent rains. The higher they rose into the Ahaggar Mountains, the moister the rivers became. The soft sand made the way difficult and at times they splashed through grass growing in water. Along the banks were old tamarisks, acacia, and other small trees and bushes.

> *Here too we saw birds and butterflies which we had not seen since before our first night in the desert. And then we saw a gazelle, unfrightened and tame, which gazed at us inquiringly. In the distance were others, grazing between thorn bushes, for in the plateau many rills descending from the higher mountains bring in water. All day long we travelled toward mountains of solid rock, and in the evening we rested at the well of Ekker which is under the shade of a great tamarisk tree.*

There, the rest-house keeper explained to them how it was that he had precious sticks to sell for firewood: they came from along the dry riverbeds. Baker explored the land and found recognizable wood chips littering the ground. His innkeeper said that they could be found all around, but only little bits too small to use. "For us they were treasures, rewarding us for all the roughness of the journey; for us they were proof that in the heart of the Sahara, within living memory, the last forest had been cut down."

A SOLITARY TREE

En route to Tamanrasset, they ascended to a large plateau; at 4,500 feet the numbers of grasses and other plants increased. In the middle of the plateau is the town, its streets lined with drooping tamarisks and Lombardy poplars. The town was irrigated, water being channelled from springs in the nearby mountains. These reached a height of nine thousand feet, where it might snow.

St. Barbe had a letter of introduction to a Mr. Claude Blangueron, director of the local schools. He had made a study of the local vegetation and had catalogued the trees and shrubs that still survived in the Ahaggar. Natural vegetation could develop here, if not for goats and camels grazing unchecked. Blangueron and his wife had a garden where the team was shown the full range of French salad greens with great pride. Gardening was part of the school curriculum. Along with the citrus, there were peaches fruiting. The gardeners were only too happy to try the variety of peaches that had been brought from England.

As the team studied the local vegetation, they were encouraged. This oasis was another place suited for tree nurseries and the development of extensive shelterbelts and microclimates, from which the 'green front' could be extended. They lost no time in organizing their new friends and pupils in the hope that they would establish a small school of 'biosylvics' in the heart of the desert. They had plenty of help in making the first nursery beds.

The next stage of the trip, to Agadez in central Niger, proved the hardest of the whole crossing: 560 miles, broken by one stop, the town of In Guezzam. At first the conditions were reasonably good. However, they could not apply the brakes or the car would dig into the soft sand, perhaps never to move again. When they had to stop they would turn off the engine and glide to a halt somewhere where the sands were hard packed.

We had been warned that over the area we were now about to tackle the quicksands were extensive. So we were up before dawn to make an early start before the intense heat loosened the texture of the sand.

The dry quicksands of the desert must not be confused with what we know of quicksands on a sea beach. The sand grains are infinitesimally small and cover the rocks to a great depth. At night in the cold they become more or less compact near the surface, but under the heat of the sun, as the grains expand, the surface becomes more fluffy and the resistance is reduced. Any object put on them will soon sink out of sight through their fine light grains.

Ordinary car tires are useless and rolls of wire netting are carried and laid in front of a car. It is a laborious way of progressing and the person who has to unroll the coil of wire sinks ankle-deep into the sand. In this part of the desert one finds many wrecks of abandoned cars.

The terrific heat adds to the discomfort of scraping sand away from sunken wheels, and bleeding fingernails are worn down to the quick by the sharp sand. If on top of all this you have engine trouble or the car is capsized, which is very easy, the traveller is in a desperate plight.

We had been warned! So I breathed a prayer and drove faster, determined to stop for nothing. At first we glided over smooth flat stretches of fairly hard sand always heading south. Though it was impossible to steer, the lightest touch of the wheel was sufficient to keep a general direction; if one attempted to do more, the car skidded dangerously. Fifty miles an hour was the best speed for this part.

Suddenly, without warning, we plunged into the quicksands and I had to grip the wheel and apply skidding tactics. After travelling at full speed on hard sand and then suddenly striking soft, the wheels turn suddenly, with the result that the car may somersault. Tyres will burst too, and that may be the end of man and machine. Luck was on our side and I gripped the wheel in time and made ever-widening curves, watching intently to diagnose the surface ahead so as to avoid calamity.

It was in the middle of this dangerous stretch that we sighted a solitary tree in the distance. It was incredible! Apart from the oasis we had not seen a tree for four hundred miles. I drove straight toward it over the quicksands, while our botanist filmed it through the windscreen. We dared not stop to identify it. It was a thorn of sorts; when the film was developed we found we had a perfect record. How that tree got there and how it survives will never be known. The chances are one in a million that anyone will come upon it again.

The solitary tree became the symbol of Sahara reclamation.

Their vehicle proved to have remarkable staying power. Despite the heat, high speeds, and tough conditions, the engine never overheated, and during this stretch of the journey they never once had to top up the radiator. On they went through rocks carved into weird shapes by the winds, over pebbles and more sand until they reached the isolated oasis of In Guezzam where huge tamarisks shaded the precious well. The rest-house keeper dictates his price for water, which sold at about half the price of gasoline. "We found it expedient to make friends with him and we each had a bath in a basin, which cost us nothing though our money vanished when we filled our petrol tank."

They now crossed into what is now Niger, then French West Africa, into a land called Aïr Massif. The vegetation became more varied. There were herds of wild camels and an occasional gazelle, as well as various birds. The land had deteriorated rapidly from the day when travel writers spoke of its tropical vegetation, fertile valleys with good water, ostriches, lions, giraffes, and, near Agadez, monkeys and butterflies. The ostriches and giraffes were long gone, but the other animals were still plentiful.

In places they found fields of wild grasses that had grown through their full cycle to seeding in just three weeks after a rare rain. The fields, looking like they were covered in corn, made an extraordinary sight, but for the most part the sand continued.

They saw a great caravan of four hundred camels, the longest they had seen on their journey, and then the massive trunk of a fallen tree, larger than any they had seen for a thousand miles, a hundred miles from the nearest forest.

It was of great significance to find it here, particularly as it was still in a state of perfect preservation. It could not have been there so very many years, possibly fifty or sixty, but much more likely to be less. The importance of this find lay in the suggestion that the forest had receded from this point within the century. Here was another link in our chain of evidence.

As they travelled on, the terrain became friendlier, the grass taller. The mud of a dried lake seemed suitable for food production. They stopped at Teguiadda, the first village in many miles, but the water was too salty to quench their thirst.

They began to see the tracks of many animals and soon cattle. There were streams of running water, the grass improved and they saw bushes—but still no trees. There were signs that there had been fires.

Here in the centre of the desert lived the Touareg people, the people of the veil, who had resisted the incursions of invaders for centuries, but had in time grown to accept outsiders. Baker found them to be a proud and distant people, somewhat intimidating, and the team made no friendships that passed the stage of a handshake, and that given slowly.

A number of stunted bushes were attempting to be trees. They saw an ostrich. There had been heavy rains and for the first and only time the car became stuck and shovels were required before the four-wheel drive could propel them out of the ruts.

Then they entered a new desert within the greater desert. There was some cultivation, but the fields were being buried by wind-blown sand. This new desert had once been a forest, slowly cleared as the farmers sought virgin land for cultivation. Having cut down the protecting trees they were in the last wedge of forest, completely surrounded by desert, cut off from habitable land and sources of food. They had no idea where to go next.

A GRAVEYARD OF DYING RACES

For hundreds of miles we had been passing through a graveyard of dying races. The solitary fallen tree we had recorded indicated the extent and speed at which the Saharan octopus had spread itself. It was hard to believe that when Livingstone was exploring Nyasaland, this area was part of the great rainforests of Nigeria. In other areas flourishing farms had disappeared within the memory of man and later during this expedition I was to trudge through sand wastes which had been my forest haunts when I had been in Africa thirty years ago. Here one could actually see the process of degradation, from high forest through the stages of orchard-bush and savannah to drifting sand.

They were standing on land where humus built over millennia had been eliminated in a single season by clearing and burning. They wondered that the French, who had such a knack for land care in their own country, had failed so miserably in this colony. The Indigenous population was defeated. They had abandoned traditional activities, such as making pottery, and now refused to bear children doomed for starvation.

There is no difficulty in diagnosing the cause of the desert. It is certainly man made. It is happening before our eyes. More often than not, climatic influences over which man has no control is given as an explanation.

Yet it seemed people could not, or would not, realize the demarcation between human and climatic causes of desertification.

They were now in a new waterless area. They found a woman grinding millet and were offered goat's milk to drink. They repaid the gift with Horlicks malted milk tablets for the children.

The landscape changed again as they drew near Zinder, close to Nigeria. It became more park-like and the track gave way to a road. "The Sahara was behind us, but desert conditions were all around. So far we had come across no sort of barrier to stop its advance!"

At Zinder, a European-style settlement contrasted with the mud houses and narrow streets typical of Saharan towns. They had enough money for a good meal and a bath. Comfort at last! The local Shell agents treated them to a full tank of gas and provided an introduction to their associates in Kano, Nigeria, their next stop.

On they went, through desert or semi-arid waste to savannah and then thorn scrub. Suddenly, they reached watered country. In two hours, they had passed from desert to rich farm- and forestland where groundnuts were the main crop, but here they were grown in amongst the trees in small patches.

Baker had seen this before:

At night their leaves would fold up like butterfly's wings at rest. When the hot air from the surrounding forest passes over the cooler patches of the groundnuts, it condenses, and in the morning there is a heavy dew equivalent to as much as a quarter of an inch of rain. As the sun rises the leaves of the groundnut plant opens out horizontally and again cover the ground with their shade, keeping it cool.

During the heavy rains, the topsoil eroded and washed into the surrounding forest, where it was held by the undergrowth and roots. Then, when new land was cleared, the good soil was reclaimed and the forest was allowed to regrow in the former clearing. This way a balance was maintained.

They found that the Nigerians' traditional sylvan agriculture was still in use. Nigeria was holding its own. In fact, when they arrived at the walled city of Kano on November 21, supplies of groundnuts were piling up, resulting in a bottleneck due to insufficient transportation.

Baker was pleased to return to Nigeria, where he had lived for five and a half years. He felt he had done his most effective work in developing a sustainable forestry system there, by advancing the use of secondary species. The lands then under his care were a great rainforest, impenetrable, with trees towering two hundred feet high, and six inches of rainfall a day feeding clear blue rivers whose sandy bottoms could easily be seen at a depth of twenty-five feet. Now, just two hundred miles to the north, was a desert so arid nothing grew.

AN INTERNATIONAL FOREST RESERVE

Baker proposed a plan to establish a three-hundred-mile international forest reserve and received support from the resident of Bornu Province, Nigeria. Baker believed that, if they could mark out a reserve in a way understood by the people and eliminate grazing, the indigenous forest would return. They had support from the British in Nigeria, but would also need that of the French colonials in order to form an adequate green front, centred at Lake Chad, where the British and French boundaries met.

Lake Chad was itself filling in with sand. Comparing modern maps with those of the last century, it appeared the lake had shrunk to one-eighth its former size in one hundred years, with the greatest shrinkage in the past forty years. The time when the great lake would disappear could easily be foreseen.

Looking for the best place to locate a shelterbelt to protect and reinforce the proposed forest reserve, the team travelled for two days, crossing several rivers by ferry before they arrived in Fort Lamy, now Ndjamena, the capital of Chad. One of these rivers was the Chari, nearly half a mile wide, deep, with a swift current. It was hard to believe Lake Chad was diminishing so rapidly with this amount of water flowing steadily into it. This observation supported Baker's assertion that the water in the lake was moving underground, as had other lakes in the Sahara.

Their first stop in French territory was with the procurateur général at Fort Lamy and his chief forest official, who gave them a warm welcome. They too were anxious about the encroaching desert. Already, the arrival of desert refugees had swollen Chad's population, which was now eight times that of any other province of French East Africa. Thus, the French authorities were very receptive.

Baker and his team were visionaries, idealists. They believed a sound and reasonable idea would translate into action; the authorities would see the sense of it and move, while there was still moisture enough in the land and air to make the reclamation project feasible. In fact, it would be many decades before concerted efforts would be made to create the Great Green Wall first proposed by Baker in 1952.

The idea re-emerged in 2002, at a special summit of African leaders in Ndjamena—where St. Barbe had first proposed it to French officials—on the occasion of the World Day to Combat Desertification and Drought. It was approved by the Conference of Leaders and Heads of States of the Community of Sahel-Saharan States held in Burkina Faso in 2005. By 2016, sixty-four years after first being proposed by Baker, about 15 percent of the planned 4,700-mile-long by 9-mile-wide green wall had been planted. That this was the realization of Baker's original vision was acknowledged in an article in *The Sunday Times* of London on July 20, 2014.

The article stated: "The idea was originally conceived by the British explorer Richard St Barbe Baker during his 25,000-mile expedition to the Sahara in the 1950s. Baker believed that tree-planting could reclaim the desert."*

SMALL FIELDS, TREE SURROUNDED

For the journey southeast, the team chose an unfrequented route for which there was no map and little information. It was at first semi-arid, but gradually becoming more fertile and treed as they entered what is now the Central African Republic.

Dotted along a five hundred mile track were happy little villages, all self-contained with their shambas for food. It was mild, primitive country, where men and women, unsophisticated children of nature, as yet untouched by European traders, had not yet discovered the need for dress of any kind.

At each village they stopped and the same pattern was repeated: first the headman would greet them, then the crowds would gather to gawk at the men and machine, then they would dole out Horlicks malted milk tablets, being the nearest thing to candy that they had. Sometimes the people would dance for them.

Though there were no signs of vehicles passing, they had no difficulty negotiating the paths between villages—though they took many risks fording streams or crossing on flimsy bridges. In little clearings the people grew cassava, plantains, and pawpaw trees.

As they travelled from one community to the next, they were always expected. Having spent many years among other Bantu people and knowing something of their ways, Baker was not surprised. There were the drums, and, Baker speculated, maybe some form of telepathy lost to 'civilized' culture. The welcome was always warm.

---

* In fact, the first trip was about 6,300 miles as the crow flies. Baker's second trip around the Sahara, visiting the leaders of every Sahara nation, involved some 25,000 miles of travel.

It was their good fortune that their journey coincided with a time of festivity. Dances went on night and day.

The lilt of the drums still haunts me and recalled other happy scenes where with the barest necessities the indigenous peoples still contrived to live a full life without being caught in the intricate machine of what we call civilization. From the point of view of the earth, they are not very destructive; although they make clearings in the forest for their food, their implements are a small felling axe and a machete....They work their land on a conservative rotation, leaving the jungle tide to cover their old farms, to which they return after resting them for seven or eight years.

Those days were a wonderful relief. Is there something in our nature that is invariably touched by primitive simplicity or is it the release from the bondage of bureaucracy? It would be easy to draw an idyllic picture of these forest dwellers in what seemed to us to be most happy surroundings. But even they have their own hard times, and should their crops fail they might be threatened with near starvation through being entirely dependent on what they produce. This is no criticism of their way of life and it is doubtful if the introduction of the so-called scientific methods of agriculture would assist them. An iron plough is a dangerous implement in Equatorial Africa because it loosens the earth to a considerable depth, allowing the soil to be washed away in the first torrential downpour. Their salvation lies in keeping to small fields, tree surrounded. So long as they only grow food for themselves they will be safe. It is only when they are tempted to clear extensive areas for the production of cash-crops such as cotton, that the balance of nature is threatened and, with it, their existence.

The team found ingenious and diversified local economies, unique almost to each village. Every one had a beekeeper, much to St. Barbe's pleasure, but each had a unique design for his hives, some of bark and others grass. Each village had its own craft styles for beds, bags, and baskets, with even the most utilitarian objects being ornamented.

"It was only when we approached the centres touched by trade from the outside world that the craftsmanship deteriorated and the article was degraded."

Local markets, which marked the four-day week, were bountiful in food and crafts; they were run on the barter system, but the people were quite happy to take their money.

They saw a leopard, but no lions, for another thousand miles. Eventually, they "came out of this dream world to the first indication of approaching civilization, some bush schools and mission churches." They were in great need of petrol, but the station was closed, since it was Sunday. Fortunately they met a contractor who filled them up. That night they slept in Bangassou. They were about to cross the River Bomu into the Belgian Congo, later Zaire, now Democratic Republic of the Congo.

CONGO

The forests were now thick and the trees met and embraced over their track. Monkeys tried to keep up with their progress, swinging from tree to tree, and often the team slowed down to help them out. Parrots called out, adding to the entertainment.

They were in a great forest of seemingly inexhaustible fertility, calling upon villagers and learning their forest ways. There was a diverse agriculture, cotton was being grown in tree-surrounded fields, and they saw women carrying huge baskets of the cotton they had gathered. The women had short plaited hair and wore cotton lengths wrapped around their waists when they worked, "one end of which they threw over their shoulders as they approached. They were a friendly people, greatly intrigued by the large blanket safety pins we gave them. We carried a lot of these for gifts."

Gradually, cotton began to take over and the forest diminished, with a great deal of feverish burning and clearing going on. At Bondo, where they had money waiting, there was little high forest left and government 'ginneries' were preparing cotton for harvest. The local people were getting their first taste of cash farming and prices the year before had been good, meaning that clearing and planting had increased dramatically. Consumer goods had been ordered, especially bicycles and cloth.

The rush didn't last long. Prices had fallen to half the last year's rate. The farmers were mystified, knowing nothing of world price, supply, and demand. Already hooked, they had to take or leave the price dictated. The solution was to plant even more cotton; consequently, more forest fell to the field.

At Langais they met a forest officer who was trying his best to plant shelterbelts, and was even moving in advance of the clearing, establishing belts for wind and firebreaks. He was pleased indeed to meet a team of ecologists, appearing as it seemed out of nowhere, to express delight in his efforts. He had thought he was fighting to save the country alone.

They now passed through an area of gold and uranium mining; as the area was used up, it was left desolate. Other areas were cleared for rubber plantations, but the growing of cotton was the greatest threat to the forest. The crop itself is very hard on the land. It was also a common practice to burn savannah to improve grazing; each time, more of the accumulated humus is lost. The government had enacted laws against this, but the people seemed willing to risk serious penalty in hope of immediate cash returns.

At Omi, they found forest plantations and, in places, fine shelterbelts. Here, in the excellent coffee plantations, shaded by larger native trees that created a fine microclimate and a permanent agriculture, was a living example of what they preached. In twenty-five years the owners had built a profitable industry and given much employment, proving the economic feasibility of what Baker had long advocated and offering a valuable example of what could be achieved on a far greater scale.

At a mission school they received the first news of Kenya and the Mau Mau rebellion that had broken out there. Baker was informed that all the loyal chiefs of the Kikuyu had been killed in the rebellion. "Not my friend Josiah," he exclaimed, instinctively feeling that they would meet again after a twenty-five-year separation. He wanted to rush to Kenya and try to play some part in settling the conflict as his friends were both native Africans and settlers, many being Men of the Trees.

Through the years that had passed I had been in close contact, and nightly had travelled back in thought to those campfire gatherings when I got to know them so well. There were some who had left us, I knew, such as the old Paramount Chief Kinanjui who at my initiation into the Kiama had presented me with the wave of his arm with fifty thousand acres of farm and forest land.

But there were demands of this current journey that had to be met. They entered the last great tropical forest in Africa, Ituri, in the northeast corner of the Belgian Congo.

Through all this ran a wide road, cutting through the dense forest complex and enabling the traveller to view a cross section. It was a superb picture of tree growth in infinite variety; trees of a multitude of species rarely seen in mixture; a paradise for botanists and plant hunters. Orchids were there too, growing high up on the trunks of tall trees, hanging in festoons amid the shade of the leaves, among cheeky little parrots, chattering monkeys and rare butterflies. On each side, in light and shadow, tree boles standing free of the usual undergrowth and entangled lianas showed clean and clear at the side of the wide road, towering a hundred feet or more, a sight such as is seen nowhere else in the world. I was thrilled! I longed for this scene to go on forever.

That was not to be. They came into a burned-out clearing and entered a large area of paw-paw plantations. The paw-paw is a small tree, with fruits growing up the narrow stalk like Brussels sprouts. There were also cotton farms and deserted farms that were rapidly invaded again by the forest.

Then, to their surprise, they found a sawmill and a carefully managed timber concession, worked by a European content to utilize the annual wood increment and not destroy the forest capital. He felled only trees of a certain girth that had reached maturity. There, in the forest, this entrepreneur had a school of apprentices making furniture.

He was a great source of information. They were tempted by an invitation to go on an expedition to pygmy territory. They had seen one troop of real pygmies; they had reddish yellow skin covered with light copper-yellow hair and stood about fifty inches. According to Baker, "the true pygmy never deserts the forest, which he protects with the blowpipe or arrow. They make contact with the outside world through their half-brothers, the products of intermarriage with other tribes." The expedition felt that they could not add this extra time to their trip, however, and carried on.

Reluctantly we went on our way, secretly hoping that we might be lucky enough to encounter again the real little people. I would particularly have liked to have seen them in their home and learnt from them the secret of living without destroying that by which they had lived. Although regarded as uncivilized and wild, they set an example to the world by their way of living conservatively, without unnecessary demands; a fine healthy agile little people, leading a fine healthy life.

They saw no more pygmies. Instead, the forest gradually disappeared and the number of farms increased. They arrived at Beni, a modern town that Baker felt had all the ugly manifestations of Western civilization at its worst. They longed for the forest again as they drove south toward the Rwenzori Mountains, the Mountains of the Moon, before passing into Uganda.

KAMPALA

There was now plenty of wildlife: elephants, the largest pod of hippopotamuses that Baker had ever seen, and a herd of buffalo grazing along the road. Recalling the days when cloth was made out of tree bark, with no damage to the trees, Baker wrote:

It was nearly thirty years since I had been in Uganda. I was much looking forward to seeing the forests that I remembered, so it was a shock to find that whole area had been deforested

in the process of cotton growing. The production of three hun-
dred and forty bales of cotton a year is poor compensation for
the valuable forest felled and burned to make cotton fields.

On meeting local forestry officials, however, Baker sensed that a
new consciousness was developing, if only because the lands were
clearly in decline. Plans had been made for proper management of
the remaining forests and there was an awareness of the threat of
desertification to the north. The game department, which had initially existed to shoot elephants, was now being reconfigured to offer
protection. Various efforts were being made to improve the environment, although emphasis was often placed on livestock and grazing.
"Surely," Baker argued, "the solution lies in turning to a silviculture
and the production of food and fruit-bearing trees, rather than in
risking the lowering of the water-table by deliberately recovering the
grazing lands and semi-arid zones."

At Kampala they stayed with a forestry friend and were pleased
to find much of his nursery given over to indigenous trees, not only
eucalyptus. Baker was concerned that most plantings used exotic
species, mainly to provide a quick financial return or fuel. He had
recommended it elsewhere, and in the past, but eucalyptus had one
great drawback: it dried up the land. Baker now felt that it should be
used mainly for planting in swamps. There were a good many suitable native species available that should be used instead.

On Christmas Eve we drove across the barrier into Kenya. The
Christmas spirit was conspicuous by its absence. Goodwill and
peace to mankind had become transformed to fear and terror.
In a passing car a women passenger was holding a rifle across
her lap with the barrel pointing at my head. Police cars with
searchlights patrolled the roads which were otherwise empty
and dark.

They had entered Kenya just after the start of the Mau Mau
revolution.

We went through the tragic town of Kakumaga, which had seen the gold rush that had brought so little profit but only dissatisfaction, both to African and settler alike. It was a scene of the betrayal of promises. The Kakumaga tribe, an agricultural and pastoral people, had been turned off their lands for gold mining. In accordance with old treaties, if land were taken for mining, they would be given the equivalent elsewhere. But an all-night session of Legislative Council had changed the law and no equivalent land was given. This was only a beginning of many later injustices, the accumulation of which had helped to bring about the tense situation which we now found.

It was around Christmas of 1952 when Baker said farewell to his travelling companions and went on alone. It felt to him like a homecoming. He discovered the whereabouts of his old gun bearer, Katootero, who was now a headman in the forest reserve. His friend, whom he had left thirty years ago with the words, "Farewell, I shall see you again," was quite unsurprised to see him, as if he had been away only a short while.

"How did you know I was coming?" Baker exclaimed. "I saw you," said Katootero. "Where?" said Baker. "In much sand," was the reply.

Baker set off to see what had become of Kenya since he had left it. He went to the important water catchment area of Elgon, which in his day had been virgin forest:

Upon it depended the fertility of extensive farmlands, now occupied by settlers. Now I looked over a landscape that for all time had been forest but which in so short a while had been replaced by coffee and wattle plantations and extensive wheat fields. I was soon to discover that this part of the country was an oasis by comparison with many areas which were suffering from steady desiccation.

Everywhere he heard the same complaint: "It's drying up!" If the locals who had lived there all along were disturbed, Baker, with the perspective of time and distance, was shocked at what he saw.

When he spoke to people about his journey, the drying of Africa, the assault of the Sahara, they were naturally alarmed, realizing that they were soon to be surrounded by desert. Even the wealthy coffee and sisal barons realized the danger. "When, however, I sought for an area of land in which to initiate experiments in biosylvics, nobody rushed to provide it."

Baker found that his efforts as conservator of forests in Kenya had been forgotten. The contemporary forestry policy was to remove indigenous forests and replace them with monoculture plantations of exotic species that were often diseased or were having detrimental effects on land and soil.

I drove on through this unhappy country toward Mount Kenya. It was a relief to come to one of the rare remaining indigenous forests and over it hung the most vivid rainbow I have ever seen. It looked as if my road went straight through the middle of the western arch, but it always kept ahead of me, seeming to move as I moved. At last it stood still and I drove right into a light shower of rain, and at that point the rainbow ended. I had come too to the end of the indigenous forest and had entered the eucalyptus world. It was the land where the rainbow ends.

Things had changed drastically for the Indigenous people. Driving along the road to Nairobi he was amazed to find that a group of Kikuyu he encountered on the road scattered and fled as his car approached them. Stopping, he called out in their own language; he asked them to come back, stepping out of the car so that they could see he was unarmed and telling them who he was, an old friend, the *Baba wa Miti*. They were amazed. He gave them a ride to Nairobi. That night a law was passed making it illegal to give a lift to a Kikuyu!

He stayed the night at Nanyuki and in the morning saw again the great peak, Karinyaga, Place of Whiteness. The mountain is over seventeen thousand feet high. At fifteen thousand feet there is a lake that freezes every night, making a good skating surface—directly on the equator. On the lower slopes of the mountain are fabulous lobelias, everlasting flowers taller than a man, scarlet lilies in profusion, and bamboos and trees of many kinds, a unique paradise of plant life. But now, as everywhere, the lower slopes were being eroded as tree cover was removed. Even where there was good rainfall, the land could be destroyed by water erosion if the ground cover was not carefully managed.

Almost everywhere he went the climate, both natural and political, had soured. At night he could hear gunshots and bodies falling to the ground; by day he saw people in police compounds, the forests gone, the land eroding. The best land was often given over to sisal, and as well managed as it was, you can't eat sisal. Nairobi had changed, surrounded now by shanties constructed of flattened tin cans, its centre filled with imposing banks and office towers. What a transformation in thirty years!

Here he ran into some of his old forest scouts, the original Men of the Trees, and was amazed that he was remembered and still called *Bwana wa miti*, Master of the Trees. He gave a talk on his findings to the local Rotary Club before heading off to Muguga, his old forestry station.

His old friend Chief Josiah had become paramount chief, one of the few chiefs loyal to the government who had not been murdered. Yet he refused police protection. Together they examined the old forest station. The old *mugumo* tree, scene of the dance of the trees, was gone, as were most of the virgin forests. Eucalyptus and pines were being grown in seedbeds. Chemical fertilizers were the coming thing and used proudly. But Baker longed to see the fruits of his old experiments with mixed species of native trees.

The trees were there, all right, over a hundred feet high, and the natural forest floor was covered with thick humus, no chemical fertilizers needed.

"It was a perfect forest, well cared for, having been periodically thinned. No wonder Josiah was proud." He offered Baker ten acres for his experiments in biosylvics and together they went over the land demarcating the boundaries. Alone, they spoke of the tensions of the moment, and St. Barbe spoke of protection, protection from the desert, the outer desert of land and the inner desert of the heart and mind; he spoke of trees against the desert, and the Tree of Life that grows within.

Little of what Baker had worked for had survived here, except for this small forest.

Here among the lovely trees I had planted so long ago and that had grown so well, my idea seemed not so unrealizable. So with pleasure and gratitude I returned to the forestry station, conscious that here, at any rate, the tradition of mixed native woods I had started had been allowed to survive.

THE 'TEMPLE OF PURE SCIENCE'

Much to his surprise, a multi-million dollar advanced research centre had been built by the East African Agricultural and Forestry Research Organization on land that had once been his, part of the plot given him by then Paramount Chief Kinanjui. The research centre had everything: laboratories, workshops, greenhouses, a complete herbarium and library, meteorological station, conference rooms, and a publishing department, as well as field plots and quarters for fifty people. It was the manifestation of Baker's dream, the means of training a cadre to direct the battle against the desert!

He rushed in to meet the director and share the vision, filled with enthusiasm and hope. But St. Barbe was in a "temple of pure science." He didn't fit in and received a cold welcome from its "high priests."

Not one to beat around the bush, he had explained his ecological survey of the Sahara and his findings. He suggested that the research centre take on sixty-four students, two from each of the thirty-two countries along the green front against the desert. With this start the centre could be the command post of a vast ecological army.

They looked at him with pity. Their plans were to accept three ecologists, and after three years one might be able to begin an ecological survey. "We are pure scientists," they said, and this refrain was repeated again and again as he met the centre's department heads.

It sounded like a slogan; all they needed was a banner with a scientific heraldic device. I thought to myself "pure science be damned." Here is a state of emergency, a state of war. The

*great Sahara desert is invading Africa along a two thousand
mile front, at a rate of thirty miles a year in some places. It
would mean another ninety miles before their three ecological students were ready to make a survey, and a hundred and
eighty thousand square miles of fertile land lost to the desert.
And then what?*

They toured the station. He saw experiments on viruses that
were damaging the groundnut industry—he had seen an area of
five hundred miles with groundnuts in small fields, tree-surrounded,
completely disease-free. He read reports on cypress canker disease—
which he knew caused little damage in properly managed forests
of mixed species. He observed experiments on agricultural chemicals and fertilizers—he had travelled the world's forests, growing for
countless millennia, with trees older than human civilization, three
hundred feet high and thirty across, produced with no need of fertilizers or pesticides of any kind.

*So much of what I saw seemed to be obsolete, in view of the
proven value of natural and ecological conditions. Today we
are learning more and more that the best method of fighting
disease is to provide the conditions in which it does not occur.
If the health of a plantation, whether it be farm or forest, is
undermined by unnatural monoculture or uneven balance,
nature hits back and provides the means of eliminating what
she does not want....I had seen a great deal and I felt that these
pure scientists had had enough of me. So I made my formal
farewells, since formality seemed to be what they wanted, and
left them. Although they had given me no encouragement for
the Green Front against the desert, I still felt that here in this
place lay the answer to the problem. It was the mode of my
approach that had been wrong. These men were but carrying
out the duties for which they had been briefed. I realized that
my approach must be to a very different quarter.
All my old friends quickly heard of my return and wanted
to see me. Next morning I gave them the only chance I could,*

owing to the local troubles; I went to the police lines behind the barbed wire, where a hundred and fifteen gathered from all parts of that location.

Many of them had been at the first dance of the trees; those distant days so full of song and dance, the beat of the drums and the joy of life. What a contrast to the barbed wire and terror! I had pictured a very different return from this. I had imagined that we would all have gathered once more under the sacred Mugumo tree, where so often we had met in the past and where, often far into the night, we had listened to tales of the 'golden age,' or danced by the light of a great circle or aromatic fires made from chips of the Mutarakwa trees.

It was difficult for me to recognize some of them. Anxiety had changed their happy carefree expressions and fear was wrinkling their once smooth brows. Many well-fed sleek bodies had shrunk. Some had become almost skeletons of their former selves.

Thauthau Thongo, the old captain of the dance, had become leader of the Kiama, the council of Kikuyu elders, which once served as a tribal parliament and court, but was now shorn of most of its power by the colonial government. He tried to recapture the good spirit of the old days, told some stories and evoked a few laughs, but it was obvious that the situation here was desperate. Why was everyone so sad?

They told Baker they were starving, that their land had been taken away, and what was left was overworked and not enough to go round. Tens of thousands of people worked on settlers' farms, where they had their gardens for food. Recently they were being rounded up without warning, and without their possessions, and dumped in the Kikuyu reserve or put in detention. On the other side, the settlers were without labour and they could no longer produce food, making the situation that much worse.

The next day he met with the Kiama. He was welcomed back and given a new staff of office to replace the one lost during the bombing of London, with the words: "'In the old days when children were fighting among themselves, the senior elder of the Kiama came and placed the staff between them and immediately the children stopped fighting. We present this Matathi stick to you and ask you to use it to bring peace to our people.' This was the first time the Kiama had ever asked me to do anything."

Receiving a new Matathi stick from Thauthau Thongo, January 1, 1953.

Baker asked how the land shortage had come so quickly; what
had become of the fifty thousand acres they had given him when he
had been joined to the Kiama? He learned how it had been eaten
away: so much for the research station, more for a veterinary station,
some for lots for European housing at Ngong. It was all gone, stolen.
The area might have supported 250,000 Kikuyu!

It should be remembered that three thousand white settlers
own over ten million acres. This works out that each white
landowner has over three thousand acres, whereas there are
over six Africans to share one acre. I was astonished that this
sort of thing could have been possible.

But what could he do? He saw the governor and explained everything that he had been told. He also explained the ecological situation,
knowing that as grievous as was the injustice in land distribution, if
would be even worse if the country were desertified. His recommen-
dation was that the Kikuyu be given work in the fight against the
desert and that the settlers should be enlisted to the same end. Instead
of fighting each other, they should fight a real enemy, the desert.

Baker imagined a Roosevelt-style CCC solution to the ecological,
economic, and social problems of Kenya. There was little more Baker
could do for his African friends than make polite suggestions.

AN UNUSUAL CONFERENCE

Before leaving Africa, he had an important engagement in Kampala.
He had been entrusted by the Guardian of the Bahá'í faith, Shoghi
Effendi, to act as host to the African delegates to the first International
Teaching Conference. The conference, held February 12 to 18, 1953,
launched a ten-year campaign that saw the spread of the Bahá'í faith
throughout the world, including a tremendous expansion in Africa.

His job involved the use of his Humber to help with trips to the
market and to deliver the African delegates to the conference in the
morning and home to their dorms in the evening. He could hold
about twenty at a time, but transporting all the delegates took several

trips. When, one night, the Humber was stolen and the police could do little to help—it was the fifth stolen vehicle reported that night— the Bahá'ís repeated the prayer, "Is there any Remover of difficulties save God...." They soon received a call that the Humber was found, undamaged. It seemed their prayers had been answered. But then the phone rang again: the policeman who had been guarding the vehicle had been knocked out and thrown in a ditch. It was gone again.

They prayed again, but there were no more calls from the police. But in the morning the vehicle was sitting outside Baker's lodgings, none the worse for its adventure!

The conference was unusual. All around them the land was in turmoil and blood was flowing, the Africans turning on the white settlers in reaction against the injustices they had endured. Yet here, at the conference, black and white got on perfectly; they could be seen embracing, united in faith and respect.

Baker's efforts for the cause of God or the cause of trees were one and the same; each served the other. On his return to Kenya, Baker shared the Bahá'í message with its governor, and also with the governors of Uganda and Tanganyika, who were meeting in conference. To each he gave the book *Bahá'u'lláh and the New Era* and explained the contribution the Bahá'í cause could make to the administration of Africa. While they were together the governor of Kenya recalled their previous conversation about employment, land, and forests and said, "By the way, Baker, your plan for employing detainees in forestry camps is coming off."

With this hope in his heart, he set off for England by plane, affording him an overview of the eastern Sahara, which he had not yet investigated in his ecological survey. From the air he retraced the steps of his journey home up the Nile thirty years earlier. The eastern Sahara was little different from the western, except of course for the Nile, but even that was no longer an intact barrier and in places the desert joined. The deterioration from the time of his first journey was evident; on the other hand, he identified many places, various oases and points along the Nile, that could serve as outposts in the coming battle against the desert.

CHAPTER NINE

The Vision Unfolds

JOIN THE GREEN FRONT!

Back in England in the spring of 1953, St. Barbe considered the lessons learned from his ecological survey of the great Sahara.

How to begin to tackle such a stupendous task as to fight seven million square miles of desert? How could I, one man, reclaim the Sahara? It is not even a project for one nation. Many nations all striving together with all the resources at their command, may be able to do something. Time and natural laws can be as much their aid as their enemy.

"Were I an all-powerful Genie," he asked himself, "able to wield a magic power over the minds of men, how should I begin to will them to tackle this great task? Where would I start?"

Education seemed the only answer. Education of the high and mighty *and* the average citizen, whoever would listen, whatever doors would open, wherever they might be.

Baker couldn't wait to set up a formal lecture, so he began at Speaker's Corner.

When I got back...the first Sunday morning I took my banner with "JOIN THE GREEN FRONT" on it to Speakers' Corner where I set up my platform between the two largest audiences; the Catholics were to the right of me and the Communists to the left. Soon curiosity was aroused and people gathered around as I warmed up to my subject.

An experienced heckler was on the attack. Baker surprised him by stepping down and giving him his place to speak his mind. That lasted only a minute and Baker resumed his speech, drawing in a couple hundred listeners, preaching the green gospel.

Among the hecklers I found some quite good speakers but managed to win them over. After only a few Sundays several of them were quite in a position to take over from me, and when I had to be away I entrusted one with my banner. Three Sundays later as I happened to be passing through London, I visited my old stand and there was a man who had been one of the worst troublemakers, pounding out the gospel of tree-planting, talking about transpiration and how trees created a micro-climate and so on. Unobserved I crept up behind him and listened, fascinated by his eloquence, now being used constructively, and by the grip he had on my subject.

On May 1, 1953, delegates to the eighth World Forestry Charter Gathering from forty-four countries met to receive Baker's report on the Sahara University Expedition. Based on this initial report, he began to work his account into a book, *Sahara Challenge*, which was published the next year by Lutterworth Press. It included an outline of an overall reclamation plan.

In brief, his plan listed the assets, such as water sources, described the measures available to prevent the desert's increase beyond its existing borders, and laid out the means to begin reclaiming it.

The assets included areas where water was available, either from some rainfall or in water bodies and wells. There was the Atlantic, the Mediterranean, the Nile, and several lakes and marsh areas. Many of the mountain ranges trapped rainfall and could be centres for reclamation; similarly, the many desert oases were potential reclamation points. To the south was the extensive forest that, if protected, could be a barrier to the desert. Also, there was evidence of underground water reserves. Finally, the desert soil was in fact fertile, for the most part, needing only some moisture to foster growth.

The first move in the battle would be to prevent further expansion of the desert. Along the northern front and down the Atlantic coast, the *banquette* system and reforestation efforts already in use in Algeria, and to some extent in Tunisia, could be intensified. In addition, the southern slopes of the Atlas Mountains should be reforested; a token planting in Tangiers demonstrated the feasibility of this idea. The aim would be to enlarge and extend the existing forests, until they formed a continuous barrier, which might then be pushed inwards along the whole front.

On the south, the forested areas formed a natural barrier. Clearcut areas needed to be replanted and the existing forests protected, especially from grazing animals. Rainfall was still sufficient to allow the forest to recover; what was needed was a continuous forest reserve in a belt thirty miles wide.

On the eastern side of the continent, the plantings might need to be irrigated due to diminishing rainfall.

In addition, agricultural methods must be changed. Clearing for cash crop production had to be eliminated, or at least reduced, and agroforestry and permaculture that employed trees to create microclimates substituted. There was ample evidence of the effectiveness of this approach in the Indigenous peasant agriculture.

The eastern encirclement of the desert was the most difficult. The approach would involve the planting of drought-tolerant species in an effort to create a more favourable microclimate, the establishment of a chain of nurseries and forests along the Nile, which could be irrigated, and the protection and preservation of the Nile itself, including its source.

Having planned and begun the encirclement of the desert, attention must be given to the oases. Here again nurseries and forest belts could be established to create better microclimates. A token effort had been made at Tamanrasset. Pilot projects should be started at each oasis, with the idea of establishing plantings between twenty thousand and two hundred thousand acres in extent.

Next was an even more experimental suggestion. There was some evidence of underground water reserves. These should be investigated, and if possible, new oases developed in places where water could be tapped. The water should be used primarily for reforestation, as the supply would not be inexhaustible and growing a forest would lead to its replenishment. The oases should be continuously expanded until they begin to grow together.

On the socioeconomic level, colonialism and inequity in land distribution intensified the problems of desertification. Desperate people, starving and without fuel, could not afford to think of a future beyond the day's meal; for them conservation could have no reality. A solution to political and economic problems had to be a part of the ecological solution.

The task was formidable, but Baker pointed out that there had been major ecological fronts opened in recent times. The American CCC program had planted a thousand-mile shelterbelt network in a ten-year period; the Soviets had an even larger project under way that was to be completed in the same time period; the new Chinese government had begun a "Great Green Wall" intended to stop the Gobi desert and increase tree cover in the country from 5 to 25 percent, to be completed in 1965; and Israel was proving that the Negev desert could be reclaimed. If these projects could be undertaken, why not a thirty-mile-wide four-thousand-mile-long forest belt in Africa?

Humanity had tried to conquer nature, but now nature was beginning to conquer humanity. Desertification was a formidable challenge to humanity, one that must be met if the human race was to survive. The drafts of the book and Baker's plan were presented to the 1954 World Forestry Charter Gathering on May 27, with representatives of fifty countries in attendance.

OTHER FRONTS

Meanwhile, there were the other activities of the Men of the Trees to keep up with. The summer school was held in Inverness, Scotland, the home of Lord Sempill, one of Baker's staunchest supporters. The school enjoyed a visit from the Queen Mother.

In September, Baker was back in Jerusalem as the guest of the Honourable Edwin Samuel to take part in the opening of the Conquest of the Desert Exhibition and Fair.

> *The horticultural development during my years of absence had been phenomenal. Groves of nut trees had been planted, and even more important, the goat population had been brought down from some two million to eighty thousand. Goats are the bane of the tree planter. They eat the young bark and kill off everything in sight....Land reclamation had been carried out and the coastal plain of moving sand dunes had been fixed by judicious planting. This sand had come down the Nile, been washed by tides onto the Palestinian Coast, and by wind had been blown inland. Thus the once fertile soil from Central Africa is enlarging the State of Israel, which by careful forestry is being made fertile once again.*

Baker saw the effect of some of the 'seeds' he had planted on his first trip to Palestine. During their tour, the head of the Israeli Forest Service asked Baker, "Do you recognize where you are?" They were on a new road from Jerusalem to Tel Aviv airport and in a small forest of native trees: Aleppo pine, Jerusalem cyprus, carob, and terebinth, along with some acacias from Australia. Among them various other native trees were returning. He answered his own question: "You planted these trees in 1929!"

From the top of Mount Carmel, they surveyed the returning natural forests.

> *Many years before I had persuaded the High Commissioner to have this area protected from the marauding goats, and the*

forest had responded by regenerating itself. I congratulated my companion on his successful conservation and before he took me down he wrote in my book: "From the summit of Mount Carmel I quote the words of the Prophet Isaiah: 'Lebanon shall be like Carmel, and Carmel shall be considered as a forest.'"

Baker also visited problem areas such as the Negev Desert, areas of which were being slowly reclaimed by the people of the kibbutzim. Already, four thousand square miles were in various stages of cultivation.

Back in England, Baker's time was now taken up in his usual activities, plus spending time with his mother and his children. His mother, at ninety-six, was near the end of her life and he felt he should be with her whenever possible. Baker's marriage had been over for some time and the children were in the custody of their mother, who was now remarried. Baker had the opportunity to be with them occasionally on holidays. Angela, the older of the two, went into boarding school. Her father paid her fees and was able to see her often. Paul remained mainly with his mother.

LAND OF TANE

In 1954, Baker was invited to New Zealand by the Men of the Trees and a group of farmers and fruit growers who needed advice on shelter-belts in their region of Central Otago. The New Zealand Forest Service simply advised that trees would not grow in the area, and if they did, that the plantings would not pay. Having followed Baker's work, the locals decided that if trees could grow in the desert, they could grow in Central Otago. However, as Baker's mother was in poor health, he declined.

At the Men of the Trees' annual general meeting a delegation from New Zealand appealed to Baker to make the trip, and when his mother insisted that he should go, he left as soon as passage could be arranged.

Aboard the *Rangitani*, he amused himself by entertaining the seventy-five children on the ship, spending an hour each evening telling a bedtime story. On his arrival in Wellington, he was given a mayoral reception attended by heads of government departments and the city fathers.

His Worship the Mayor referred to my previous visit, twenty-three years before, when I had prepared plans which were now resulting in returns of twelve million pounds a year. In my reply I requested that a tree be planted along the new road between Auckland and Wellington for each of my young fellow passengers and that in future a tree should be planted for each young New Zealander whether he or she arrived by sea, air, or stork!

A full program of lectures and advisory work had been arranged. At a garden party given in his honour, he met Catriona Burnett and her mother. Catriona's father had been a member of Parliament, and together the family had a large sheep farm at Mt. Cook Station. As Baker recalled, "I fell for them both at first sight and invited them to come and stay with me in England."

The big meeting at Central Otago drew an impressive crowd of local dignitaries and farmers from far and near. A local branch of the Men of the Trees was formed and an executive elected.

Following the meeting Baker received a telegram that his mother had died. Grief-stricken, he felt great remorse that he had not been with her. Nevertheless, his response was to rededicate his life to tree work on her behalf. So at sixty-six, at the time when most people are thinking of retirement, Baker's activities redoubled.

Baker re-embarked for England on the *Rangitani* and set to work on a book called *Land of Tane: The Threat of Erosion*, essentially a report on his recent trip with recommendations as to conservation and tree planting. A fellow passenger typed the manuscript for him. In his foreword to the book, Viscount Bledisloe, the former governor general of New Zealand, wrote: "Richard St. Barbe Baker has earned for himself the reputation of being the greatest living authority in the English-speaking world on the supreme value of silviculture from the standpoint alike of scenic beauty, economic importance, dominant climatic influence, and human health. He is a man of wide knowledge, exceptional culture, and penetrating vision."

While still on board, Baker also began a second manuscript, titled *Horse Sense: Horses in War and Peace,* and dedicated it to his two favourite horse lovers: his children Angela and Paul.

With his mother.

AT THE FIRS

As soon as he landed, Baker went to the family home, The Firs, and took up residence, doing his best to keep the family tradition of nursery work alive. He now enjoyed more frequent visits with the children, who spent Christmas with their father at The Firs and enjoyed the rare snowfall, playing snowman leapfrog.

His literary life during this period was quite active. *Land of Tane* was published, and with the help of Evelyn Harbord, he wrote two novels, published by George Ronald a couple of years later. *Kabongo* and *Kamiti* were sympathetic portrayals of African village life, intended in part to support the plight of his Kikuyu friends in Kenya. In his foreword to *Kamiti*, Dr. Kwame Nkrumah, prime minister of Ghana, recommended the books to all who wish to understand the African people, stating that, having himself grown up in a small African village, he found Baker's effort to introduce the ordinary African to the world true to life and a valuable contribution to the literature.

Efforts to promote the Sahara project were intensifying. A Green Front pamphlet was circulated in Germany. Contributions were coming in; one donation of £1,000 was received in the summer of 1954.

Baker wanted to begin the Sahara Reclamation Programme by making small experimental plantings in each of the countries concerned. Megaprojects had made him cautious. He had seen many effective smaller efforts, such as the groundnut farms in Nigeria, where the farmers' traditional small fields surrounded by trees resulted in a sustainable and productive system. However, the British colonials, seeing this productivity, had decided to send in the bulldozers, chained together, to clear huge tracts of land for groundnut production. The scheme ignored the smallholders' methods, resulting in the creation of a new desert approximately two hundred by one hundred miles in size.

There were other unintended negative impacts. The men who were brought in for the project were the hard-drinking, gambling type and had a deleterious influence on the people. Small, he thought, is beautiful.

A woodcut illustration from Baker's novel Kamiti.

BAN THE BOMB!

Baker made several trips to the Sahara. In 1957, he returned from a trip that supported creative reconstruction and harmony with nature to find that on the other side of the world hydrogen bombs had been exploded on Christmas Island. "This seemed to me utterly opposed to the goodwill that I had been trying to build up through reclaiming the deserts," commented Baker. Surely the time had come to turn from a destructive to a creative way of living.

Baker turned his efforts to peace work and launched a petition against bomb testing that drew eight thousand signatures. This he presented to the Queen. But the testing continued and he decided to bring the matter before the World Forestry Charter Gathering of ambassadors and diplomats, which took place on May 23, 1957.

On August 21, 1957, Catriona Burnett from New Zealand came to The Firs for a visit, with her aunt. The children joined them a week later. Baker was invited back to New Zealand. As he had a pressing invitation to attend the World Vegetarian Union Congress in Bombay, India, he decided to set out by boat. Passing through the Suez Canal, and impressed by the new plantings made since Nasser had taken power, he sent the president a copy of one of his books and invited a contribution for the journal, *Trees*. Never pass up an opportunity!

On his arrival at Karachi, he was met by the local Bahá'ís, who reported that Shoghi Effendi, the Guardian of the Bahá'í faith, was critically ill in London with the Asian flu. They asked him to conduct a prayer meeting that night. The next day was a full one. He lectured on the Sahara and showed a film to the British consul. As fortune had it, he had arrived in Karachi in the middle of a United Nations symposium on arid zone research. Many of the delegates came to his lecture and he was invited to their reception to meet the others from Rome and the Near East.

It had long been my desire to meet the authorities on Arid Zones and Desert Reclamation, but I had not realized that my arrival in Karachi would coincide with this Symposium. In fact, since I was first introduced to the Bahá'í Faith it has been my experience

*that whenever I have put their cause first, my work for the Men
of the Trees and land reclamation has prospered enormously.*

He was able to advise the Pakistani Ministry of Agriculture on
desert reclamation before going to Bombay for the World Vegetarian
Union Congress. On arrival, he was greeted by grief-stricken Bahá'ís
who informed him of the death of Shoghi Effendi. They invited him
to conduct an all-night prayer vigil. Despite his exhaustion, he felt
he must consent. He accompanied them to their headquarters and
found the room full of stricken, sobbing Bahá'ís, their hearts completely broken.

From the conference, Baker went to New Delhi by train and was
taken to see Prime Minister Nehru.

"Baker, I have read your book, *Sahara Challenge*, three times," were
his first words. "Now what are we going to do about the Indian desert?"

"The answer is the same," Baker said. "Trees against the desert.
The fields must be tree-surrounded and reduced in size. Trees are
needed to fix the soil and lift the spring water table and keep the land
cool." Nehru called in the minister of agriculture and asked the two
to spend time together.

Next was Ceylon, where he met the publisher of *Green Glory*,
which had been translated into Sinhalese and published with a foreword from the Ceylon high commissioner in London. In Colombo
he surveyed the results at the chena plantations, which had been
prompted by his previous visit in 1931. He then set off for Australia,
presenting lectures and film screenings on board the ship, and was
met in Sydney by the Men of the Land, who had changed their name
to attract more farmers.

Around the beginning of the 1958, he made it to Mount Cook
Station in New Zealand to visit Catriona and her family. After a
pleasant stay, and after he had moved on to visit other friends, he
realized that he missed Mount Cook, more specifically Catriona, and
wrote to ask her to marry him.

*In the letter I said that I would ring up at ten o'clock on Monday
morning to get her decision. It was a long distance call and the*

last thirty miles was single line. At the time there was a furious storm raging, which was causing considerable interference on the line; it was as much as I could do to hear her shouting back, 'Yes, Yes!' It seemed strange to her that although there had been plenty of opportunities for proposing under idyllic conditions a Man of the Trees should wait until he had gone away and then expect to get an answer on a bad line in the middle of a storm.

Baker was now sixty-eight, Catriona in her early forties.

WEDDING BELLS, AGAIN

Another marriage, again to a much younger woman. In 1959, Baker set about detaching himself from England since he planned to reside at Catriona's home in New Zealand. The decision was made to sell the family home, The Firs, for which he received about £2,200.

Baker and his first wife had divorced in July 1953. The children were in schools, with Angela primarily in Richard's care and Paul in Doreen's. Baker applied for custody of both children as he wished to take them to New Zealand. The courts denied this, but allowed the children to visit New Zealand on holidays.

It was decided to move the British headquarters of the Men of the Trees to the estate of Lord Bessborough, its president. The headquarters and activities of the Sahara Reclamation Programme would move to Mount Cook with Baker. On August 20, 1959, a farewell gathering was held prior to his departure and 'retirement.'

The wedding was held in New Zealand on October 7, 1959, two days before Baker's seventieth birthday. There were four hundred guests, only a quarter of whom could fit in the little church, built by Thomas Burnett. But everyone attended the wedding breakfast. The cake was topped with a living western red cedar that would be planted afterward in a ceremony at a Sunday school built by Catriona in memory of her mother.

Catriona had promised St. Barbe a horse for a wedding present. She drove him out to pick up the horse, letting him ride it home— eighty miles away! Tui, a chestnut cob mare, met with an accident shortly thereafter and had to be put down; she was replaced with a beautiful palomino with a long silver mane and tail.

Baker was soon back at work.

I soon found that I had to rise at four to cope with my writing, as this gave me four uninterrupted hours before breakfast, after which I threw myself into the day's work at the station. When I was not needed to help with the animals I devoted myself

Marriage to Catriona Burnett, the wedding cake crowned with a western red cedar.

to the garden, where I erected three bins to provide organic compost for the vegetables that were my special care. My wife and her brother had given me a kit set greenhouse as a birthday present. I erected this with a boy's help and was able to raise all sorts of vegetables...

After a good deal of wrangling with the children's mother, Paul and Angela came for a vacation during their school holidays—New Zealand's winter—and enjoyed skiing and skating. Together, the family then set out for the Redwood Reunion in California, reuniting many of those who had been involved in redwood conservation efforts in the past years, including many of the British Men of the Trees. It was also an opportunity to attend the Fifth World Forestry Congress in Seattle and renew international forestry contacts.

It was a happy time for Baker, especially having his family together and sharing with them the ultimate tree experience, the California redwoods. Afterwards, Paul and Angela flew back to England while he and Catriona returned to New Zealand to resume the routine of station life. It was the only time she would travel with him on what would become annual world tours.

Baker's departure from England had thrown the Men of the Trees for a loop; some thought that they no longer had any direction or drive without St. Barbe. Nevertheless, memberships kept coming in and people were joining at a rate of two per day, according to a letter from the organization's secretary.

Meanwhile, Baker was working on a series of books, a library of famous trees that he had begun with his book on New Zealand. He began work on *Famous Trees of India* and *Famous Trees of Australia*. Letters flew back and forth from the famous and humble: a personal letter from Prime Minister Nkrumah of Ghana; a packet of seeds from trees in the Garden of Gethsemane; a bundle of horse stories; a series of letters from a Mr. Cawcutt, bus-driving tree poet, each lovingly answered by Baker; a request from Vinson Brown, publishers of his book of Indigenous prophesies for information on Maori prophesies; letters from Marion Hofman, publisher at George Ronald, occasionally with a payment of royalties tucked inside.

Baker notes in one letter that his first novel *Kabongo* was a "complete flop." Despite Nkrumah's positive review, it had bad reviews from the British press, due to the backlash against liberation movements and his sympathies with the Africans. Other reviewers described it as defeatist because the author allowed the protagonist, the elder Kabongo, to go off into the forest to die.

RETIREMENT?

The children returned to New Zealand for Christmas, 1962. Baker notes in his diaries that Angela had read his latest manuscript and had some suggestions. He also notes Catriona's encouragement that he resolve to rest a little each afternoon, but on January 2, 1963, his diary records that he rose at 4:00 a.m., prepared orange juice for the family, fed the horses, had breakfast at 4:45, and then began gardening. He also notes his efforts to learn Chinese, Italian, and Maori vocabulary.

Baker's children, Angela and Paul.

Life was full, yet for Baker, Mount Cook was something of a retirement. He was now seventy-four, but wrote that he was

beginning to feel that I was living a selfish life, enjoying superb mountain scenery and all the comfort of a perfectly run home at Mount Cook, without being of much use to my fellow-men and women. True, I had been kept in touch with Africa and my Sahara Reclamation Programme and had managed to interest one hundred and eight countries in this work of regeneration by tree-planting, and many billions of trees were well and truly planted and growing. I realized that there had to be periods of rest and refreshment in between intensive endeavour. But I knew in my heart that the time had come to launch out once more into the world of humanity.

After consulting with the National Spiritual Assembly of the Bahá'ís of New Zealand, a lecture series was set up in collaboration with the chairman of the United Nations Association. Since the UN FAO had launched the Freedom from Hunger Campaign in 1960, Baker's Sahara work, films, and slides could easily be turned to good account suited to that purpose. As a lecture series was planned throughout New Zealand, it came to St. Barbe to undertake the tour on horseback.

After consulting Catriona, he decided to ride the full 1,200 miles of the planned tour. He found a good horse in Rajah, "an aged dark bay and a famous jumper." A young Dutchman had tried the record ride before, but all his horses had been lost in accidents and the ride had been terminated. This seemed a good challenge to Baker, aged seventy-four, and a fine opportunity to speak to the children of New Zealand about trees and conservation to fill in the time between UN lectures. He decided to ride from the northernmost kauri tree to the southernmost.

Rajah, unbeknownst to Baker, was not used to journeys. Bets were laid that he wouldn't get more than twenty miles down the road. However, "the first day I did thirty-two, ending up in the rain. I had given talks to six schools on the way and Rajah seemed rather tired. So we decided that twenty-five miles and five schools would be better."

St. Barbe decided to avoid publicity at first until he felt more certain he would be able to achieve his goal. However, in Auckland he was noticed by a television crew and from then on his visits were anticipated by school children along the way.

Near Invercargill, the most southerly city in the world, he finally found what he thought to be the southernmost kauri tree on the island. He had spoken to about ninety-two thousand people, between schools and UN Association meetings, in addition to media coverage, "a good travel teaching trip all told."

With the New Zealand trip under his belt, Baker looked for new adventures. One of his greatest desires was to visit China, and efforts were made to obtain permission. Baker was greatly impressed by Chinese efforts in forestry and desert reclamation. He had himself sent tree seeds to China to support these efforts and wished to see first-hand, in the Gobi Desert, what might be useful in the Africa work. His dream was to ride across the Gobi on horseback. These plans were frustrated by the Chinese authorities, who, on the eve of the Cultural Revolution, were not interested in foreign travelers.

However, soon after Baker returned from his record ride he received a cable from California, alerting him to a new threat to the redwoods. A six-lane highway was proposed, one that would cut through the heart of the forest, including the Grove of Understanding that he had fought so hard to save and that had been handed over to the State of California in 1939 "to be preserved for all time." A prize of $80,000 had been offered to anyone who could come up with an alternative route that would cause as little destruction as possible.

Three days later he was in California, in conference with the Garden Clubs of America Conservation Committee. There he was deputized to meet with the Department of Natural Resources to study proposals for alternate routes. After new routes were agreed upon, the next step was to lobby the secretary of the interior in Washington, as the federal government was providing most of the funding for the project. The suggestion was made that Baker go to Washington, which he agreed to do.

The Sierra Club was championing the idea of a Redwood National Park of some two hundred thousand acres, and had outlined the area

Baker spoke to ninety-two thousand people, including many school children, on his great ride.

Hoping to visit China, Baker took every opportunity to make connections with Chinese officials.

they had in mind. This caused the lumber companies to wade in and cut the choicest groves with the object of killing the project. They were stopped only by an injunction, but by then much damage had already been done. Meanwhile, others were proposing other areas for conservation, and this rivalry risked the unity of the conservation movement.

In Washington, Secretary of the Interior Stewart Udall had just returned from West Germany, and despite a long line of people waiting to see him, agreed to meet Baker first. They spoke for about twenty minutes, and Udall agreed to the new proposal, but said, "We must keep our fingers crossed, as this will have to go before Congress and many committees."

In New York, Baker again went on the air with Lowell Thomas and *World News* and was able to speak of the redwoods, the Sahara, and the prevention of desertification in the American grain belt.

"THE WORLD'S GREATEST CONSERVATIONIST"

The Sahara Reclamation Programme was launched in Rabat, Morocco, early in 1964, with supporting cables received from the various African heads of state. On February 19 Baker set out on a twenty-five-thousand-mile trip around the circumference of the Sahara, visiting each of the leaders of the twenty-four African nations in and around the desert. He had the feeling that now that the five colonial powers were gone, the new African states could unite on the great scheme of desert reclamation, aimed at adding two million squares miles of agricultural and forestry land to Africa—equivalent in size to a new continent. The journey by land, sea, and air was completed on June 3.

Baker worked on any front he could think of to promote the Sahara Reclamation Programme, which was to have a resident representative working on the spot in Africa and the Middle East to build support. One of Baker's tasks would be to find Arabic-language publishers for *Sahara Challenge* and its sequel, *Sahara Conquest*, which told the story of Baker's circumnavigation of the desert. Another avenue was to form a Sahara Corporation that would become involved in resource development, the profits to be used in reclamation.

On yet another front, Baker approached Britain's composers to produce a Saharan symphony.

By February of 1965 he had returned to New Zealand and Mount Cook. In contrast to his first marriage, in which his wife (understandably) resented his dedication to the causes that kept him away from home and family, Catriona was entirely sympathetic; both caring and

The twenty-five-thousand-mile journey around the Sahara attracted considerable media attention.

supportive, she managed his schedules and handled correspondence while he was away.

That year, he was named patron of the Tree Society of South Africa and formed links with a Swiss NGO called World Service Locarno, which proposed to promote Baker's goals in Europe.

On March 3, 1966, Baker left New Zealand for Los Angeles and again made his rounds, speaking to individuals and groups—networking, in today's terminology, and what a master of that art he was. On March 14, he again met with Secretary of the Interior Udall, who dubbed Baker "the world's greatest conservationist."

The Sixth World Forestry Congress, which was held in Madrid beginning on June 6, 1966, provided an opportunity to present the twenty-four countries in and around the Sahara to the world forestry community. St. Barbe hosted a dinner for the representatives of these countries in order to promote social contact and break down old prejudices, paving the way for cooperative action in the Sahara.

In mid-July he toured Switzerland, meeting with his friend Badi Lenz, who was attempting to promote Baker's ideas in Europe. Baker met with Swiss forestry officials, professors, and students, as well as the Bahá'í community. Then he was back to England.

In October of 1966 I was invited by Henry B. Stevens of New Hampshire to a vegetarian lunch in London where I was presented with the Millennium Guild of New York M.R.L. Freshel Award of one thousand dollars for Sahara Conquest. This is an award presented annually to a writer of the book making the greatest contribution to humanitarianism. On my return to New Zealand I was pleasantly surprised to be welcomed by the Lord Mayor of Wellington, the British High Commissioner, the Canadian Trade Commissioner, and a number of professors from the University. It was the first time this particular award had come to New Zealand and this was their way of honouring me. I was particularly pleased that my daughter Angela was able to obtain special leave to come and meet my boat. At the time she was taking the Community Nursing Course at Nelson, having already taken her University entrance examination.

A GLOBAL NETWORK

In 1967, St. Barbe turned his attention back to New Zealand, which he thought had a bright future in forestry. He often pointed out that for every substitute found for wood, ten new uses for forest products were found, and observed that with the spread of education and literacy, increasing amounts of paper would be required. St. Barbe was convinced that sustainable forestry was more profitable that most other forms of land use, especially grazing:

Forty-two years before my father-in-law had planted half a million trees on Mount Cook Station, and as a forester I found it interesting to work out the wood increment and see how the returns compared with sheep farming. The returns from the shelterbelts and plantations proved to be forty times higher than those from wool. In that country five acres supports one sheep which brings a return of ten shillings a year; in other words the return amounts to only two shillings per acre as compared to four pounds under timber. Inspired by these figures, I started out on a forestry fact finding mission throughout New Zealand to discover how much more land might be devoted to forestry. It was heartening that, as a result of my endeavour I was able to persuade the government to double the planting programme.

An interesting footnote to Baker's fact-finding mission comes from Doreen Ellis, general secretary of the Auckland YMCA, who was making arrangements for Baker's Auckland lecture on this tour. She notes in her letter of June 5, 1968, that "thirty or more years ago Mr. Baker visited Southend-on-Sea high school in Essex, England when I was still a pupil and gave a talk on trees and the Men of the Trees, illustrated by pictures on the school's Epidiascope. I still recall the impression he made upon me!"

This small episode illustrates the ripple effect of Baker's activities. His never-ending campaign of public education reached hundreds of thousands of people everywhere, and some of these people would in time begin to create a little—or a large—ripple of interest in the natural environment and trees in particular. It may be that these humble contacts, building a global network of interest and love for trees among average citizens, was the most lasting and effective—though immeasurable—impact of Baker's life work.

Next on the agenda was a similar tour in Australia:

> *Journeying through Queensland I was shocked to find miles and miles of eucalyptus forest being felled to make cattle runs. Small farmers were being encouraged to take land newly broken up and sown to grass. With the removal of the forest the water cycle was broken, rain and dew were becoming less and less and desert conditions threatened the country. I managed to give some press and television interviews which sparked off interest in desert reclamation, before returning to New Zealand.*

Baker's efforts, lectures, travels, and books on desert reclamation had created a vast network of interest in the subject and barely a day passed without offers of help. It was the kind of visionary project that could attract idealists to dedicate their lives to the effort. Not infrequently, these people were somewhat eccentric and held extreme views on health, diet, social policy, or religion, although they were just as likely be notable leaders and officials. For example, the secretary general of the World Muslim Congress, Inamullah Khan, became acquainted with Baker's work and provided introductions to the sheik of Kuwait, recommending that the sheik's private secretary finance a visit from Baker and arrange an audience with the sheik. He noted that Baker was a person of international fame, a friend of Islam and of Africa, who might be able to assist in Kuwaiti development.

Despite many small victories, it must be said that Baker was never able to establish a well-organized, financed, and centralized office that could coordinate reclamation efforts in a systematic way, making the best use of the many people willing to help. His objective was always to inspire others to carry out his vision and schemes, especially at the governmental level. His diplomatic work through the World Forestry Charter Gatherings, the push to generate interest, enlist, and unite the African states, and the effort to establish organizations such as the University of the Sahara and the Sahara Corporation never materialized.

The African states did indeed show interest, and many heads of state were at least nominally interested in Sahara reclamation. However, Baker's attempts to hand the project over to them, as a vehicle of African unity, evaporated as many of the new nations degenerated into internal conflicts, such as the Biafra-Nigeria war. Narrow self-interest superseded the visionary opportunity that desert reclamation offered to an emerging, independent Africa.

Baker felt that he had failed in his efforts in Africa and that he must return to try again. About this time, he became aware of the pressures on the Indian community in Kenya and wanted to recommend that they might be given employment in Sahara reclamation. He went to the high commissioner for India in New Zealand with the suggestion. Instead, the commissioner invited Baker to India to help solve its desert problems. Baker agreed: a desert is a desert, after all, and India *is* halfway to Africa!

Some weeks later in Delhi, I was met by the Inspector-General of Forests, who used my visit to create interest for land reclamation and increased food production by tree-planting. I was invited to meet various Ministers in the Government, including the Minister of Planning, the Minister for Food, and the Deputy Prime Minister, Mr. Moraji Desai. After discussing these problems with the officials I gave a broadcast intended to create interest for the implementation of the plans which I had proposed.

While in India, he also met with Sir Sarvepalli Radhakrishna, the president of India, who had popularized the life of the great Indian poet Tagore.

Next stop, Pakistan, to consult with President Ayub Khan, a great tree-lover who was well aware of their ecological contribution. "I was heartened to see that some of my suggestions of eleven years previous had been followed with some success."

I wondered whether the religious background of Islam was influencing the material welfare of the people. In Morocco, before the King had announced his successful planting programme for youth, known as the Forêts Jeunesse, the Muezzin had broadcast passages from the Koran referring to the rewards in store for the planters of trees. In Pakistan I was once more reminded of the fact that every Moslem treats the Koran not only as a guide to Heaven, but also as a handbook for daily living. As I expected to see more of the North African countries in the future, I took the opportunity of learning more about Islam.

On to Kuwait, where he took advantage of the introduction provided by the secretary of the World Muslim Congress. A cabinet minister and the personal secretary of the sheikh were there to meet him. He was greatly impressed with Kuwait and was able to make a broadcast praising the efforts of the government to reclaim the desert through shelterbelt plantings fertilized with municipal sewage.

In Egypt, "I was quite unprepared for the affectionate reunion awaiting me in Cairo where I was met by Hussein Zeid, Director-General of Public Relations. Later I was received by General Hassan Sobeh, Director of the Desert Organization." A full-day visit to view the newly reclaimed areas in Tahrir province exceeded Baker's expectations as he found "wide areas of the desert, which two thousand years ago had been the granary of Rome, were now being made fruitful again."

THE POPE AND DR. SEN

Baker went on to Rome with the purpose of meeting both Pope Paul and Dr. B.R. Sen, the secretary general of the UN FAO, which was also in charge of forestry. His first stop was the British embassy to register for a ticket for the Vatican; he learned that at least three weeks' advance notice was required. Sad, he retreated to his hotel room. The next morning he encountered a couple waiting to leave for their audience. "Lucky you," he said, explaining his situation. Chance had it that the couple had two extra tickets and offered him one—but he had to leave in five minutes. "Needless to say I was ready in no time at all."

At the end of the audience the Cardinal, Master of Ceremonies, said that the Holy Father would be pleased to bless anything we treasured. I had no rosary or crucifix, not even a prayer book, but I had one precious copy of Sahara Challenge, which I had brought to present to the Director-General of the FAO. As the Pope passed I knelt with my book raised in front of me as he blessed it. After the audience I telephoned the Cardinal and said: "Monsignor, I have a confession to make." I told him what I had done and continued: "Is it too much to ask that in a future encyclical the Holy Father will mention that the most pressing need of the world today is to reclaim the deserts and feed the people?"

The cardinal replied that he could hardly expect to dictate the statements of the Church, but that he would tell the pope about Baker's work and was sure that His Holiness would pray for his efforts.

Baker was now late for his appointment with Dr. Sen, but hopeful that since he had come all the way from New Zealand, he would still be given a few minutes.

"Come in, Baker," said Dr. Sen, "I have been waiting for you. We met last in New Delhi when you were working out your shelterbelt scheme for my country with Nehru. What is on your mind, Baker?" he asked quietly. I said: "On Tuesday next, fifteen countries of the Sahara will be appealing to you for help in planning to contain the desert threatening them. The last chapter of this book, Sahara Challenge, has an overall plan for Sahara reclamation and I want you to have this before your Symposium on Tuesday. This is the only copy I have in Europe and it has just been blessed by the Holy Father. I feel you should have it."

It was some time later when Baker noticed a report on the Pope's 1965 address to the United Nations in New York, in which he had said:

It is not enough to feed the hungry. Each man must also be assured a life in keeping with his dignity, and that is what you are striving to do. Is this not the fulfillment before our eyes, and thanks to you, of the prophet's words that apply so well to your Institution: "They shall beat their swords into pruning-hooks" (Is. 2:4)? Are you not employing the prodigious forces of the earth and the magnificent inventions of science no longer as instruments of death, but as instruments of life for the new era of mankind?

For Baker, the Pope's biblical "pruning-hook" reference in relation to food, peace, and employment was a confirmation of a growing consciousness of the role of trees in the world's future.

AN EVER-WIDER CIRCLE

From Rome, Baker returned to England, which he used as a base of operation through much of the year. His correspondence and diaries indicate an ever-widening circle of contacts and interests. By 1969, what was becoming the largest and most influential environmental organization, the World Wildlife Fund, appointed Baker its first member of honour, a list that later included such figures as the aviator Charles Lindbergh, who had become a noted conservationist later in life, and the famed astronaut Neil Armstrong.

Late in 1969 he made his first contact with the Findhorn community in Scotland, perhaps the first and most renowned of the New Age groups then springing up around the world and also one of the first ecovillages. Baker had a long connection with the Findhorn area. In 1952 he tested his Humber along its sandy coast before starting the Sahara survey. The next year he and his family had a sailing holiday there.

Findhorn had become famous primarily because of its phenomenal garden, grown on a barren stretch of sandy coastline. The founders of Findhorn attributed the success of their garden to their connection to plant spirits, or *devas*. Local people attributed their gift for gardening to a favourable microclimate and heavy applications of horse manure. Regardless, the caravan community attracted worldwide attention and eventually became home to thousands of residents from more than forty countries. It has housed many successful educational initiatives and some forty community businesses, including the Findhorn Press, which published an edition of Baker's *My Life, My Trees* in 1977. Over the years, Findhorn has also gained credibility outside New Age circles. Its ecovillage, for instance, has received a UN Habitat Best Practice designation.

A few words with a giant lily in the fabled Findhorn garden.

Findhorn's residents lived in caravans, the originals of which were designed and built by Baker following the First World War. Back then he had imagined such caravan communities dedicated to natural living. In a letter to Baker dated May 23, 1970, Findhorn founder Peter Caddy noted that "When Sir George [Trevelyan] visited Findhorn he was tremendously enthusiastic about the implications of the Findhorn Garden and felt that it was the answer to the re-afforestation of the world's deserts and said at the time, 'if only St. Barbe Baker could come to know of this work.'" Baker became a frequent visitor to Findhorn over the next twelve years and even used Findhorn as a mailing address on his letterhead. In the introduction to *My Life, My Trees*, Findhorn's Dorothy McLean claims to have received the following message "channelled" from the tree *devas*:

> There is high rejoicing in our kingdoms as the Man of the Trees, so beloved of us, links with you here. Is it not an example in your worlds, that it is one world, one work, one cause under God, being expressed through different channels? I am speaking on behalf of all the tree devas, who have long been overlighting the Man of the Trees, and we wish to express our deepest thanks to him. We hope he has always known of our gratitude for what he has done for us....He brings hope for all the world's future. What contribution could be greater?

Regardless of one's opinion of spiritualism, the Findhorn connection is another indication of the wide reach of Baker's global network, ranging from religious and spiritual organizations to the realms of science, academia, business, government, and NGOs. He had no problem collaborating with *deva* channellers, while at the same time publishing "The Sahara: An ever-present challenge," an article on trees and desert reclamation in UNASYLVA (No. 93), the official FAO scientific journal. He used any opportunity, without prejudice, to raise awareness of trees to heal the planet.

In 1970 he began another international tour, stopping in Tripoli, Rome, and Geneva. He then revisited his old forestry stations at Benin and Sabopa in Nigeria. He was pleased to see that the work had been taken up by the University of Ibadan, the first to be established in Nigeria, and that many of his old forest rangers and their children had taken important government posts.

In the fall, he visited the United States before returning to New Zealand. Toward the end of 1970, he received a warm letter from an old friend from his university days in Saskatchewan, John Diefenbaker, who had gone on to become prime minister of Canada. He was now chancellor of the university and the two alumni renewed their friendship:

Dear Richard,
I am delighted to receive the autographed copy of your new book My Life, My Trees and the message you inscribed touched me deeply. You may be sure that at the next meeting of the Senate I shall advise the members of your words "the University

Baker hosting a luncheon for the delegates of sixteen Saharan nations at the World Forestry Congress, 1972.

*of Saskatchewan, the best treed campus in Canada." After all
the years that have passed since first we met I would greatly
enjoy a chat with you and hope you may be visiting Canada
before too long. With my very best wishes.*

Yours sincerely,
John Diefenbaker

Baker had returned home for Christmas, but was soon building
an itinerary for his next trip, this time to South America. While there
he would be looking for a special horse to use on a planned goodwill horseback ride through the USSR and Mongolia to China via
the Gobi Desert. In early March, 1971, he arrived in Puntas Arenas
in Chile to begin the tour. In addition to looking for just the right
horse, he hoped to make local contacts in advance of the 1972 World
Forestry Congress in Buenos Aires.

Back in England by the end of the month, he was hard at work,
first following up the Argentine trip with a luncheon for its ambassador, then engaging in work for the Men of the Trees. With 1972
being the fiftieth anniversary of the Men of the Trees in Kenya, Baker
began plans to take a British delegation to Africa from April 21 to
May 6, 1972, to coincide with Kenya's National Tree Planting Week
and to hold golden jubilee celebrations. To make arrangements on
the Kenyan side Baker approached Chief Josiah Njonjo's son, now
the attorney general of Kenya.

Baker was beginning to enjoy more recognition for a lifetime
of conservation work. On May 12, he received a letter from Cyril
Clemens, Mark Twain's cousin and the editor of *The Mark Twain
Journal*, stating simply:

Dear Richard Baker,
*In recognition of your outstanding contribution to World
Peace, you have been elected A KNIGHT OF MARK TWAIN.*

The Clemens family had presented this award to such figures as
Sigmund Freud, Ernest Hemingway, and George Bernard Shaw.

In 1971, he received an honorary doctor of laws from his alma mater, the University of Saskatchewan. One of its first one hundred students, he had kept in touch with the university since 1910, returning every so often to check on Saskatoon's growth. It had now increased a hundredfold in population and the old university had become a significant institution. Its president was a well-known chemist, Dr. John Spinks, who became a close friend.

Baker arrived in Saskatoon on November 6 for convocation and a dinner in his honour. At convocation, much to the surprise of those attending, he and Chancellor Diefenbaker joined in a lusty version of the university yell, which Baker had penned back in the day.

After speaking in cities across Canada and the eastern United States, he arrived in Rome on December 11 to again consult with FAO officials. From Rome, Baker went to North Africa, where he spent the early months of 1972 on Sahara Reclamation Programme activities, including trips to Benin and then to Kenya to make preparations

Receiving an honorary doctorate from his alma mater, his old friend Chancellor Diefenbaker presiding.

for the golden jubilee. Twenty-one Men of the Trees left London on April 21 for Nairobi. Through their participation in National Tree Planting Week activities, they contributed to the planting of half a million trees in three days! There was a great reunion between Baker and Chief Josiah Njonjo, whom Baker considered among his closest friends, his confident, and his ally.

WORLD CONFERENCE ON DESERTIFICATION

In 1974 Baker envisioned even more grand and visionary projects. His correspondence includes, for example, plans for a new movement that would encompass peace activities, globalism, development, and ecology, called the Movement for World Reclamation. It would begin by bringing together "ten just men," including religious and political leaders, as well as leaders of thought, including E.F. Schumacher, the celebrated author of *Small Is Beautiful*.

Perhaps the most significant event of the year in relation to Baker's work was the resolution of the United Nations General Assembly calling for "international co-operation to combat desertification" and investing the executive director of the United Nations Environment Program (UNEP) with the responsibility to call an international world conference on desertification. A small secretariat was established in Nairobi, a mere seventeen miles from the location of the first dance of the trees fifty-two years previous. The General Assembly called for a more profound understanding of the process of desertification and the adoption of concerted action to arrest and, where possible, reverse these processes.

Late in 1974, Baker suffered a ruptured appendix and was laid up in hospital for a long stay. He had another operation on March 12, 1975, after which his surgeon had given him one year to live. Undaunted, Baker was soon busy again, recommending that the French government name a forest in memory of Jean Giono, who wrote the fine reminiscence of Elzéard Bouffier titled *The Man who Planted Trees and Grew Happiness,* a story which had become an international phenomenon. Baker was the first to have this story translated and published in the journal of the Men of the Trees. It has since been republished numerous times and was made into an animated film that won an Academy Award.

That fall, he returned to Mount Cook for the winter. In his Christmas 1976 letter, he described the highlights of that year's activities:

> *Early in the New Year we had a visit from my American publisher, Martin R. Haase, Founder of Friends of Nature, affiliated to the Men of the Trees. He and his oldest son... had come by way of the Redwoods in Northern California, where they had been shocked to see the destruction of many of the finest groves adjoining the Redwood National Forest.... The Conservationists had become despondent, and the State of California seemed unable to act without an independent report. Rudy Haase insisted I should investigate the situation and prepare that report.*
>
> *Flying out of Auckland on 30 March we sat next to a young merchant in precious stones, who was checking the contents of a package. When he had finished I spoke of my life of tree planting and said that friends had often asked me how many acres of tree planting I had been responsible for in my lifetime. Perhaps he, with the help of his computer could help me answer that question.*
>
> *He went through my curriculum vitae, and after three and a half hours work pronounced that the grand total was 23 billion acres or 23 trillion trees in 108 countries, islands or states, between 1889 and 1975.*

Baker had a lively imagination, to say the least. The total forested acreage of the planet is less than ten billion acres, containing some three trillion trees. It is just this sort of 'statistic' that, while attracting the young, the hopeful, the idealist, the utopian, and the dreamer, might get Baker in trouble and lessen his credibility with scientifically minded people. And yet it seems that his incredible enthusiasm—easily given to such flights of fancy—was the kind of impetus he needed to remain steadfast, to inspire others, and to sustain his noble obsession.

The Christmas letter continues:

In April, with the help of Dr. Edgar and Mrs. Weyburn of the Sierra Club, Save the Redwoods League, State and National Park Rangers, we were able to complete the report on the eve of the State Enquiry. The Attorney General thanked me in person and said that he would be able to act. Later, when visiting the Secretary of the Interior in Washington, D.C., I learned that an injunction had been served on the three major lumber companies to stop felling in the region of the National Redwood Forest until the matter had come before Congress. The Secretary of the Interior assured me that there would be no more clear felling of Redwoods.

The next summer he was in England, speaking at the Health and Healing Conference in London. He then devoted himself to international projects, working with VEGFAM—a kind of a vegetarian Oxfam—to establish funding for nursery projects in Kenya, and

A warm welcome to Nairobi from Chief Josiah Njonjo, co-founder of the Kenyan Men of the Trees.

with Jocelyn Chase of Chase Organic Products of Argentina to promote alternative Amazon development based on food-bearing trees instead of forest clearing and cattle grazing—an early effort in what would become the fair trade movement.

In early October, his novel *Kamiti* was published in German. Later that month he flew to Nairobi to present a cheque from VEGFAM to the Kenyan branch of Men of the Trees. He wrote:

> *The Men of the Trees in Kenya are most grateful for a generous donation of 500 pounds from* VEGFAM, *and are using it to grow avocado pears, walnuts and Macadamia nuts to feed the people who are natural vegetarians living on their organic gardens. We had a memorable reunion on the afternoon of the presentation with Chief Josiah Njonjo, father of the Hon. Charles, Attorney General, and representative Men of the Trees from England....*

Chief Njonjo donated the land for the orchard.

As usual, Baker was already acting in advance of the world; a year later he would be back in Nairobi for the first World Conference on Desertification where the nations had at least agreed to talk about the problem and would hopefully resolve to act collectively—as Baker had first proposed some fifty-five years earlier, from the same location.

Following the Kenya trip, he visited Iran to promote a seventeen-year, seventy-thousand-trees-a-year planting program. After following up on desert reclamation work being undertaken in Pakistan and India, it was on to Sydney and then to Townsville to stay with his daughter Angela and her husband, Ken Barnes. "Angela met me at the airport with her small son David Paul, who, after a few minutes was all smiles. We called on Ken at his work." Young David, Baker's first grandchild, had been born earlier that year, on April 15.

One might have expected Baker, at eighty-seven, to finally relax in the bosom of his family. It seemed, however, his destiny was, as Diefenbaker had put it, to "keep up the good work to the end."

CHAPTER TEN

Earth Healer

THE HEADWATERS OF CONSCIOUSNESS

In 1977, the Chipko tree-hugger movement became one of Baker's central concerns. The conservation movement among the Indigenous women of the Himalayan region of India started in response to the clear-cutting of mountain slopes. This caused landslides and other problems that were threatening the hill people's way of life while doing untold damage to the land and watershed of northern India. A letter dated January 22, 1977, by a Chipko supporter from the Lakshmi Ashram in the Himalayas, outlines the situation:

Dear St. Barbe,
I have thought of you often in the time we have been here, because of tree work. This past week there was a seminar on the forest in Dehra Dun. It was a meeting point between government and people...at first head on, but developing into a common understanding for what they termed Social Forestry—the realization that the fates of the hill people and the forest is

inseparable. The state of affairs is appalling as I am sure you well know....

Can you help? I believe you can and know you can if there is a way....The problems facing such an endeavour are enormous. For instance nobody knows the kind of trees that will meet the environmental needs and the peoples' need and benefit. So the Government sticks with the pine for the money and the water table goes on disappearing. Then there is the matter of doing it, which in India is a nightmare to do anything.

His answer was "yes." St. Barbe would visit Chipko later in the year to lend his voice to their struggle.

Baker had begun 1977 by working on a book of reminiscences of "275 great ones and friends who have inspired and helped me and the Men of the Trees." At Catriona's suggestion it was to be called *Tall Timber*, but the manuscript would not be available in print until 2010, when it was published by the Men of the Trees of Western Australia with Barrie Oldfield as editor. Around the same time, however, Baker published *Trees for Health and Longevity* privately. He subtitled the book *An Introduction to Tree Therapy*, describing himself as its "first student and teacher."

Also in progress was a one-hour documentary on Baker's life, proposed by Canadian filmmaker and Academy Award winner Christopher Chapman. Considerable work was done on the film, but due to lack of funds the project was not completed.

In January, Baker's friend and American publisher Rudy Haase nominated Baker for the Nobel Peace Prize, based largely on his efforts to unite the world in "One World Purpose" to create in the Sahara desert a "Peace Garden of the World," by utilizing the twenty-two million members of the world's standing armies. In his letter of January 31, Haase wrote, "You certainly deserve the award, much more so than Kissinger, but I'm afraid it takes lobbying in high places, and the decision is political in nature rather than on strict merit." He also suggests that Baker take the opportunity presented by the incoming Carter administration in Washington to urge that a Redwood National Park finally be established with high priority.

In New Zealand, Baker received due recognition with his appointment as vice-patron of the Tree Society, a group similar to Men of the Trees.

Meanwhile, various preparations were underway for aspects of Baker's annual world tour.

On April 4, Baker arrived at San Diego airport and was met by an assistant of Edmond Bordeaux Szekely, the foremost proponent of natural health and healing at that time. The California segment of the trip involved the usual series of meetings and personal contacts, as well as the presentation of a report on the Redwood National Park before hearings of the Congressional Sub-Committee on National Parks in San Francisco.

The hearings were stormy, the rooms filled with loggers protesting plans to protect trees, shouting in unison, "No More Parks!" The loggers' main concern was the loss of jobs; to them, the conservationists threatened their livelihood. In his presentation, Baker pointed out that those wanting to save the trees were not preservationists, but conservationists. Quoting John Ruskin's passage, that the earth is not ours but is lent to us, as much for our children as for the next generation, he argued that forest management preserves jobs in perpetuity and that while all out exploitation may be advantageous for the present generation, it undermines the economy for our children and their children.

Now a venerable conservation elder, Baker made a strong impression on the congressional sub-committee, as indicated by a series of glowing tributes penned into his daybook by several congressmen and their staff.

Baker then continued through the redwoods, up the West Coast to Victoria, where he was provided with introductions to a group of First Nations people who wanted to hold a ceremonial dance in his honour, which was to be featured in Chris Chapman's film. On May 22, he touched down in Saskatoon, the guest of University President Emeritus John Spinks. In a conversation I had with Dr. Spinks, he recalled with a wry smile how Baker had a way of taking command of situations. On his visits to Saskatoon Baker would arrive at Spinks' office, where a huge stack of mail from correspondents around the world would already be waiting for him. After a welcoming chat,

Baker would ask if he might briefly prevail upon the president's secretary to help him respond to a letter from some prime minister or other. Before long, the whole office would be working full time for Baker, typing letters, perhaps a brief to the United Nations, and the president's work would grind to a halt. Baker was a charmer.

He also visited the University of Regina—where I met him for the first time—and after a hiatus of sixty-seven years returned to the Indian Head Tree Nursery, which was now pumping out millions of trees each year for farm shelterbelts.

In Toronto, he appeared on Peter Gzowski's popular national radio program, *Morningside*. After an interview with the Toronto *Globe and Mail*, the journalist Cameron Smith wrote in Baker's book, "Dear Dr. Baker, as the forests are the fountain of life, so you stand at the headwaters of consciousness. May we all join you there one day."

Next he visited his friend, Dr. Stuart Hill, a noted advocate of ecological agriculture at McGill University in Montreal. Dr. Hill once told me something that shed light on the nature of Baker's tours. Baker was Hill's houseguest. He loved the old man, but after several days felt compelled to ask what was next on his itinerary. Baker said he planned to go to New York but shared no details of when and how he would leave Montreal. Eventually Hill realized that Baker had no way or means to continue his trip, so he bought him a ticket and took him to the airport.

The next week was spent at the United Nations and in Washington, among other stops. "In New York on 9 June the Bahá'í International Community arranged for me to take part in a gathering of NGOs at the UN Headquarters, making final arrangements for the first UN Conference on Desertification to be held in Nairobi 29 August to 9 September. I was appointed senior advisor to the Bahá'í delegation."

A press release from UNEP at that time confirmed what Baker had been trying to bring to global awareness since the 1920s: that man-made deserts covered nine million square kilometers; that arid and semi-arid lands, which were home to 628 million people, covered 36 percent of Earth's land surface; that two thirds of all nations were affected; and that, based on soil and vegetation data, the total area of endangered lands was 43 percent of the world's surface.

On June 15, Baker followed up his presentation to the congressional hearings on the redwoods earlier in the year with a visit to the secretary of the interior, who penned the following into Baker's book: "Dr. Baker, your enormous concern for the future has contributed to mankind's survival. Best wishes, Cecil D. Andrews." Baker later commented: "Three days later, Andrews got out by plane and helicopter to inspect the area in Humboldt County covered by my report. Three weeks later, President Carter got the thirty-nine and a half million dollars needed to save the first National Redwood Park."

THE KENYA CONFERENCE AND MAATHAI

Baker now had renewed reason to be hopeful for his big vision, Sahara reclamation:

We of the Sahara Reclamation Programme and Friends of Nature are humbly grateful that fifty-eight countries and international organizations have agreed to concerted action to stop the Sahara spreading over more of Africa. The first phase is estimated to cost $3000 million dollars and is expected to be completed in 1982, and will be financed from grants from donor countries and the Organization for Economic Cooperation and Development. We are profoundly grateful to the Ottawa Conference Chairman Boulama Manga, Minister of Rural Development in Niger, and Jean Pierre Goyer, the Canadian Minister responsible for relations with francophone countries, as well as my old classmate, John G. Diefenbaker, and of course the Canadian Government who generously lent me a plane to demarcate lines of shelterbelts between Chad and Niger and draw attention to the urgency of accepting the challenge of the Sahara.

In Nairobi by the end of August 1977 for the UN Conference on Desertification, the now eighty-eight-year-old Baker wrote:

1500 delegates from 110 countries attended. I have never worked so hard in all my life keeping in touch with all these

countries, many leaders of whom I had known intimately through the years and had been working with them for Desert Reclamation by tree planting. This historic conference was held at Kenyatta Centre only 18 miles from Muguga, my old forestry station where with my old interpreter, Chief Josiah Njonjo, I had started the Men of the Trees 55 years ago....
History was again made when the National Women's Council of Kenya became Men of the Trees and planned to plant 15 million trees a year for the next five years and then 30 million a year for the following five years. The Forestry Department nurseries are helping and 800 illiterate Maasai Market Women have presented 15,000 acres of land which they purchased for this purpose. Anyone who wants to help combat the oncoming desert can become a life member of the Men of the Trees, Kenya, for 100 shillings....

In *Wangari Maathai: Visionary, Environmental Leader, Political Activist*, a biography of the 2004 Nobel Peace Prize winner and founder of Kenya's Green Belt Movement, Namulundah Florence notes the connections between Baker, Chief Njonjo, the Men of the Trees, and Maathai, who was also Kikuyu. She was involved with the National Council of Women of Kenya (NCWK) at the time of the UN conference. Florence notes that, while the Men of the Trees had limited success in Kenya, Maathai's Green Belt Movement, which later branched off from the NCWK, was considerably more successful in fulfilling the vision first articulated in the 1920s. Elsewhere, Maathai and the Green Belt Movement noted the early work of Baker and Njonjo. Maathai's vision of employing women in large-scale tree planting, which later became a pan-African movement, was reminiscent of Baker's schemes.

At the conference, Baker, Njonjo, and Maathai—who first came to the public's attention for Chipko-style tree-hugging—came together for a ceremonial tree planting. Baker celebrated his eighty-eighth birthday with Njonjo, who was born on the same day.

Maathai went on to inspire UNEP's Billion Tree Campaign. When an American corporate executive boasted that their corporation was planning to plant a million trees, she responded: "That's great, but what we really need is to plant a billion trees." That goal was achieved in 2007. Another billion trees were planted as part of the UN World Food Programme agroforestry initiative, after which the target was raised to seven billion trees. By 2016, over 14.2 billion trees had been planted as a result of this initiative.

It is difficult to evaluate the contribution that Baker's work made to the emerging global recognition of the problem of desertification. It can be said with certainty, however, that Baker was far ahead of the

A tree planting ceremony at the first World Conference on Desertification; Wangari Maathai planting the tree; Josiah Njonjo on the far left; Baker holding his Matathi stick.

field in his understanding of desertification as a fundamental world problem, and that Baker made relentless, even heroic efforts to bring the problem to the attention of the world. If only the world had the sense to listen to Baker and to acknowledge the severity of the problem fifty years before it did, untold damage could have been prevented.

The next notable stop for Baker was the 1977 World Wilderness Congress in South Africa late in October, where Baker spoke to a packed hall on "The Wilderness and Trees." The group behind his visit was working on publishing an expanded version of *Sahara Conquest*, which would be retitled *Desert Conquest*. The South Africans hoped that building common cause around environmental protection might help build racial understanding in their country.

Later, Baker visited Soweto to initiate the planting of nut and fruit trees for every child born. As he recounted, "A very brave woman drove me. The highlight of my visit to this frightening all black

At eighty-eight, joining another dance of the trees.

concentration city was to a nursery school where the tiny tots sang with me: 'The more we are together the happier we'll be.'" As part of his tour, Baker visited various parts of South Africa and other southern African countries, including Swaziland.

INDIA'S TREE-HUGGERS

Before leaving for India, Baker received the following letter from Sunderlal Bahuguna, the Gandhian supporter of the Chipko and one of India's first and most prominent environmental activists, outlining for Baker the situation as it stood in northern India:

Respected St. Baker [sic],

Jai Jagat! Kindly allow myself to introduce as a humble servant of your noble mission, working in far off Himalaya villages along with a small dedicated group of Gandhian workers. Due to indiscriminate felling of trees, the Himalayan hilltops have become bald, the topsoil has been washed away, water resources are fast drying up. Landslides have become a regular feature taking hundreds of lives. Government and the timber merchants both need money. Our fine pine forests have turned into funeral grounds of pine trees due to excessive resin extraction to feed rosin and turpentine factories. We became conscious about this devastation when a flood in Alaknanda River, a tributary of Ganges, took many lives and turned the green fields into heaps of sand. I wonder, whether you have heard about 'chipko' (hug to the trees) movement launched here by the people and inspired by the Sarvodoya group. There has been some impact, but the government has not yet succeeded [sic] to our demands to declare the Himalayan forests as preservation forests and stop all commercial operations forthwith. Every year the green trees are sold through public auction. This year there were demonstrations in front of auction halls. I and a friend took a three days prayer and fast.

When I heard about your visit to India in connection with International Vegetarian Congress, I felt the silent prayers of

Himalayas pines and other trees have been heard by the Almighty. He is sending you here to relieve them of the brutal behaviour of men. I could not contact you earlier as I recently got your address from The Ecologist. Kindly spare at least two weeks time in India to visit Himalayan forest areas, meet the people and forest officers. I will take you around and arrange your tour with our limited resources. I am anxiously waiting for your reply and meeting with you in Delhi to finalize the programme.

Ever at your feet.
Yours, Sunderlal

Accompanying the letter were various articles and resolutions further describing the Chipko situation. The villagers of the area, realizing that their way of life and future were facing extermination as commercial interests were destroying their forests, vowed to hug the trees, placing their bodies between tree and axe. The loggers said that they would kill the men who stood in their way, so the women marched into the forest to tie sacred threads on the threatened trees symbolizing the spiritual relationship between human and tree, a theme which recurs again and again in the folk songs and literature of this region.

In his annual letter later that year Baker commented:

In India I was side tracked for the 24th International Vegetarian Union World [Congress] where I spoke on "Feeding the Millions—Forward the Trees" and was taken into the Himalayas where the women had started the "CHIPKO, HUG TO THE TREES" Movement to save the Char Pines from being stripped from their mountains. Students tried to stop a Forestry Department auction selling felling concessions to contractors and 500 police were sent to cope with them. Twenty-one students were arrested and jailed! On my return to Delhi I gave a lecture to University professors and heads of Government Departments, the Minister of Petroleum and Chemicals presiding. The Government accepted my proposal to serve an injunction on felling all trees above 4000 feet altitude for ten years. This will have a wonderful psychological effect upon the mountain people.

The presentation mentioned was a speech to the national seminar on "The People and Forests" in New Delhi on December 21–22, 1977. Prime Minister Desai and other cabinet ministers were in attendance. The seminar introduced the theme of social forestry, involving the relationship between people and the forest—just what Baker had long appreciated.

In his annual letter, he notes that when he left the Royal Hospital Sheffield on April 15, 1975, following two surgeries, the senior surgeon had given him only one year to live. It was almost two years, so far, and Baker said he had a few more appointments to keep.

That year, 1977, Alan Grainger, a young scientist, friend, and protégé of Baker's, who had been assisting him since 1973, was appointed secretary of the International Tree Crops Institute (ITCI). Grainger was appointed by Lawrence Hills, the renowned expert

A radio broadcast in India, in support of Chipko.

on organic gardening who had founded the institute earlier that year with Henry Esbenshade, a carob expert from California. Hills and Grainger in turn invited Baker to be the institute's Honorary President, and Baker promptly agreed.

At the beginning of January 1978, at Mount Cook, Baker received a letter from a friend who commented that Baker had never received the recognition for his work that he deserved. "Not being recognized was probably the greatest thing that ever happened to you....You built up your treasures in heaven and did not wait for the world's acclaim. Maybe if you had been recognized, your passion and one-pointedness would have been lost on the way with the trivia of pomp and circumstance."

Ironically, a second letter from another friend, which arrived simultaneously, noted that Baker's name was on Prime Minister James Callaghan's list to receive the Order of the British Empire. In a letter from 10 Downing Street, Callaghan's principal secretary states that the "Prime Minister was glad to be able to include your name in his recommendations to the Queen for the award of OBE in the New Years Honours List. As you requested, a reference to the Men of the Trees was included in your citation which was: Forestry Adviser. Founder, Men of the Trees."

He wasn't long at home before he was again preparing for yet another world tour.

Lucas Mangope, president of the new nation of Bophuthatswana, had invited Baker to his country to advise on tree planting, stating: "We are now on Page Number One of our history books. Your visit at this stage of our development could provide the opportunity to have your name inscribed on that page as the man whose expertise brought the trees to our country." China also remained on his agenda, as Baker was still planning to survey the Gobi at age eighty-nine!

Baker returned to England in the spring of 1978, where a variety of engagements were being planned by a small troop of supporters including Hugh Locke, Michael Thompson, and Alan Grainger.

I arrived in England for the first AGM of the Men of the Trees under Royal Patronage. It was of the greatest possible encouragement to have HRH *The Prince of Wales as patron. This gives us high expectations that the work of restoring tree cover to the British Isles and establishing a Coastal Defense program will be given priority in a national campaign to protect the environment.*

Baker had the privilege of an audience with Prince Charles at Buckingham Palace on June 11. Baker had hoped this would reinforce his conservation-employment proposal.

It is worth noting again that women were often the mainstay of the Men of the Trees, in many cases working at the grassroots to effect the global vision at the local level. Baker used to recount with amusement that on one occasion a female listener at a lecture asked the question, "Do the Men of the Trees embrace women?" The name Men of the Trees was certainly 'generic' given that women were actively involved at all levels from the beginning. But the organization remained, like the society it emerged from, male dominated.

The lecture tour of the Scottish Highlands (including Findhorn) and islands, Ireland, and Wales, included ninety lectures and radio or television interviews with local sponsorship by the local Men of the Trees, Bahá'ís, or vegetarians.

A FEW WORDS TO HER MAJESTY

The summer tour included a week in Northern Ireland in June and the remainder of the month in England, where he was involved in a minor car accident. Much of July was spent in Scotland. However, July 12 was set aside for his investiture into the Order of the British Empire by Queen Elizabeth at Buckingham Palace. Of course, Baker managed to slip in a few words on trees to Her Majesty, as mentioned in the letter of July 13 written on her behalf:

Dear Dr. Baker:
The Queen has commanded me to thank you most warmly for the kind gift of your book yesterday [Famous Trees of Bible Lands]. Her Majesty was particularly pleased that you were able

to attend the Investiture and was also delighted to see you in such
good health. She very much looks forward to reading your book.

With the OBE attached to his name, and a future king as patron
of the Men of the Trees, Baker decided to appeal to Prince Charles
to use his influence to advance the cause, suggesting that the unemployed be given work in tree planting and thinning pine forests in
order that they might be underplanted with broadleaf trees. He suggested that the pine poles be used to build a special floating sea wall
to prevent the erosion of coastal lands; this erosion was shearing off
up to fifty feet of coast in a year.

On October 9, 1978, his eighty-ninth birthday, Baker left for the
Eighth World Forestry Congress in Jakarta, which was to begin on
October 15. He had met the environmental economist E.F. Schumacher
and at the congress he had arranged to show Schumacher's last film,
On the Edge of the Forest, which had moved him deeply. To his
great disappointment, the film was not allowed to be shown, on the
grounds that it was "a one sided view and that it would cause a furor
and alienate the lumberman." Baker wrote in a letter to his friend
Harry Kurth of the World Union for the Protection of Life:

I am still suffering from delayed shock at the refusal to show the
Schumacher film. It seems that the art and science of silviculture
has been prostituted to short term economics and forestry is
becoming a matter of money, machines, and manpower, in that
order. To have experienced this terrible insight into the ruthless-
ness of those controlling money, riding on the bandwagon of
forestry when undermining its very basis, sustained yield and
maintenance of earth's green mantle: trees...a bitter blow!

Baker's involvement at the conference was cut short when he
was forced to leave due to a bout of malaria and heat prostration.
He returned home. In February 1979, his daughter Angela remarried and he attended the wedding. In the meantime, he caught up on
correspondence and writing, including a plan for a book on cente-
narians—which category he intended to join.

It was the fiftieth anniversary of the Men of the Trees in Palestine, now Israel, and Baker planned to visit and celebrate the jubilee. The Jewish National Fund (JNF) agreed to sponsor a celebration with school children, in part to re-enact the scene of Baker's plantings with children on the New Year of the Trees, 15 Shevat, 5689, according to the Jewish calendar. In its letter of February 7, 1979, the JNF points out that Baker's memory of the date in 1929 must have been mistaken, as the date he mentioned was not in fact the correct day for the celebration and was, as well, a Sabbath day, meaning that no rabbi would have led the event as Baker described. No doubt Baker had a tendency to find the dramatic and the synchronistic element in every event—if the tree planting ceremony he was involved in in 1929 was anything like the traditional Jewish Tree Festival, then he had been the one to revive it after thousands of years!

Who can say for sure what the whole story is?

The letter points out that the Tree Festival was indeed revived and annually involved thousands of children. It states: "Last year, and this year too, approximately 120,000 children gathered in different ceremonies to plant trees. They came in groups, classes of between 20–40, whole schools of up to 400 children, as well as mass ceremonies making up between 3–5,000 children at a time. They came with flags, banners, children's orchestras and choirs....School children have a half day off school and it is devoted to tree planting, the study of trees, forests, nature and environmental ecology. The fruits traditionally eaten on the 15th of Shevat, are mentioned in the Talmud in connection with the day it names 'The New Year of the Trees'."

Baker had planned his trip for March 15, the day he believed to be the fiftieth anniversary, but which was, in fact, about a month late for the real Tree Festival, which fell in February. He was met at the airport in Tel Aviv by David Hofman, his old roommate from the 1930s, now a member of the Universal House of Justice, the international council of the Bahá'í community.

This visit was a triple jubilee for Baker, marking his first meeting with the Guardian of the Bahá'í faith, who had become the first life member of the Men of the Trees, the jubilee of the Men of the Trees in Palestine, and the jubilee of the revival of the Festival of the Trees. Messages of congratulations came from around the globe, from old friends and supporters, as well as prominent figures, including Prince Charles.

With the advent of the UN Year of the Child in 1979, Baker began to shift his attention to children, feeling that educating children in ecological consciousness was the only lasting hope that sustainability would become a new ethic for humanity. He proposed that a tree be planted for every child born that year.

Around the beginning of April, Baker was not well, but on April 13, after a round of antibiotics and natural remedies, he spoke at the World Symposium on Humanity, an inter-continental conference, held simultaneously in London, Toronto, and Los Angeles. Baker contributed to sessions on the future of the planet in the London conference, held at the Wembley Conference Centre. The sessions, organized by Alan Grainger, brought Baker together with other leading environmental thinkers, including Aurelio Peccei, founder of the Club of Rome; Edward Goldsmith, editor of *The Ecologist*; Lawrence D. Hills, founder of the Henry Doubleday Research Institute and the International Tree Crops Institute; and Amory Lovins, the pioneer of "soft energy" strategies. This put Baker on the same platform as other leading global thinkers of the modern environmental movement.

DECLINING HEALTH

Baker's robust health was at last in decline. On the back of a letter dated May 12, 1979, he painstakingly lists a number of his problems. Nevertheless, he was well enough to pass a medical examination for a driver's license! He continued to work long hours and maintain a schedule that would tax a man of thirty, maintaining his travel schedule, writing dozens of letters a day, using local contacts to write, type, and post them—and often pay for the postage—as he really had no money at all and no source of income beside his modest pension.

There were many small victories. His contacts in South Africa wrote on May 1 about their organization GROW, of which Baker was patron:

You must really be wondering what happened to operation GROW.... We are incredibly busy and are being called to many places. Thank you again for recommending our project to VEGFAM. *The donation they sent helped a lot. We were involved in a number of tree planting ceremonies in Soweto schools toward the end of last year and have distributed hundreds of fruit trees, especially loquat, mulberry, fig and apricot, plus some almond and pecan nut and a few walnut trees. Nut trees are very expensive and we are trying to get some of the black co-workers to grow almonds and pecans from the nuts.... Wherever we can we plant food bearing trees and try to make people aware of their great potential. We have started orchards at many little schools, nursery schools, institutions and other suitable situations, as well as a few home gardens.*

An accompanying clipping quotes a participant in the GROW project: "It is such a relief to be able to have something to eat without begging for it. The time when we used to stampede over one and other rushing for dumped vegetables is over. We now live like decent human beings again." Penned onto the clipping are the words: "This is our reward!"

On another front, plans were made, with the support of Hugh Locke, for Baker to visit Bophuthatswana at the invitation of the president, to prepare a national tree-planting program. Locke wrote: "Dr. Baker has been collecting tree seeds from Australia, New Zealand, and China to bring with him. However he will better know your requirements when he views the country and sees sites, in addition to studying the climate and rainfall." Baker recommended a forester who might carry through with his planting program.

Lack of money was ever a block to the work. Everything depended on donations and in-kind contributions of hospitality. Rudy Haase was much beloved of Baker for his support, including his financial contributions. One American member of the Men of the Trees offered his estate of $100,000 upon his death, but despite such intentions, money was never equal to the mammoth tasks envisioned.

On the Sahara front, Prince Charles replaced the deceased Emperor Selassie as patron, but the Sahara programme was really going nowhere. Baker met for over an hour with Prince Charles at his palace and found him to be deeply concerned about trees and the work of the Men of the Trees in North Africa.

Baker now refocused much of his concern on the Amazon. He had long recognized that its deforestation was among the most serious environmental problems facing the planet, with more immediate significance even than the Sahara project. From his base in Hugh Locke's apartment, Baker travelled Europe and lectured widely on this topic.

NINETY YEARS, NINETY TREES

After celebrating his ninetieth birthday on October 9, 1979, by giving ninety trees as gifts, Baker addressed the One Earth Conference at Findhorn and then flew to Kenya for another celebration with Chief Njonjo, born on the same day. Adding the dates together, they celebrated on the 18th. He had a meeting with the ambassadors of Saharan countries before going on to Bophuthatswana and Soweto to view tree projects. He was back to Mount Cook for Christmas, from where he sent a letter to all of his contacts suggesting all governments establish an International Children's Tree Day, much in the style of the Jewish New Year of the Trees.

As usual, Baker's visit to Mount Cook in 1980 was given over to communication with his global contacts. Christopher Bird, the author of the bestseller, *The Secret Life of Plants*, became a close friend and planned an article on Baker.

Being the original tree-hugger, Baker remained a figurehead for the Indian Chipko movement, for whom conservation had become a life-and-death struggle. The hill people were willing to give their life for trees, having come to understand that their life was dependent on them. The following excerpt from a lengthy letter from the spiritual leader of Chipko, Sunderlal Bahuguna, refers to Baker's role in the continuing Chipko struggle:

Respected St. Baker,
Yesterday was the happiest day of my life, when I got two letters...both mentioning your anxiety about the progress of

CHIPKO *movement. Do you remember the moment we parted at Vinoba Bhave's Ashram, we promised to be with each other in our prayers and work for the Service of Mother Earth and the trees? I always feel your presence during my prayers.*

Our struggle continues. This year we have been successful in driving out 300 Nepali imported axe men of the contractor. The shameless forest officers came to help them with police. Our movement is becoming popular and people in other parts of the country are getting inspiration. But the vested interests are there. For them the value of the trees is for timber and raw materials for the industry.

I am optimistic. Indira Gandhi is back in power and the new forest policy is to be discussed in Parliament. I wish you to write her, conservationists in India and abroad, and foresters to save the Himalayas. Declare Himalayan forests as protection forests.

I am eager to meet you. Is there any chance of that? Send me one of your slides hugging the tree. I have got a projector now. Send your blessings. I read your book, My Life, My Trees, during my prayerful fast. It was a scripture for me.

Always with you in your prayers and mission, ever yours, Sunderlal

Already Baker was planning yet another world tour, one that included a foray in India. One of his favourite quotes, from Masefield, seemed to have been written for Baker:

My road calls me, lures me, East, West, South, and North,
Most men's lead them homewards, but my road leads me forth
To add more miles to the tally of the grey miles left behind
In search of that one Beauty, God put me here to find.

Baker began preparing for a trip through Argentina, Paraguay, Uruguay, and the highlands of Brazil to investigate Amazon deforestation, before traveling through North America. He would leave

The original tree-hugger meets a Himalayan forest friend.

Auckland April 1, travel through California for a redwoods reunion, through Portland, Seattle, and Vancouver, and on to Saskatoon, at all times focusing on public education on the Amazon issue. In a letter, the organizer of the Vancouver portion of the tour provides an insight into what was a typical local schedule for the now ninety-year-old forester: four media interviews, two public meetings with people "hanging from the rafters," and an impromptu visit to the local forestry school.

CHILDREN OF THE GREEN EARTH

After a tour through Canada, he returned to Britain, where he intensified his focus on children. Baker began to promote the adoption of the principles of a new organization he had started, the Children of the Green Earth.

By August he was in Switzerland visiting the Swiss Federal Institute of Forestry Research, which was investigating social forestry and interested in the Chipko movement. He attempted to arrange study projects for Indian foresters in Switzerland through the offices of the Indian prime minister, and the Indian Department of Agriculture later agreed to send a four-member team.

Before returning to New Zealand for the winter, Baker was able to visit the Chipko movement again.

In 1981, he increased activities in Australia and with several friends launched a chapter of Children of the Green Earth at Peak Crossing in Queensland. Meanwhile, on the American West Coast, Michael Soule and Ron Rabin filed papers to found Children of the Green Earth as a non-profit organization and started mixed-media presentations for school children, along with tree plantings, in a number of Oregon communities and in Canada.

In a letter of February 11, 1981, Alan Grainger was able to report that the branches of the International Tree Crops Institute in Australia and the USA were thriving and an advisory council for ITCI India had been formed. The *International Tree Crops Journal* had been well received, and its second issue had, following earlier permission from Baker and the publishers, reprinted his 1928 paper in the *Empire Forestry Review* describing his pioneering experiments in agroforestry at Sapoba in Nigeria.

The edition of *My Life, My Trees* published by Findhorn had received a tremendous response and Findhorn were now interested in publishing both *My Health, My Wealth* and *My Horse, My Kingdom*. Grainger had suggested that they also publish *Richard St. Barbe Baker's Book of Tree Poetry*, an anthology of Baker's favourites; he had arranged for Baker to record the poems at Findhorn studios.

An extensive global schedule was arranged for 1981, beginning with interviews and public meetings in New Zealand and Australia.

On May 8, Baker at last arrived in Beijing and was hosted by the Chinese Academy of Forestry. He spent much time planting trees with children—all of them dressed smartly in white shirts and bright red scarfs—with banners flying. All did not go well, as Baker contracted double pneumonia while on a visit to the Great Wall. Yet, at age ninety-one, he managed to fight it off, making it to London for the fifty-ninth AGM of the Men of the Trees on May 15. Later in the summer, he travelled to Nairobi and Bombay, followed by another tour of Australia and New Zealand.

In November, Baker wrote to his close friend Dr. John Spinks, at the University of Saskatchewan, and his wife Mary, suggesting a new idea for the university:

> *I was impressed by a paper by Bob White on "Rural Planning with Earth Care." I would like to help found a chair in Deep Ecology at the University and have him appointed to this position. Bob White was the first plant pathologist to receive the Men of the Trees bursary to the top student of the year; nine others have followed and I would like to enlist their help in holding a workshop or seminar for a day in May 1982, convenient to you, to them, and to the University.*

Robert (Bob) White is one of many examples of those who were influenced by Baker. A Saskatchewan farm boy, Robert studied agriculture at the University of Saskatchewan. After receiving the Men of the Trees Bursary, he looked up Baker on his travels, was inspired

Preparing to plant trees with several Children of the Green Earth.

Baker, aged 91, in China preparing to plant trees with a group of children.

to do post-graduate work in deep ecology, and has maintained his passion for trees throughout his life. It was he who provided care for Baker in the final days of his life.

In the letter to Spinks, Baker goes on to mention a new Australian film on his life, titled *Man of the Trees*. A premiere in Sydney attracted 1,100 people. Another showing in Melbourne had attracted 1,450 people.

A FINAL TOUR

Late in 1981, Baker was back in New Zealand with Catriona. He had now reached the ripe old age of ninety-two. His health was failing and, though mentally strong, he was now often in a wheelchair. Nevertheless, his planning proceeded undiminished. In the letter to Dr. John Spinks mentioned above, he goes on to outline some of his plans for the year:

> *I expect to be supervising the planting of fruit trees in poor Mexican villages, presented by* VEGFAM, *and after a few days holiday over Easter as a guest of Mrs. Bordeaux Szekely at Rancho la Puerto, Tacata, Mexico, I am holding a meeting for conservationists at the Sierra Club, San Francisco, to study the Redwood situation in connection with a new threat by the Reagan administration—to consider what we can do to check further exploitation by lumbermen. While in Canada I shall devote as much time as possible to Christopher Chapman, who for some time past has been working on a film with the working title "Green Glory." In this I am co-operating with the Arbor Day Society of Canada, and planting trees with children. C.C. has already done some shooting and recording in British Columbia in the Douglas and Cedar Forests....I am looking forward to returning to Canada in September to address 15,000 Bahá'ís expected to attend their World Conference at Montreal....*

A festival of trees was planned for the spring, which would give a good start to the diamond jubilee of the Men of the Trees and strengthen the new movement, the Children of the Green Earth.

On the March 27, 1982, he left New Zealand, arriving in San Diego on April 1, after a brief stopover in Hawaii. The next two months were spent touring for Children of the Green Earth, participating in tree plantings, and resting on the West Coast. One of the main highlights of the trip was the dedication of the Redwood National Park as a World Heritage Site on May 22, 1982.

Baker had become exceedingly weak. His friends in Children of the Green Earth settled him in a cabin in the redwoods, the pilgrimage site where he had so often found healing and inspiration, in the hope that his health could again be restored. Michael Soule cared for Baker for several weeks, fully expecting the old man to slip away at any time.

One morning, Michael woke and heard nothing from Baker, who had always awoken before anyone else. Entering his room he discovered him completely quiet and at peace. Michael immediately began to plan how he would inform Catriona, Paul, and Angela, and all of Baker's friends worldwide. He was thinking of funeral arrangements as he leaned over Baker's body to offer his personal respects. Baker's eyes flashed open as he shouted "Surprise!" His sense of humour, at least, was intact.

Though Baker was extremely weak, it was decided he would continue his journey in a wheelchair. He flew to Saskatoon where plans had been made to plant a tree near the grave of John Diefenbaker on World Environment Day, June 5. His Saskatoon friends, including Robert White, were shocked to see his extreme frailty and were at a loss as to what to do: whether to cancel the events and confine Baker to bed or to let him have his way and maintain the schedule as ever.

The morning of the tree planting came with rain and wind—certainly he could not head out under these conditions to plant a tree. Then miraculously, it seemed, just as they were deciding to cancel, the sky cleared and the sun shone. The tree planting was on.

Baker was distressed when a mechanical planter was brought in to place the aspen poplar, but once it was settled in the ground he somehow found the strength to get up from his wheelchair and stand with a group of children around the tree, chanting with them the slogan of Children of the Green Earth: "From our hearts, with

Robert White helps Richard St. Barbe Baker make his way to his last tree planting, at the Diefenbaker Centre on the banks of the South Saskatchewan River.

our hands, for the earth, all the world together." The tree properly blessed, he was taken home. Just as they entered the house, the clouds and rain returned.

Baker rested for several days. His flight to Toronto was scheduled for the morning of June 9. His friends and supporters realized he was extremely weak and were uncertain what to do. At 8:30 a.m. that day, Richard St. Barbe Baker decided his life would end in Saskatoon, where his life's work had first taken shape. He had planted his last tree.

In his diary, a final notation was penned, a quote from Psalm 1: 2–3:

Whose delight is in the law of the Lord,
and in his law doth he meditate day and night.
And he shall be like a tree planted by the rivers of water,
that bringeth forth fruit in his season;
his leaf shall not wither, and whatever he doeth shall prosper.

Epilogue

At the foot of a friendly tree let my body be buried,
That this dust may rise and rejoice among the branches.
— from "The Friendly Trees," Henry Van Dyke

Baker often quoted these lines, making it clear this was exactly how he wanted to be buried. Specifically, he had said, "if I die in Saskatoon, I want to be buried under a tall tree overlooking the river and the University." Even more specifically, he had informed Hugh Locke that he wanted to rest at the foot of *two* tall conifers. Saskatoon's Woodlawn Cemetery seemed ideal; however, there were no longer any burial plots available in its well-treed older areas. In the new areas, ease of cutting grass took precedence over trees.

Karma, it seems, was on his side. The noted Saskatoon artist, Otto Rogers, was asked to go to the cemetery, explain the situation to the superintendent, and ask him to look again for a suitable plot. While waiting, Rogers wandered about the cemetery and found what he considered an ideal burial spot. Soon he saw the superintendent heading toward him. He reported that a body had recently been exhumed. The empty grave was precisely where Rogers was standing. It was at the foot of impressive twin conifers that would, in due course, raise Baker's dust to "rejoice among the branches."

This final bit of serendipity capped off a serendipitous life. Again and again, chance put Baker in the right place at the right time to effect change. But "chance favours the prepared mind," and Baker's unwavering focus on trees prepared him to seize every opportunity.

What became of his endless travels and talks and broadcasts? Seeds were sown. Some failed to take root, others grew impressively.

Looking back from today's vantage it is clear that the forest conservation movement of which Baker was a forerunner did not stem the tide of deforestation. Nigeria, for example, lost more than 90 percent of its primary forest due to practices initiated in the colonial era. Some 17 percent of the Amazon forest has been liquidated in the last fifty years. Since 1990 there has been a net loss of 129 million hectares of forests all told, an area about the size of Peru. In the first ten years of this century, fifty countries experienced net losses in forest area, and today some 7.6 million hectares of forest still disappear annually.

Fortunately, it is not all bad news. From 2000–2010, forest cover increased in forty-four countries, including Baker's beloved Kenya, as well as Algeria, Morocco, and Egypt. Forest cover remained stable in some thirty countries, including Canada and Russia, which contain the largest expanses of boreal forest, as well as a number of highly populated countries such as India, Mexico, Congo, South Africa, and Papua New Guinea. And while Baker would rejoice that the Save the Redwoods League has preserved more than two hundred thousand hectares of his favourite trees in dozens of redwoods parks, he would no doubt be raising the alarm about new threats, from climate change to burl poaching, were he with us today.

While Baker's grand sylvan vision did not receive the support he had hoped for in his day, some of his dreams are now being realized. His vision of a green front against the Sahara ultimately came to fruition in the twenty-one-nation effort to plant Africa's Great Green Wall. On completion, it will be the planet's largest living structure, spanning an area three times the size of Australia's Great Barrier Reef.

Baker always had high hopes for Chinese forestry, which he saw as a model for the world. Forest cover in China had fallen to a historical low of less than 10 percent of land area by 1949, but as a result of major reforestation and afforestation programs had recovered to

The twin conifers overlooking Baker's Saskatoon gravesite.

nearly 20 percent by the end of the twentieth century. This trend continues today. In 2018, China announced plans to plant new forests that will cover at least 6.6 million hectares, an area roughly the size of Ireland. China's State Forestry Administration's target is to increase forest cover from the current 21.7 percent of the country to 26 percent by 2035, drawing closer to Baker's prescription for sustainability: one third of every nation forested.

Perhaps his greatest impact was felt through the influence he had on individuals. For example, when Scott Poynton was fifteen, in 1979, he chanced to hear one of Baker's countless radio interviews. Mesmerized by his use of poetry and science to tell stories, Poynton determined to dedicate his life to becoming a forester. He gained a master of science in forestry from Oxford University, where he was awarded the prestigious Oxford Forestry Institute's Jubilee Prize. He went on to form The Forest Trust (TFT) in 1999. Its first goal was to ensure that the furniture trade used only wood from sustainably managed forests. TFT helped make that goal a reality, demonstrating that industry can be transformed for the better. The impact of TFT's change model led the organization to expand its approach to a total of thirteen forest commodities. TFT is now taking action all over the world to transform supply chains, creating change from boardrooms to factories to forests. Today, like his erstwhile mentor, Poynton is heavily involved in writing and speaking about protecting forests and other natural resources.

Tony Rinaudo leads one of the world's most successful agricultural development self-help programs. Since the 1990s, millions have benefitted through the afforestation of millions of hectares of desertified farmland in Niger and other nations using Farmer Managed Natural Regeneration (FMNR), an approach Rinaudo developed. FMNR is a low-cost reforestation method that regrows trees from existing live stumps and seeds in the ground to support ecosystem repair and improve yield. Rinaudo was profoundly influenced by Baker after a "chance" visit with a friend. In the middle of this friend's shed was a big pile of clearance library books, unceremoniously dumped on the floor. Two non-descript covers caught his attention, Baker's *Sahara Challenge* and *I Planted Trees*. Baker's story emboldened him "to think and do the unthinkable," says Rinaudo. "His approach of listening to people, loving and respecting people from other cultures and having awe and walking in step with nature instead of trying to dominate it has been built into my approach to life and work."

Wilderness champion Vance Martin, who was mentored by Baker in all things trees, was also deeply impacted by Baker's loving attitude toward nature and people. He met St. Barbe at Findhorn, where Martin started the organization Trees for Life. Infected by Baker's "indefatigable-ness," he went on to become president of the WILD Foundation, chairman of the Wilderness Specialist Group of the World Commission on Protected Areas, and international director of the World Wilderness Congress, before launching the Nature Needs Half movement. Like Baker, he has specialized in bridging the interests of people and nature and championed the special role of cultural interests and Indigenous peoples in sustaining wild nature.

Numerous letters, from women and men, young and old, who were touched and many times changed by their chance encounters with Baker can be found in his extensive papers. A good example is a letter from Julian Boles, who had once helped Baker to establish the mythical tally of twenty-three trillion trees planted in his lifetime. Though in itself astounding, Mr. Boles's memory of the sum was dramatically different. The letter provides another example of the impact of a chance encounter with Baker:

> I was very happy to see your name on a list of speakers at this year's Festival of Mind and Body....You may remember a 17-hour period in 1976, in February of that year, when we were sitting together high over the Pacific Ocean discussing the state of the world and your work with trees over the 84 years of your life to that day. We were calculating the number of trees you had assisted in planting (was it 11.2 billion?) in the various countries, and your philosophy of life in the eyes of a Bahá'í.... It would not be an exaggeration to say that our shared plane journey together from Auckland to San Francisco (you were dealing with a threat to the California Redwoods) had an immediate effect on the course of my actions. The purpose of beautifying the world became the most important.

Another of Baker's chance encounters pops up in a cult classic film by Louis Malle, of which the critic Roger Ebert said, "Someone asked me the other day if I could name a movie that was entirely devoid of clichés. I thought for a moment, and then answered, *My Dinner with Andre*." In the film, the character Andre mentions a remarkable conversation with a figure who can only be Baker:

And when I was at Findhorn, I met this extraordinary English tree expert who had devoted his life to saving trees. Just got back from Washington, lobbying to save the redwoods, he's 84 years old, and he always travels with a backpack cause he never knows where he's gonna be tomorrow. And when I met him at Findhorn, he said to me, "Where are you from?" and I said, "New York." He said, "Ah, New York. Yes, that's a very interesting place. Do you know a lot of New Yorkers who keep talking about the fact that they want to leave, but never do?" And I said, "Oh, yes." And he said, "Why do you think they don't leave?" I gave him different banal theories. He said, "Oh, I don't think it's that way at all."

He said, "I think that New York is the new model for the new concentration camp, where the camp has been built by the inmates themselves, and the inmates are the guards, and they have this pride in this thing they've built. They've built their own prison. And so they exist in a state of schizophrenia where they are both guards and prisoners, and as a result, they no longer have, having been lobotomized, the capacity to leave the prison they've made or to even see it as a prison." And then he went into his pocket, and he took out a seed for a tree and he said, "This is a pine tree." He put it in my hand and he said, "Escape before it's too late."

Baker was primarily a catalyst, a wedge, a collaborator. He accomplished what he did mainly by inspiring others. His *modus operandi* was often reflected in their work.

Nobel laureate Wangari Maathai is an interesting example. Although not directly influenced by Baker, the seeds of her efforts to mobilize African women to plant trees were sown in the 1920s when

Baker collaborated with Josiah Njonjo in the dance of the trees. Maathai's Green Belt movement was a more successful manifestation of Baker's vision of mobilizing citizens to plant trees.

Through his efforts, and those with whom he collaborated or inspired, billions of trees have been protected and planted. The work goes on. In 1992, the Men of the Trees in the United Kingdom was renamed the International Tree Foundation (ITF). ITF has supported local community organizations to grow and protect trees in more than thirty countries. Today, it is focussed on continuing Baker's mission to combat desertification and deforestation in Africa. In addition to supporting sustainable community forestry and agroforestry projects across Africa, it is organizing a global effort to celebrate the centenary of the Men of the Trees by planting twenty million trees in Kenya's forests. ITF also works with children through Tree Power, an educational program that supports teachers and schools to inspire new generations about the importance of trees and forests, and through Fruit-full Communities it works with young people in England and Wales to design and plant orchards in their neighbourhoods.

Men of the Trees organizations are still active in Australia. In Western Australia, for example, the organization continues to engage thousands of members and volunteers. It has planted over fifteen million native trees and understorey plants since its inception in 1979. On July 25, 2014, with the support of two thousand people, it broke a Guinness World Record by planting over one hundred thousand trees in an hour. Recently, the organization has been renamed Trillion Trees to reflect its new focus: a challenge to the world to plant a trillion trees.

Many threads come together in the efforts of Felix Finkbeiner and Plant-for-the-Planet. Felix was a fourth-grade student in Bavaria in 2007 when his teacher assigned a classroom presentation on climate change. His research brought him to the stories of Wangari Maathai and Richard St. Barbe Baker. Taking a leaf from their books, Felix challenged his classmates—and ultimately, children throughout the world—to plant a million trees in each country, an idea that grew into the international children's organization Plant-for-the-Planet. Its initiatives were so effective that in 2011 the United Nations turned its Billion Tree Campaign over to the organization Felix started.

Plant-for-the-Planet now has 67,000 Ambassadors for Climate Justice between the ages of nine and twelve training other children to share the sylvan vision with people of all ages. So far, fifteen billion trees have been planted in 130 countries. Plant-for-the-Planet now aims for one trillion trees, enough to capture twenty-five percent of anthropogenic carbon emissions every year.

Shortly after Baker's passing, his friend Edward Goldsmith, the late great environmentalist and long-time editor of *The Ecologist*, eulogized Baker in his magazine. No one said it better, so he gets the last word. Here, in part, are his comments:

> *I like to think of St. Barbe as a prophet, in the Old Testament sense of the term; that is to say, as a wise man, a teacher and an inspirer. Alan Grainger describes St. Barbe's "unique capacity to pass on his enthusiasm to others. Many foresters all over the world found their vocations as a result of hearing 'The Man of the Trees' speak. I certainly did, but his impact has been much wider than that. Through his global lecture tours, St. Barbe has made millions of people aware of the importance of trees and forests to our planet."*
>
> *St. Barbe, besides being a wise man, a teacher and an inspirer, was a tireless fighter for the values and ideas that he held to be so important and on whose acceptance by the world at large, he felt sure, must ultimately hinge the fate of our planet and of all those who inhabit it. Those who have looked seriously at the problems that we and future generations must face realize that St. Barbe's values and ideas are quite as important as he made them out to be.*
>
> *St. Barbe knew decades ago that global reafforestation was essential. In his book* Green Glory, Forests of the World, *he proposes, "that all standing armies everywhere be used for the work of essential reafforestation." But such action, he realized, could not be successful unless we first obtained the full cooperation of local people everywhere. More so, it is they, rather than governments and international institutions, who should take the lead. In the New Earth Charter, he writes:*

We believe in the innate intelligence of the villagers, the country men and the workers, that they should be allowed to manage their own affairs. We believe they will put into their work not merely their hands and their feet, but their brains and their hearts. Each can experience the transcendental joy of creation, and can earn immortality and bestow immortality.

We have here a confrontation between two conflicting world-views. The one sees nature as but a source of commodities to be sold on the world market. The other sees nature as St. Barbe's "vast sentient being" and, as the Chipko villagers put it, "the basis of our life." The one reflects the ingenuity of science and technology: the other the wisdom that is only embodied—as Eugene Odum, the father of modern ecology, admits—in the culture of traditional peoples, the wisdom that itself reflects, as St. Barbe would have put it, "The Divine Law and the Laws of Nature," whose violation can only lead to destruction and annihilation.

Almost everywhere in the world man has been disregarding the Divine Law and the Laws of Nature, to his own undoing. In his pride, he has rampaged over the stage of the earth, forgetting that he is only one of the players put there to play his part in harmony and oneness with all living things. St. Barbe realized that to stop the destruction we must abandon our present goals and move our society on to a very different course. As he writes in Land of Tane:

Man has lost his way in the jungle of chemistry and engineering and will have to retrace his steps, however painful this may be. He will have to discover where he went wrong and make his peace with nature. In so doing, perhaps he may be able to recapture the rhythm of life and the love of the simple things of life, which will be an ever-unfolding joy to him.

He realized that if we did not do this soon, it would be too late. In The New Earth Charter, he warned:

This generation may either be the last to exist in any semblance of a civilised world or it will be the first to have the vision, the bearing and the greatness to say, "I will have nothing to do with this destruction of life, I will play no part in this devastation of the land, I am determined to live and work for peaceful construction for I am morally responsible for the world of today and the generations of tomorrow."

What is required is nothing short of a spiritual renewal, a new religious worldview and one very much closer to that of our forest dwelling ancestors. To begin with, we must learn once again to regard Nature as "holy," as a vast "sentient being," a phrase that occurs again and again in St. Barbe's writings. St. Barbe undoubtedly saw nature in this way:

It is with a spirit of reverence that I approach God's creation—this beautiful Earth. We may climb mountains or wander through field and forest, intoxicated by loveliness through the changing hours and seasons recorded by the length of shadows cast by the trees—and as we watch the pink, opalescent fingers of the dawn reaching up from beneath the dark horizon, so we wait for the sunrise of our awakening to the realisation of our kinship with the earth and all living things.

He was a unique figure whom we shall never replace. Nevertheless I feel sure that in death, as in life, he will continue to teach and inspire us. It is up to us, his disciples and his friends, to celebrate the life and work of Richard St. Barbe Baker. It is up to us too, to carry on the fight—as tirelessly as he did in the past; to assure that his vision is realized and that his ideas live forever.

TWAHAMWE!

A portrait by Ian Anderson, Baker's nephew.

‑❧‑

Notes on Sources

Most of the source material for this book was found in the R. St. Barbe Baker fonds, University Archives & Special Collections, University of Saskatchewan (http://sain.scaa.sk.ca/collections/r-st-barbe-baker-fonds). The extensive collection, 4.5 metres of textual and other records, includes Baker's thirty-plus published books and several unpublished manuscripts. Most of these books are auto-biographical, and three in particular were the main sources for his personal story and most of the quotes covering the period up to 1970. Quotes from Baker's books and other writings are used liberally to convey a sense of Baker's voice. The innumerable clippings, diaries, notebooks, newsletters, circular letters, correspondence, articles, etc. in the collection supplemented the material from Baker's books and provided most of the information on his life post 1970. The story is pieced together from all of these and where the various narratives are contradictory or off sequentially, I did my best to sort them out.

Permission to quote liberally from Baker's books—all now out of print—and other archival material was graciously granted by his literary executors.

The following notes mainly provide sources for quotations. Any other material quoted from and not referred to specifically below is from the R. St. Barbe Baker fonds. Information obtained from inter-views I conducted and other sources is also noted.

PROLOGUE

The excerpt at the end of the prologue is from one of Richard St. Barbe Baker's favourite poems, "The Friendly Trees," from *Songs Out of Doors* by Henry Van Dyke (Scribner's, 1922.)

CHAPTER ONE

Information about Baker's childhood and youth comes primarily from his autobiographical books, especially *My Life, My Trees* (Findhorn Publications, 1979) and *I Planted Trees* (Lutterworth Press, 1944). The lengthy quote about his first gardening experiences is from *My Life, My Trees*. Another autobiographical book, *Dance of the Trees* (Oldbourne Press, 1956), was a good source on his early Canadian experiences, including his encounters with Charlie Eagle and the Moose Woods community and his overnight stay en route to Beaver Creek.

CHAPTER TWO

Sources for this chapter include the three books mentioned above, plus Baker's first book, *Men of the Trees* (George Allen & Unwin, 1931), *Africa Drums* (The Adventurers Club, 1942), and his little book, *Caravan Story and Country Notebook* (self-published 1969). *Dance of the Trees* provided the two lengthy quotes in this chapter about being lost in the bamboo and the first dance of the trees.

CHAPTER THREE

Sources for this chapter include the books cited above. The long quotes regarding Baker's work in Nigeria and Benin are from the chapter "Life's Changing Patterns" in *I Planted Trees*.

CHAPTER FOUR

Baker's travels in Palestine are covered in his autobiographical books. The longer quotes are from three chapters in *I Planted Trees*: "Planting in the Holy Land," "The Feast of the Trees," and "The Rebirth of Palestine." Additional material was found in Baker's *Famous Trees of Bible Lands* (H.H. Greaves Ltd., 1974).

CHAPTERS FIVE AND SIX

Sources and quotes related to Baker's travels in America, New Zealand, Ceylon, etc., his work to save the redwoods of California, and involvement with the Civilian Conservation Corps are from his autobiographical books, as well as his books *The Redwoods* (Lindsay Drummond Limited, 1943), *Green Glory: The Forests of the World* (A.A. Wyn, Inc., 1949), and *Land of Tane: The Threat of Erosion*, (Lutterworth Press, 1956). I interviewed David Hofman, a long-time friend of Baker's and a leading figure in the Bahá'í community, in Saskatoon circa 1989. The quote about Baker's encounters with Martha Root and the king of Sweden is included in his manuscript for *Tall Timber*, which recounts his encounters with outstanding women and men.

CHAPTERS SEVEN AND EIGHT

Sources and quotes are from the autobiographical books, as well as the two books Baker wrote specifically about his work on the Sahara expedition and reclamation campaign, *Sahara Challenge* (Lutterworth Press, 1954) and *Sahara Conquest* (Lutterworth Press, 1966).

CHAPTERS NINE AND TEN

Baker's autobiographic books continue to provide source material and quotes for the early portions of chapter 9. *My Life, My Trees* covers Baker's life to 1970. From 1970 on, the material comes from correspondence, diaries, circular letters, and other materials from the R. St. Barbe Baker fonds.

EPILOGUE

The excerpt from the poem is from "The Friendly Trees," from *Songs Out of Doors* by Henry Van Dyke (Scribner's, 1922). I interviewed Otto Rogers and Hugh Locke regarding Baker's burial. The selection from the script of *My Dinner with Andre* is widely available online, including in the article "A Chilling Description of Our World from a 1981 Movie," by Daniel Lattier, posted March 28, 2016, at www. intellectualtakeout.org/blog/chilling-description-our-world-1981-movie. The lengthy quotation from the eulogy by Edward Goldsmith is from his article "The Vision of St. Barbe Baker," in *Richard St. Barbe Baker, Man of the Trees: A Centenary Tribute* (The Indian National Trust for Art and Cultural Heritage, 1989.)

Photo Credits

(by page number)

Source: University of Saskatchewan Library, University Archives & Special Collections, Richard St. Barbe Baker fonds

217   mg071_baker_m16_Dominion_and_Rural_Rides_Talking_to_
      Students_001
217   mg071_baker_m6_1971-1982-1_Forest_congress_001
219   mg071_baker_m1_1920-1950_Baker_in_garden_001
227   mg071_baker_m1_1951-1980_with_lily_001
229   mg071_baker_m6_1971-1982-1_With_delegates_of_16_Sahara_
      countries_001
231   mg071_baker_m6_1971-1982-2_Graduation_with_Diefenbaker
234   mg071_baker_m12_Africa3_Meeting_Njonjo
243   mg071_baker_m12_Tree_Planting
244   mg071_baker_m12_Africa3_Women_dancing
247   mg071_baker_m6_1971-1982-2_in-India_on_the_radio
256   mg071_baker_m5_folder3_Hugging_tree_001
259   mg071_baker_m11_Sahara1_Baker_with_children_in_wheelchairs
259   mg071_baker_m1_1920-1950_with_a_group_of_Chinese_children
275   mg071_baker_m1_by_fence_with_tree

Other Sources:

16   The literary estate of Richard St. Barbe Baker
20   id #lh-4070 courtesy of Saskatoon Public Library
34   The literary estate of Richard St. Barbe Baker
97   The literary estate of Richard St. Barbe Baker
164   The literary estate of Richard St. Barbe Baker
168   The literary estate of Richard St. Barbe Baker
195   The literary estate of Richard St. Barbe Baker
208   The literary estate of Richard St. Barbe Baker
262   Photo by David van Vliet
267   Photo by Paul Hanley

-ᚼ-

Acknowledgements

I wrote a first draft of this book, circa 1989, with the support of an Explorations Grant from the Canada Council for the Arts. The Council's generous support at that time was and is appreciated.

While the project was set aside for several decades, my interest in and affection for St. Barbe was sustained by several friends and fellow admirers of the Man of the Trees: Robert White, David van Vliet, Hugh Locke, and Paul Mantle. Paul encouraged me to revive the project.

Hugh Locke provided encouragement and support along the way. Hugh and Michael B. Thompson, as Dr. Baker's literary trustees, granted permission to quote liberally from his books, all now out of print. Hugh also made arrangements for HRH The Prince of Wales to provide the foreword.

I am particularly indebted to the University of Saskatchewan Library, University Archives & Special Collections, Richard St. Barbe Baker fonds, and its staff, both in the 1980s and currently, for providing me the opportunity to sift through their extensive collection of Baker's papers, which yielded most of my material.

University Archives & Special Collections generously provided digital copies of most of the photographs used in this book, which are used with their permission. Several photographs were extracted from Baker's books by Paul Mantle; these are used with the permission of Baker's literary trustees. Some of the photographs were taken many decades ago. While they are not in excellent condition, their inclusion enhances the story of Baker's life nonetheless. A few of the photos were taken by Dr. Baker. A photograph of Charlie Eagle and friends was provided by the Saskatoon Public Library and is used with their permission.

I am humbled by the support for this project from HRH The Prince of Wales and Jane Goodall. Many thanks to both of them. And thank you to Ryan Walker for connecting me to Dr. Goodall.

Nancy Ackerman of AmadeaEditing massaged the manuscript, offering many helpful suggestions.

Many thanks also to the University of Regina Press, who brought the project to fruition.

Haleh Samimi, my wife, helped me in so many ways; she makes everything worthwhile.

Books by Richard St. Barbe Baker

Men of the Trees: In the Mahogany Forests of Kenya and Nigeria, 1931
The Brotherhood of the Trees, 1931
Among the Trees, 1935
Magic in the Woods, 1935
Trees, 1940
Among the Trees, Vol. 2, 1941
Africa Drums, 1942, 1951, 1954
The Redwoods, 1943, 1959
I Planted Trees, 1944
Trees: A Book of the Seasons, 1948
Trees: A Reader's Guide, 1948
Green Glory: The Forests of the World, 1949
Tambours Africains, 1949
Famous Trees, 1952
Sahara Challenge, 1954
Kabongo: The Story of a Kikuyu Chief, 1955
Dance of the Trees: The Adventures of a Forester, 1956
Land of Tane: The Threat of Erosion, 1956
Sahara Conquest, 1956
Why I am a Vegetarian, 1957

Kamiti: A Forester's Dream, 1958
Horse Sense: Horses in War and Peace, 1962
Famous Trees of New Zealand, 1965
The True Book About Trees, 1965
Sahara Conquest, 1966
Caravan Story and Country Notebook, 1969
My Life, My Trees, 1970, 1981
Famous Trees of Bible Lands, 1974
Trees for Health and Longevity, 1981
Man of the Trees: Selected Writings of Richard St. Barbe Baker,
    1989, 1993
Tall Timber, 2010

Index

PAUL HANLEY is a writer with a special interest in the natural environment, agriculture, and the future of civilization. He is the author of *ELEVEN* and the coauthor and editor of *The Spirit of Agriculture and Earthcare: Ecological Agriculture in Saskatchewan*.